T0330081

# Uncertainty and the Environment

NEW HORIZONS IN ENVIRONMENTAL ECONOMICS

**General Editors:** Wallace E. Oates, *Professor of Economics, University of Maryland, USA* and Henk Folmer, *Professor of General Economics, Wageningen University and Professor of Environmental Economics, Tilburg University, The Netherlands*

This important series is designed to make a significant contribution to the development of the principles and practices of environmental economics. It includes both theoretical and empirical work. International in scope, it addresses issues of current and future concern in both East and West and in developed and developing countries.

The main purpose of the series is to create a forum for the publication of high quality work and to show how economic analysis can make a contribution to understanding and resolving the environmental problems confronting the world in the twenty-first century.

Recent titles in the series include:

Designing International Environmental Agreements
Incentive Compatible Strategies for Cost-Effective Cooperation
*Carsten Schmidt*

Spatial Environmental and Resource Economics
Selected Essays of Charles D. Kolstad
*Charles D. Kolstad*

Economic Theories of International Environmental Cooperation
*Carsten Helm*

Negotiating Environmental Quality
Policy Implementation in Germany and the United States
*Markus A. Lehmann*

Game Theory and International Environmental Cooperation
*Michael Finus*

Sustainable Small-scale Forestry
Socio-economic Analysis and Policy
*Edited by S.R. Harrison, J.L. Herbohn and K.F. Herbohn*

Environmental Economics and Public Policy
Selected Papers of Robert N. Stavins, 1988–1999
*Robert N. Stavins*

International Environmental Externalities and the Double Dividend
*Sebastian Killinger*

Global Emissions Trading
Key Issues for Industrialized Countries
*Edited by Suzi Kerr*

The Choice Modelling Approach to Environmental Valuation
*Edited by Jeff Benneett and Russell Blamey*

Uncertainty and the Environment
Implications for Decision Making and Environmental Policy
*Richard A. Young*

# Uncertainty and the Environment

Implications for Decision Making and Environmental Policy

Richard A. Young

*Consultant, Arthur Andersen Business Consulting, London*

NEW HORIZONS IN ENVIRONMENTAL ECONOMICS

**Edward Elgar**
Cheltenham, UK • Northampton, MA, USA

Published by
Edward Elgar Publishing Limited
Glensanda House
Montpellier Parade
Cheltenham
Glos GL50 1UA
UK

Edward Elgar Publishing, Inc.
136 West Street
Suite 202
Northampton
Massachusetts 01060
USA

A catalogue record for this book
is available from the British Library

**Library of Congress Cataloguing in Publication Data**
Young, Richard, 1973–
    Uncertainty and the environment : implications for decision making and environmental policy / Richard Young.
        p.    cm. — (New horizons in environmental economics)
    Includes bibliographical references and index.
        1. Environmental policy—Decision making.    2. Environmental policy—Economic aspects.    I. Title.    II. Series.
    HC79.E5 Y69    2001
    333.7—dc21

                                                                        00–067690

ISBN 1 84064 626 8

Typeset by Manton Typesetters, Louth, Lincolnshire, UK.
Printed and bound in Great Britain by Biddles Ltd, *www.biddles.co.uk*

# Contents

# Figures

# Tables

# Preface

This book is concerned with the issue of uncertainty in environmental decision making. The focus on uncertainty stems from the premise that uncertainty is a key issue which must be addressed, if sustainability objectives are to be met at a project or policy level. Using an alternative conceptualization of uncertainty, it is contended that there are a number of different modes of uncertainty and that many environmental decisions are largely characterized by what is termed 'hard uncertainty', in which the set of possible actions or future states is unknown or where the probability distribution for such outcomes is unknown or not fully definable. The presence of hard uncertainty radically alters the way in which environmental uncertainty can be dealt with at both an epistemological and a practical level and poses a number of problems for traditional decision-making frameworks based on probability.

Consequently, a critique is advanced of the use of traditional models, such as expected utility, in environmental decision making and it is argued that there is a need to evaluate decision-making models in relation to the rationality of the way that decisions are made. Building on this, an alternative model of decision making under uncertainty derived from the work of George Shackle is outlined and applied to environmental decision making. The model is operationalized in terms of both explaining the way that decisions are and should be made, and applied to a case study of the Belize Southern Highway Project.

By analysing data derived from interviews conducted with decision makers in the Government of Belize, the Inter-American Development Bank, the Department of Foreign and International Development (DFID) and the World Bank, the relevance of the Shackle model is demonstrated. In particular, its applicability as a means of explaining the way that hard uncertainty is evaluated within the decision-making process is highlighted. The research suggests that the behaviour of individual decision makers is broadly consistent with the key propositions of the model regarding the way decision makers evaluate uncertainty and the way that the outcomes of a policy are evaluated. At an institutional level, however, it is argued that although a sifting out of the possible outcomes of a project or policy does occur, hard uncertainty is often not explicitly recognized in the decision-making process. In response, a normative framework for dealing with hard uncertainty in environmental decision making is advanced as a means of ensuring that hard uncertainty is explicitly considered in the decision-making process.

The views expressed within this book are mine and do not reflect the views of Arthur Andersen.

# Acknowledgements

The research which forms the basis of this book was carried out as part of my Doctorate at the University of Glasgow and there are a number of people and institutions that I would like to acknowledge. I would like to thank my supervisors Professor Chris Doyle and Professor Arthur Morris for all their comments and encouragement, which were crucial in the writing of the thesis. I am grateful to Professor Jim Ford who encouraged me at the initial stages of my thesis to develop my ideas with respect to the work of George Shackle. Additionally I would like to thank Nick Hanley, Simon Zisman, Silvana Dalmazzone and Charles Perrings as well as all the post-grads at the Department of Environmental Economics and Environmental Management, University of York, for their help and feedback. My research was funded by way of a University of Glasgow Science Scholarship, with additional funding for my fieldwork coming from the Department of Geography, The Cross Trust and the Carnegie Trust.

During my period of fieldwork I was fortunate to gain the help of a number of people whom I would like to acknowledge. I am grateful to all those in the Government of Belize, The Inter-American Development Bank, DFID and the World Bank who spared the time to allow me to interview them.

I would also like to thank Cambridge University Press for kind permission to reproduce material from the following publications: Barbier *et al.*, 'The Economic Value of Biodiversity' (ed. Perrings) Figure 12.1 in Vernon H. Heywood (ed.) *Global Biodiversity Assessment*, 1995; Mooney *et al.*, 'Biodiversity and Ecosystem Functioning: Basic Principles', Figure on page 315 in Vernon H. Heywood (ed.) *Global Biodiversity Assessment*, 1995.

Above all I would like to thank my parents for the support which they have always provided me.

# 1. Introduction: Dealing with uncertainty in environmental decision making

## 1.1 INTRODUCTION TO THE PROBLEM OF ENVIRONMENTAL UNCERTAINTY

*On the whole, men are more good than bad; that however isn't the real point. But they are more or less ignorant, and it is this that we call vice or virtue; the most incorrigible vice being that of an ignorance that fancies it knows everything and therefore claims for itself the right to kill.*

Albert Camus, *The Plague* (1972)

At the core of this book is the assertion that many decisions surrounding the environment are conditioned by the presence of uncertainty. The recognition that there are a number of different modes of uncertainty radically alters the way in which environmental uncertainty can be dealt with both at a epistemological and practical level, and necessitates an alternative approach to that encompassed by traditional probability-based models. However, while there is an extensive literature on probability-based models of risk in decision making (Perrings *et al.*, 1995), the literature on dealing with environmental uncertainty and in particular with what will be termed 'hard uncertainty'[1] in decision making is rather limited. It is this issue of dealing with environmental uncertainty in decision making that provides the impetus for the research carried out and presented in this book.

The uncertainty that decision makers are faced with in many environmental problems is derived from three main sources. First, uncertainty exists about the resilience of ecosystems and the consequences of human induced change for ecosystems, particularly when the action could result in a ecosystem threshold being exceeded. Second, uncertainty is often present with regard to the value of those changes. The third source stems from uncertainty as to future supply of vital ecosystem functions and services that may be of unanticipated importance in terms of human welfare. The prevalence of uncertainty in environmental problems raises questions about how uncertainty is and should be evaluated in the decision-making process.

While current models can claim some virtues in dealing with risk or what will be termed soft uncertainty,[2] it is argued that they are limited in terms of their applications to hard uncertainty problems of the sort often encountered on a regular basis in environmental decisions. A central hypothesis of this book is therefore that decision models based on risk or soft uncertainty and in particular the notion of probability cannot be expected to deal either adequately or explicitly with issues of environmental uncertainty such as biodiversity loss. Given the need for an alternative and novel decision-making framework for dealing with environmental uncertainty, the Shackle model will be proposed and interpreted in the context of environmental uncertainty. The question of whether this model is useful in explaining the way in which decisions are made under environmental uncertainty will be addressed. In addition a key element of the research aims to assess the extent to which the Shackle model can be adapted to serve as a decision-making framework which allows explicit attention to be given to uncertainty.

The research therefore aims to provide a contribution in five main areas. First, an important step will be in developing criteria for defining the nature and the different modalities of environmental uncertainty, and for assessing the implications of the different levels of uncertainty in terms of decision making. Second, on the basis of these criteria traditional models for dealing with risk will be critically assessed in terms of their suitability for dealing with environmental uncertainty. Third, an alternative model for dealing with uncertainty based on the work of George Shackle will be interpreted and applied in relation to environmental uncertainty, and fourth, the practical application of a model that will aid decision makers to deal adequately with uncertainty will be advanced.

The final contribution centres on a reassessment of how we rationalize decision making when faced with the realities of uncertainty. The interpretation of the resulting model of uncertainty necessitates a departure from the use of the traditional criteria used to assess decision rules in terms of their rationality. Consequently models of environmental uncertainty need to be assessed more in terms of their procedural rationality and their application at the *ex ante* stage of decision making rather than purely in terms of their optimality or usefulness in providing *ex post* explanations of human behaviour in decision making.

In attempting to deal with the realities of uncertainty in environmental decision making, a practical as well as theoretical approach has been employed. It was this reason that motivated the use of a case study to apply the Shackle model of decision making in a real world experiment. The fieldwork and subsequent data that were collected focused on the way that uncertainty about the environmental effects of development projects was dealt with by a developing country, Belize, and by the Inter-American Development Bank. The interviews conducted allowed the practical application of an alternative model of uncertainty, as well as providing valuable observations on the more general nature of dealing with uncertainty in development agencies such as the Inter-American Development Bank, the British Development Division in the Caribbean and the World Bank. The quantitative and qualitative data collected have also provided a useful insight into questions surrounding whether or not the Shackle model is useful in explaining the way that decision makers deal with uncertainty. To the author's knowledge this is the first major application of the Shackle model in the context of environmental uncertainty[3] and is the first application to a real world decision rather than a laboratory experiment.

Before dealing with the problem of uncertainty in environmental decision making, however, it is necessary to outline the research framework that is chosen, what such a framework implies and the theoretical issues that will need to be addressed. Consequently the rest of this chapter will be concerned with positioning this research within the overall context of sustainable development and biodiversity. The first part of the chapter will be concerned with some of the theoretical issues that sustainability and biodiversity pose for this research. After a brief outline of some of the origins and the main issues posed by sustainability, the notion of the interconnectedness between the ecological and economic systems will be highlighted. Having a greater understanding of key characteristics of this system is important in the debate regarding the form of sustainability advocated, and in particular in emphasizing the difficulty in assuming the substitutability of natural and other forms of capital. The key issue of the uncertainty raised due to the public good nature of many environmental services will also be reviewed and the problem of irreversibility and the appropriateness of equilibrium analysis tackled. The implications of the precautionary principle in the context of sustainable development will be briefly considered, before a framework for research is outlined and the main hypotheses to be addressed are formulated.

## 1.2   INTRODUCTION: SUSTAINABLE DEVELOPMENT

The problem of uncertainty in environmental decision making stems from growing concerns about the impact of human activity on the environment, encapsulated in the ever growing discourse on sustainable development. The significance of this debate for the research is that it makes the issue of dealing with environmental uncertainty in decision making imperative and it is within the context of meeting sustainability objectives that the problem of environmental uncertainty will be addressed. Understandably the complexity of the relationship between humans and their environment has produced a wide set of interpretations of sustainability, all with a number of either implicit or explicit implications that merit careful consideration. However sustainability is defined, it will inevitably involve making trade-offs between a number of concerns, which are often competing. It is the making of the trade-offs and the role that uncertainty plays in some of the main concerns of sustainability that form the focus of this chapter.

### 1.2.1  The Research Context: Sustainable Development and Biodiversity

With the publication of the Bruntland Report in the 1980s the sustainability discourse came to the fore of the world political agenda (Common, 1995). The report tried to reconcile some of the earlier development failures based purely on economic growth with a development paradigm in which social and inter-generational objectives were recognized as distinct and were given equal weight to economic efficiency, and in which the long-term degradation of the environment was seen as a barrier to development (Munasinghe, 1993b). Thus, according to the report:[4] 'Sustainable Development seeks to meet the needs and aspirations of the present without compromising the ability to meet those of the future' (WCED, 1987).

Inherent in the concept of sustainable development is therefore an ethical condition that future generations have a right to have handed on to them the capacity to generate for themselves a level of well-being no less than that enjoyed by the current generation (Barbier *et al.*, 1995). Another important issue is whether at present rates of consumption it is indeed possible for economic growth and sustainability to go hand in hand. For Herman Daly it is crucial to distinguish between development in terms of qualitative change and growth which is defined purely in quantitative terms (Daly and Cobb, 1989). What is most important is that the sustainable development debate represents an attempt to focus on the nature and type of economic growth that would be compatible with sustainable development and on how traditional development objectives could be reconciled with concerns for environmental quality and inter temporal equity.

The promotion of environmental concerns in the sustainable development discourse is itself perhaps best manifested in the increasing prominence given to biodiversity. One of the first calls for this link can be seen in the First World Conservation Strategy which argued that:

> the maintenance of essential ecological processes and life support systems, the preservation of genetic diversity, and the sustainable utilisation of species and ecosystem have the overall aim of achieving sustainable development through the conservation of living resources. (IUCN/ UNEP/ WWF, 1980 in Barbier *et al.*, 1994)

The issue of biodiversity gained international recognition as a result of the Biodiversity convention signed under the auspices of the UNCED at Rio in

June 1992. The concept of biodiversity involves a complexity of meanings, although all imply some measure of distance (Barbier *et al.*, 1995). Based on this principle, three main perspectives can be seen. The first is that of genetic diversity, which refers to the heritable variation within and between populations, or the sum of the genetic information contained in the genes of plants and micro-organisms. The second is that of species diversity, which refers simply to the number of species in a particular habitat. The third, ecosystem diversity, refers to the diversity both within and between ecological processes, such as habitats, biotic communities and ecological processes (such as photosynthesis, nutrient cycling and nitrogen fixing) (Blaikie, 1996) and is based on the concept of the functional role of species in supporting critical structuring processes. Arguably it is this concept of functional diversity that is the most crucial to the sustainable development debate. Unfortunately it is more difficult to classify than the other categories of diversity. Functional diversity can be defined in two main ways: first in terms of the diversity of ecological functions performed by different species; and second in terms of the diversity of species performing a given ecological function (Barbier *et al.*, 1995).

A rationale exists therefore for linking biodiversity and the sustainable development discourse on scientific, economic and moral grounds, in that biological diversity is the underlying component in our life support system, that biological diversity provides us with many direct and indirect economic benefits and that all species require respect regardless of their use in humanity. As will be highlighted in this and future chapters, the large degree of uncertainty inherent in decisions regarding biodiversity, means that the issue merits particular attention in the context of environmental uncertainty.

However operationalized, the concept of sustainability necessarily involves making a number of trade-offs between, for example, ecological objectives such as the maintenance of biodiversity, economic objectives such as economic growth, and social cultural objectives such as wealth distribution. Figure 1.1 highlights some of the trade-offs that may be required to be met, with the boxes contained in the middle of the arrows indicating issues that need to be resolved in order to facilitate the making of trade-offs. The context for this book is restricted, however, to focusing on the uncertainty which arises as a result of the interactions between the highly interconnected and complex economic and ecological system, and the accompanying trade-offs between the economic and ecological objectives, within sustainable development.[5] Inevitably, especially when the role of uncertainty in decision making is considered, socio-cultural and political issues will be raised, but due to the scope of these issues, the bulk will remain outside the consideration of this book.

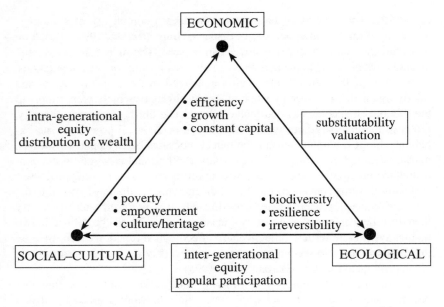

*Figure 1.1    Trade-offs among the three main objectives of sustainable development*[6]

## 1.3    SUSTAINABLE DEVELOPMENT AND UNCERTAINTY: KEY ISSUES

One of the pivotal arguments in this book is that uncertainty is central to the sustainable development discourse and will need to be addressed if sustainability objectives are to be met. Indeed given certainty about the future, the attainment of sustainability goals would arguably be relatively straightforward. The next section considers some of the most important uncertainty issues raised by the sustainable development discourse. As will be seen, it is in stressing the importance of these issues within the sustainability debate that such a potentially explosive mix for environmental decision making is implied (Facheux and Froger, 1995).

### 1.3.1    The Complexity and the Interconnectedness of the Ecological–Economic System

While academically it may be more convenient to analyse the economic and ecological systems separately, increasingly many environmental and ecological economists have begun to emphasize the fact that the economic system is both highly connected with and dependent on the ecological system. Increasing evidence points to linkages between economic activity and the environment which are pervasive and complex. The more highly connected ecological and economic systems are, the more change in one implies change in the other, or as Norgaard (1984) terms it, the more they 'coevolve'. The implication of this is that it is necessary to look at the economy not as a closed system but as a component of a wider system. Thus matter and energy used up in human production and consumption activities must eventually end up in environmental systems and result in significant forms of environmental and economic damage, such as pollution, (Perman *et al.*, 1996). Furthermore the entropic nature of the system ensures that, while the total amount of mass or energy remains the same, its structure does not. The consequence of this is that economic–ecological interactions may lead to irreversible losses (see Section 1.3.5).

The recognition of the possibility that there may in fact be limits to the impacts of economic activity on the environment is based on the realization that environmental resources provide a number of both direct and equally crucial indirect services and functions which do in fact affect human welfare. Moreover, it can be argued that the regulatory functions performed by ecosystems, such as waste assimilation, indirectly support all economic activity (Barbier *et al.*, 1995). The processes among and within the physical, biological and chemical components of an ecosystem result in specific types of ecosystem function or property, such as nutrient cycling, biological productivity, hydrology and sedimentation. These interactions or life support functions in turn generate many ecological resources and services that are of fundamental value in that they sustain human societies (see Table 1.1).

The highly interconnected nature of the economy and of the environment and the complex series of feedbacks between the two, further complicate the sustainability problem. Thus meeting an ecological objective such as the maintenance of key ecological functions and services is complicated by the uncertainty surrounding the effects of increased economic activity on these ecological functions. This fundamental issue of uncertainty boils down to the problem of ecosystem thresholds and resilience. It is sufficient to remember that the effects of economic activity have very real consequences for the environment, which due to the complexity of the interactions pose considerable problems in defining quantitatively the extent and type of economic activity that is consistent with ecological sustainability. As Michael Common argues:

> the level of human impact on the national environment is now such that its capacity to support future economic activity at the level required by the human population and its aspirations is questionable. The issues arising are characterised by ignorance and uncertainty. (Common, 1995: p. 4)

*Table 1.1    Ecosystem functions and their uses in the economic system*

| Regulation functions | Production functions | Carrier functions | Information functions |
|---|---|---|---|
| Providing support for economic activity and human welfare through: | Providing basic resources such as: | Providing space and a suitable substrate *inter alia* for: | Providing aesthetic, cultural and scientific benefits through: |
| – protection against harmful cosmic influences | – oxygen | – habitation | – aesthetic information |
| – climatic regulation | – food, drinking water and nutrition | – agriculture, forestry, fishery, aquaculture | – spiritual and religious information |
| – watershed protection and catchment | – water for industry, households | – industry | – cultural and artistic inspiration |
| – maintenance of evolutionary potential to adapt to change | – clothing and fabrics | – engineering projects such as dams and roads | – educational and scientific information |
| – erosion prevention and soil protection | – building, construction and manufacturing materials | – recreation | – potential information |
| – storage and recycling of industrial and human welfare | – energy and fuel | – nature conservation | |
| – maintenance of biological and genetic diversity | – minerals | | |
| – biological control | – minerals resources | | |
| – providing a migratory, nursery and feeding habitat | – biochemical resources | | |
| | – genetic resources | | |
| | – ornamental resources | | |

*Source*:   Adapted from Barbier *et al.*, 1995

Although ecosystems contain hundreds and thousands of species interacting amongst themselves and with their physical system, the consensus is that the system is driven by a relatively small number of biotic and abiotic variables, on whose interactions the overall balance of the species within the ecosystem depends (Holling, 1992). This idea has led to the distinction between species which are drivers and those which are passengers. The implication is that the loss of only certain species could have a massive effect on the viability of an ecosystem and the ecosystem functions that it supports. Thus only a small set of structuring processes made up of biotic and physical processes are seen as critical in influencing the structure and overall behaviour of the ecosystems; processes that are supported by different groupings of animals and plants with often complementary functions (Holling *et al.*, 1995). A major problem, however, is that there is a significant lack of information on which species are in fact key, due to the lack of long-term ecosystem studies (Barbier *et al.*, 1995).

It is this issue of uncertainty that lies at the heart of the biodiversity problem and results in the conclusion that at present the consequences of reductions in the number of species and specific combinations of species in terms of human welfare is often unclear. The argument that a reduction can be presumed to be negative can be presented on two counts. First, while certain species may appear to be redundant in a present ecological state, they may be of crucial importance in providing ecological functions of use to man in future evolved states. Second, genetic diversity is the basis on which the process of natural selection works, so that any reduction in biodiversity in effect hinders the evolutionary process which can be regarded as a key life-supporting function of the biosphere. Thus, under the assumption that the environment is dynamic and will change over time, the reduction in the evolutionary potential of an ecosystem limits its ability to adapt to change and most importantly to external shocks (Common, 1995). In effect such a process can be seen as reducing the options of future generations to adapt to future changes in environmental conditions. This problem of ecological uncertainty and its implications will be further developed in Chapter 3.

An important point to stress is that, with the realization of the interconnectedness and co-dependence of the economic and environmental system as a joint system, it is evident that the joint system responds very differently to perturbation depending on where the economy and the environment are relative to the local system equilibria, as well as the characteristics of those equilibria. The dynamics of the joint system will reflect the structure of the connections between each subsystem. The existence of multiple locally stable equilibria (or basins of attraction) which are separated by unstable equilibria means that, as economic and ecological systems pass from one basin to another, the central characteristics of the system may undergo a profound change. If a system is in the neighbourhood of a particular unstable equilibrium or threshold, minor perturbations of its state variables may have catastrophic consequences for its structure and organization. The capacity of the system to absorb such shocks without losing stability is captured in the concept of resilience, which was briefly introduced earlier. The main implication of this characteristic is that the joint system dynamics may not be either continuous or gradual, but may flip in the face of particular shock. It is in the maintenance of the resilience of the joint system that biodiversity has been given central stage (Perrings *et al.*, 1995). A key factor for the research presented in this book is that there is a high level of uncertainty surrounding the propensity and implications of particular phase changes, which may indeed only be recognized after they have occurred.

While the ecological and economic systems can be seen to be highly interconnected, a further source of uncertainty is derived from the fact that the two different systems do not interact evenly over time or space. Taking the latter issue, it is evident that many ecosystems cut across the structure of human society, for example the Amazon Basin spans several countries and interacts with many economic sectors (Munasinghe, 1993a). Often, therefore, the situation arises that the spatial extent of the environmental resource is more limited than the ecosystem from which it is derived. This problem of the juxtaposition of different spatial scales poses considerable questions for the sustainability debate, such as how we should evaluate changes in the scale of an economy *vis-à-vis* its ecological and physical context. The issue of time similarly causes difficulties for sustainability. Uncertainties over time lags in the cumulative environmental consequences of economic activity, present and future preferences and values as well as future possible substitution possibilities all pose significant constraints for meeting sustainable development objectives. As Perrings (1987) points out, it is therefore possible for components of the joint ecological–economic system to be entirely unconnected over one temporal or spatial horizon, but highly connected when viewed over some other spatial or temporal horizon.

### 1.3.2  The Public Good Nature of the Environment and Uncertainty

The public good nature of many environmental resources and the problems that this poses in relation to market failure is well documented in the environmental economics literature. It is important to note that as the environmental service or function tends towards that of a public good, familiarity decreases and information surrounding its value is often absent (Turner, 1993). Consequently the level of uncertainty is often greatest when the environmental service in question is a pure public good (see Figure 1.2).

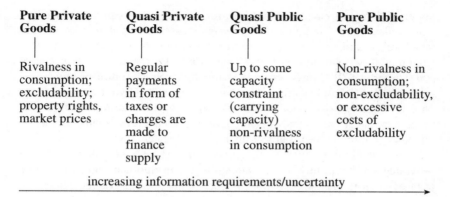

| Pure Private Goods | Quasi Private Goods | Quasi Public Goods | Pure Public Goods |
|---|---|---|---|
| Rivalness in consumption; excludability; property rights, market prices | Regular payments in form of taxes or charges are made to finance supply | Up to some capacity constraint (carrying capacity) non-rivalness in consumption | Non-rivalness in consumption; non-excludability, or excessive costs of excludability |

increasing information requirements/uncertainty

*Source*:   Adapted from Turner, 1993

*Figure 1.2   The environmental commodities continuum*

The existence of public goods and the resulting problem of market failure lead to a gap between the market price of environmental resources and the true value to individuals and societies. It is this absence of a market price that is one of the main problems in terms of defining environmental/economic trade-offs for sustainable development objectives. One of the main causes of this gap is ignorance or uncertainty regarding the social consequences of private actions with respect to the environment. The implication of the disparity between the market price and the 'true' social costs of environmental change creates difficulties for meeting sustainable development objectives, due to uncertainty about the value of environmental change on human welfare. While the environmental economics literature has made significant developments in this field through the use of valuation, as will be shown in Chapter 2, significant uncertainties remain which are due in part to the pure or quasi public good nature of many environmental problems such as biodiversity. This is essentially because the burden of the negative effects of uncertainty with regard to many environmental services will lie with society as a whole rather than with the individual or private company carrying out the activity.

### 1.3.3   Uncertainty and the Substitutability of Ecological Functions

The question of substitutability between the elements of man-made and natural capital in the sustainable development discourse is a core component of the uncertainty problem. Neo-classical economics tends to assume away the question of uncertainty regarding substitution policies, implying that uncertainty about the supply of essential environmental functions and services is not crucial, as lost environmental functions and services can be replaced by man-made capital (Common, 1995). Recent reassessments about the extent to which substitution possibilities do actually exist refute this (see: Daly, 1986; Common, 1995; Costanza 1991; Mason, 1996; Pearce *et al.,* 1990; Pearce and Turner, 1990). Moreover, any assumptions about future technological advances and possibilities for substitution are pervaded by uncertainty. Likewise uncertainty exists about which elements constitute critical capital, due to the fact that elements that appear not to be critical currently may in fact be critical in future evolved states or unanticipated states. It is in this sense that the issue of biodiversity plays a crucial role. The role of biodiversity, in providing an opportunity set in maintaining the evolutionary potential of the joint ecological–economic system, is once again seen as crucial. There is a large degree of uncertainty over whether it is possible to substitute for the role that individual species play in the functioning of critical environmental services, in present and future unanticipated states. Subsequently the structures and processes of physical systems are seen as vulnerable to incremental human choices. These changes may not have an immediate impact, but at some spatial or temporal scale the destruction of critical ecological systems will result in direct impacts on human welfare (Norton, 1995). As Common argues, there 'remain great uncertainties regarding substitution possibilities' (Common, 1995: p. 47). While it can be conceded that some substitution possibilities do in fact exist, there remain some critical elements of natural capital, for which substitution is either not technically possible or would be too expensive, and a reduction in this critical base of natural capital in effect reduces the opportunity set on which future generations can adapt and evolve in response to stress and shock exerted on the joint ecological economic system.

The need to sustain an adequate level of natural capital means that there is therefore a need to deal with uncertainties regarding the effects of economic activity on natural capital, uncertainty over future values and preferences as well as uncertainty over the impact of future technological change. Although some argue that the question of substitutability will only be resolved empirically, many of the most important issues will only be resolved *ex post.* Furthermore due to the fact that many critical elements of natural capital are subject to irreversibility, by the time the uncertainty has been resolved it will be too late. It is to the issue of irreversibility and its role in the uncertainty problem that the discussion now turns.

### 1.3.4  Irreversibility and Uncertainty

The irreversibility of the damaging effects of economic activity with respect to many critical environmental functions is one of the most important problems to be faced in the sustainable development and biodiversity discourses. Indeed it is the issue of irreversibility that necessitates the need to recognize uncertainty. If irreversibility did not in fact exist, then the question of uncertainty would not be of such paramount importance. If a mistake was made, it would be possible to reverse the effects of a particular decision, in effect giving another opportunity to roll the dice that constitutes economic activity. However, unlike financial markets, for environmental problems it may not be possible to absorb and eventually reverse previous losses. The presence of irreversibility therefore requires that sustainable development explicitly deals with the issue of uncertainty.

The importance attached to the issue of irreversibility relies on the argument that has been put forward that substitution possibilities for critical environmental services and functions are in fact limited. On this basis it is therefore important to maintain the crucial set of ecosystem properties that form the basis of the essential life supporting functions (Barbier *et al.*, 1995). It is apparent that, if the ecosystem is pushed beyond the stage at which it is able to cope effectively with externally induced shocks, then its capacity to support the flow service may be severely diminished or removed. For example once a large area of rain forest is removed, then although over a very long period the action may be slowly reversible, the course of action over at least a time period of one generation is irreversible.

An example of an action that at present appears to be completely irreversible is the destruction of the ozone layer, as it is thought that this process cannot be reversed nor the ecosphere repaired by human effort (Hinterberger *et al.*, 1997). In the case of biodiversity of species, the extinction of species is by definition irreversible. The argument that transformations of natural capital are for all intents and purposes irreversible is also derived from Georgescu-Roegen (1973). From an economic perspective the fact that a process may be reversible upon the expenditure of infinite energy is of no relevance if the costs are beyond the means of the decision maker. In which case in the joint ecological–economic system, it is economically irreversible. This form of irreversibility reflects the fact that the cost of rehabilitation or restoration exceeds the resources available (Perrings, 1997a).

The issue of irreversibility has attracted a wide-ranging literature in environmental economics, which, in contrast to traditional economics, does not tend to assume that resource use decisions are irreversible. The literature on irreversibility (Krutilla and Fisher, 1975; Arrow and Fisher, 1974) has tended to focus on the option of development. In particular a fundamental asymmetry has been identified that, while a decision to develop in the presence of irreversibility can not be reversed, a decision not to develop can be reversed. Thus taking the latter option leaves open the opportunity to develop in the future. While such approaches provided innovative and valuable insights into the problem of irreversibility, the linking of irreversibility and uncertainty is through the reliance on probability and the concepts of option and quasi-option value. As Chapter 3 will go on to argue, however, this linking of irreversibility to the use of probability may only be applicable to certain cases of risk or what will be termed 'soft uncertainty'.

An additional aspect of irreversibility is in relation to the decision-making process in which, as Vickers (1994) points out, each decision moment is itself not only unique but is also embedded in the unidirectional flow of time. Shackle (1961) views such decisions as 'self destructive' in that by taking them, this forever changes the possible structure of future decisions. Georgescu-Roegen (1973) and Perrings (1987) highlight this aspect of the irreversibility with respect to the entropic processes at the heart of economic activity. Accordingly in a world governed by the laws of thermodynamics, the irreversibility of entropic processes ensures that the system will necessarily evolve through a sequence of states that are not predictable from its history. In the case of ecological–economic relationships the dynamic nature of both domains will reinforce this inherent irreversibility as an essential element of uncertainty. The impact of economic decisions on ecosystems necessarily involves changes in ecosystem structure that, however small, force acceptance of a new set of decision events which in themselves will be unique and irreversible. The uniqueness and irreversibility of the decision context and its implications for decision making under uncertainty will be looked at in more detail in Chapters 4 and 5.

### 1.3.5   Equilibrium Analysis in Economic and Ecological Systems

The issue of equilibrium and its assumptions plays a crucial role in the analysis of the economic–ecological system. A key factor in the recognition of the importance of uncertainty in ecological–economic analysis is the shift from an equilibrium framework to one which emphasizes concepts of disequilibrium. If we take the issue of equilibrium in the ecological system, it is evident that while there was a traditional tendency to use an equilibrium or static stability concept, increasing evidence has shifted the focus to that of a dynamic system. The traditional view advocated for example by Clements (1905) and Forbes (1880) was that in the case of species populations, while the populations oscillated, the oscillations were kept within bounds, tending towards an equilibrium. Although these views were firmly in the equilibrium or balance of nature camp, they did contain within them the seeds of a more modern conception of equilibrium based on the concept of resilience mentioned in earlier sections.

The weight of evidence against a static balance was such that by the middle of this century the idea of dynamic balance gained emphasis. However, even this concept has become discredited (see Shrader-Frechette and McCoy, 1993). It has been argued by Shrader-Frechette and McCoy that it may be better to move away from employing stability terms such as 'balance', 'equilibrium', 'homeostasis' or 'stability' and towards the notion of resilience or what they term 'persistence'. The emphasis on the persistence or resilience of the system highlights the notion of a dynamic rather than a static system, in which the ecosystem or community may not in fact return to some 'normal condition' (Shrader-Frechette and McCoy, 1993). Recent contributions have reinforced the notion that ecosystems are not in fact equilibrium systems but rather dynamic systems, in which the presence of large-scale dynamics and ecosystem organization indicates that ecosystems behave in a non-linear rather than a linear manner (Norton, 1995).

While in ecology there has been a shift away from equilibrium analysis, in economics there has been a tendency to rely on the notion of static equilibria, such as those which form the basis of neo-classical models. Although there has been a recent break with this, shown by the approaches of evolutionary and ecological economic modelling (see Faucheux *et al.*, 1996), the emphasis has remained on the use of an equilibrium framework. Equilibrium analysis, which Georgescu-Roegen sees as largely transferred from classical mechanics is essentialist or reductionist in nature and is based on the modelling of all variables and relations which are assumed to be (at least probabilistically) known and stable over time (Katzner, 1995). This reduction of uncertainty in equilibrium models to probabilistic measures will be questioned in Chapter 3.

Christensen (1996) has pointed out that the deterministic equilibrium structure not only does not admit to the interdependence of individual tastes and preferences, but perhaps more importantly for environmental problems, the neo-classical framework assumes that resources and factors of production are given, independent, and physically disconnected from other resources. In short, such a paradigm lacks a specification of the physiological and ecological structure of economic activity. In this sense an alternative non-essentialistic approach highlighted by Katzner (1995), can be extended to ecological–economic issues, in which explanation is based on the idea that every conceptual phenomenon exists only as the combined result of the interactions of all other conceptual entities. Concepts cannot be said, therefore, to have single causes since they are understood to co-determine each other. This is very much in line with the notion put forward earlier of the co-evolution of economic–environmental relationships with the emphasis being on out-of-equilibrium positions in which the ideas of transition and non linearity have key roles to play (Faucheux *et al.*, 1996).

### 1.3.6    Uncertainty and the Precautionary Principle

This chapter has put forward the arguments that highlight the nature of uncertainty in the sustainable development problem. It is clear that the extent to which uncertainty is given importance is crucial in the way that sustainable development is defined. The argument put forward here is that if sustainable development objectives are to be met then the role of uncertainty must be recognized and tackled explicitly within the decision-making process. One of the concepts that has been put forward in relation to uncertainty in terms of sustainable development and in particular the issues of biodiversity is that of the precautionary principle.

The precautionary principle has evolved as a concept due to the presence of uncertainty and in particular irreversibility. The precautionary principle, which is similar to the principle of safe minimum standards (Ciriacy-Wantrup, 1963), in essence is a kind of insurance problem that will allow for a higher margin of error and act as a buffer against hard uncertainty. The principle states that rather than await certainty, regulators should act in anticipation of any potential environmental harm in order to prevent it from occurring and stresses the need to avoid potentially damaging outcomes (Costanza, 1994). Like sustainable development its adoption in many international environmental resolutions (for example the Rio Declaration of June 1992) has seen it evolve as a basic normative concept within many environmental discourses. The precautionary principle does recognize the problem of uncertainty as central to sustainable development by stressing our inability to predict all the future consequences of economic activity in relation to human welfare. If, as has been posited, it is the case that the dynamics of ecological systems are not in fact smooth and continuous, then the underlying notion of the precautionary principle is one that seeks to avoid the thresholds around which the resilience of the system may in fact be lost.

O'Riordan (1995) suggests a number of meanings that can be ascribed to the precautionary principle in its simplest form.[7] For the purpose of this book there are two of particular interest:

1. Thoughtful action in advance of scientific proof of cause and effect based on principles of wise management and cost effectiveness. Namely that it is better to pay a little now than an awful lot later. In this sense, precaution is a receipt for action over inaction where there is a reasonable threat of irreversibility or of serious damage to life-support systems.
2. Leaving ecological space for ignorance, meaning that we should not extract critical resources, even when they are there for the taking, because we do not know what the longer-term consequences of their removal are (O'Riordan, 1995: p. 9).

Like sustainable development, however, a number of grey areas exist in relation to the application of the precautionary principle. In particular it does not offer much in the way of guidance as to how the problem should be dealt with (Common, 1995). Foremost is the fact that, if a precautionary principle were to be applied, then it necessarily implies an opportunity cost. As Barbier *et al.* (1995) point out, the question soon becomes one of what things should be set aside, and whether this should be at any cost. Moreover the precautionary principle does not tell us which adverse future outcomes are the most important. Consequently, while the principle advocates a precautionary approach in the face of hard uncertainty, it does not identify how to determine the circumstances in which uncertainty is such that a precautionary approach outweighs the opportunity cost of its implementation to society.

This concern can be exemplified with the problem of biodiversity. While it may be argued that maintenance of biodiversity is an essential element in sustaining the opportunity set for future generations in the face of perturbations to the ecological–economic system, it has also been the case that biodiversity loss, through natural resource selection such as in agriculture, has in many cases improved human welfare (Perrings, 1994). Clearly, therefore there is a need for a means of assessing the trade-offs between adopting a precautionary approach to uncertainty about the environmental implications of development and the social benefits of development. It is the need to deal with this type of uncertainty within a decision-making framework that will be highlighted in the following chapters.

## 1.4   A RESEARCH FRAMEWORK

This chapter has stressed the crucial role that uncertainty plays in the research context of the sustainable development and biodiversity discourse. Identifying uncertainty as a crucial factor immediately poses a number of challenges for traditional scientific research due to the very nature of the uncertainty problem at hand as well as the subjective nature of human behaviour in the face of uncertainty. Indeed rather than reducing the level of uncertainty surrounding the ecological–economic system, it should be realized that the progress of science has in fact uncovered more rather than less uncertainty (Costanza, 1994). As a consequence, given that for many environmental problems a large number of the facts are uncertain, and that value will be in dispute, it is often 'soft' scientific information which will end up serving as the inputs for 'hard' policy decisions to be made.

In this scheme of things it may be, as Norton (1995) argues, time to 'loosen the intellectual hinges, to try many different models and engage in disciplinary crossovers to increase communication across disciplines' (Norton, 1995: p. 122).

Funtowicz and Ravetz (1991) argue that such a new approach might be termed 'post normal science' in which scientific method would no longer necessarily imply anything about the precision of the results achieved, and in which the concept of the scientific explanation and of what constitutes a good decision is being changed. What it does imply is a forum for open inquiry which has no preconceived answers and which is aimed at exploring the extent of our knowledge and the magnitude of our ignorance (Costanza, 1994). By creating a new relationship between retaining the basic principles of scientific method and adapting to the reality of uncertainty, a new place for science in human affairs can be fashioned. It is this philosophy that will underlie this research.

### 1.4.1   Aims, Hypotheses and Outline of Research

Although the topic of uncertainty and accompanying research framework would suggest the difficulty of making testable hypotheses which can be verified as true or false, it will be useful to outline some broad hypotheses or research questions which this book aims to answer and to formulate the nature of the problem to be addressed. There are four main hypotheses or concerns which are the focus of the research presented in this book:

1. Existing conceptualizations of uncertainty and in particular environmental uncertainty do not reflect the full range of uncertainty faced in decision making.
2. By recognizing that there are in fact a number of different modalities of uncertainty, it is argued that the use of utility maximizing models, based on the notion of probability, do not adequately deal with the range of environmental uncertainty faced by decision makers.
3. The Shackle model better explains the way that decisions are made in the face of uncertainty and in the context of improving the procedural rationality of the decision-making process can be fruitfully employed in a prescriptive sense.
4. Building on this, it is hypothesized that the Shackle model can be operationalized in a real world decision context, as is done in a case study which focuses on the Belize Southern Highway Project.

As well as the theoretical contribution that this book aims to make, a core element is the application of the Shackle model to environmental uncertainty in respect of a road development project in Belize. The case study not only demonstrates examples of the type of uncertainty that is faced in such decisions, but also demonstrates the application of the Shackle model as a means of explaining decision making in the face of hard uncertainty. As well as developing a model of decision making under uncertainty, the interviewing of decision makers and the collection of additional information provides a rich source of qualitative data, in which to contextualize the application of the model. The case study also provides the practical basis on which the model is used to develop a prescriptive decision-making framework capable of explicitly dealing with environmental uncertainty.

This chapter has given an introduction to the problem of uncertainty in the context of sustainability and has outlined the research framework that is to be adopted. In the following chapter the decision-making context of cost–benefit analysis, and the valuation of environmental resources will be briefly reviewed. After that, Chapter 3 takes the important step of conceptualizing uncertainty at an epistemological level before providing a framework for defining the different modalities of uncertainty. Using this framework a theoretical basis is developed, highlighting the dimensions of environmental uncertainty. Building on this, a critique of the use of probability in environmental decision making in the face of hard uncertainty will be made, and the need for an alternative framework to that of expected utility forwarded (Chapter 4). In Chapter 5 the Shackle model will be introduced as an innovative alternative in the context of environmental uncertainty and its application in decision making analysed. Chapter 6 introduces the case study of the Belize Southern Highway and Chapter 7 describes the methodology adopted to carry out the fieldwork. Chapter 8 assesses whether the evidence suggests that the model is useful in explaining decision making under uncertainty. Chapter 9 looks at the way that uncertainty is handled at a more general level in the decision-making process and develops a normative framework for dealing adequately with uncertainty. In Chapter 10 conclusions are drawn.

## NOTES

1. *Hard uncertainty* can be defined at this stage in terms of situations in which a) the set of possible actions or future states is unknown or b) where an exhaustive set of future states can be specified, the probability distribution for such outcomes is unknown or not fully definable. A more comprehensive definition of hard uncertainty and the different modalities of uncertainty is left until Chapter 3.
2. *Soft uncertainty* or *risk* is used to define situations where 1) the set of all possible outcomes of an action are known and 2) the probability distribution of all possible outcomes is also known (see Section 3.2.1).
3. The only exception was its use by Perrings (1989) in a theoretical paper, see Chapter 3.
4. The report is officially titled *Our Common Future* (World Commission on Environment and Development, 1987) but derived its popular title from the name of the chairman of the Commission, Gro Harlem Bruntland.
5. While attention is focused on the economic and ecological sustainability aspects of this

framework, it is important to emphasize the important contribution of the socio-cultural view to the sustainability debate. (See for example O'Connor, 1988, 1989; Escobar, 1996; Oslender, 1997).

6.  Figure 1.1 is based on the structure of the diagram contained in Munasinghe (1993b: p. 2) but has been subsequently adapted to take into account the author's own views.
7.  Also see O'Riordan and Cameron (1994) for greater detail on the precautionary principle.

# 2. The decision-making context

## 2.1 INTRODUCTION

An important step in dealing with environmental uncertainty is the choice of the framework which will provide the basis for the decision-making procedure. While there are many techniques and approaches for appraising policies and projects which have an impact on the environment, the focus of this book is restricted to that of dealing with environmental uncertainty within what will loosely be termed a cost–benefit framework. The use of such a framework reflects two factors. First, decision making, which considers any investment in relation to a policy or a specific project, will involve an assessment, even at the most rudimentary level, of the costs and benefits of such a decision. Second, decisions made by society involving the allocation of environmental resources or services will necessarily imply valuation. Although criticisms have been made regarding the top-down decision-making structure implied by the use of cost–benefit analysis, a complete rejection of such an approach ignores the realities of decision making.

The aim of this chapter is to raise some important concerns surrounding the use of cost–benefit analysis which have an important effect on the way in which a decision is made. In particular it considers whether cost–benefit analysis should be interpreted as a decision criterion or alternatively whether it should be seen more as a general framework. In order to do this, a very brief description of cost–benefit analysis, and some of the more important stages is first provided. After that some of the main theoretical issues underlying the cost–benefit framework and the valuation of environmental resources will be highlighted. While the focus of this book is not environmental valuation *per se*, it is an important topic because valuation plays an important part in the use of a cost–benefit framework for decisions affecting the environment. Furthermore, almost all models of decision making under uncertainty utilize estimates of the values of the different outcomes considered by the model. From a practical view, although the Shackle model could be used operationally without values for the outcomes, operationalizing the model in the case study of Belize required the use of valuations of the different outcomes. What is important in relation to this chapter, is how values and in particular environmental values can be interpreted in the context of uncer-

tainty. The purpose of this chapter is therefore to review some of the major
issues raised and to develop a suitable decision-making framework, which
can provide the basis for the interpretation and analysis of the model of
decision making under uncertainty proposed.

## 2.2  COST–BENEFIT ANALYSIS

Cost–benefit analysis (CBA) is usually introduced at the appraisal stage of
the decision-making process and is thus a crucial element in the project cycle
in that it is often one of the key determinants as to whether or not the
government or institution financing the project will go ahead with the pro-
posal. Normally the analysis takes a number of stages, starting from the
definition of the project through the identification of the project inputs, deter-
mination of which impacts are economically relevant, the carrying out of the
physical quantification of the relevant impacts, the estimation of the monetary value of relevant effects, the discounting of the costs and benefits to
finally the application of the net present value test. Externalities such as
environmental costs or benefits for which no market prices exist should be
incorporated by the use of environmental valuation techniques where possible, although in reality this is often not attempted (Munasinghe, 1993b).

The basic criterion for comparing the costs and benefits of a project relative to the baseline case, is the Net Present Value (NPV) test, where NPV is
defined as:

$$NPV = \sum B_t(1+r)^{-t} - \sum C_t(1+r)^{-t} \qquad (2.1)$$

Where $B_t$ and $C_t$ are the respective benefits and costs of the project at a given
time period and the expression in brackets is the discount factor where the
rate of discount is assumed to be the real rate of interest $r$ at a given time
period $t$. $B$, $C$ and $r$ are defined in economic terms using appropriate shadow
prices. The rule is therefore to maximize NPV and the criterion for the
acceptance of a project is if NPV > 0. If projects are to be ranked, the one
with the highest NPV is chosen.

An alternative criterion is that of the internal rate of return (IRR) which
may be defined as:

$$\sum_{t=0}^{T}(B_t - C_t)/(1+IRR)^t = 0 \qquad (2.2)$$

In effect the IRR is the discount rate which reduces the NPV to zero. The
project is acceptable if IRR > $r$, which in most cases implies NPV > 0.

### 2.2.1 Efficiency and the Use of CBA

The purpose of CBA in its narrowest sense is to select projects or policies which imply an optimal allocation of resources, with the main criterion being that of efficiency. In such a Pareto optimal state, where prices reflect the true marginal costs, scarce resources are said to be efficiently allocated for a given income distribution, if no one person can be made better off, without making someone else worse off (Bator, 1957). This principle of efficiency is built into the Kaldor–Hicks potential compensation test which is at the heart of the welfare basis of CBA. The test implies that the potential (via compensation) should exist for a proposed project to make at least one person better off and none worse off. The use of the NPV as a criterion for optimality, however, is only valid in cases where there is a relatively high degree of certainty surrounding the costs and benefits of a project. The issue of the optimality and rationality of the decision will be raised further in Chapter 4.

### 2.2.2 Sensitivity Analysis

While the use of sensitivity analysis is often cited as the means by which CBA 'deals' with uncertainty it does not deal explicitly with uncertainty *per se*. For instance, although sensitivity analysis is useful as a means of demonstrating the effect of a variation in key parameters, it is more limited in relation to dealing explicitly with uncertainties at the *ex ante* stage of the decision process. While, as will be highlighted in the next chapter, it may be possible adequately to predict probability distributions for some of the variables within a cost–benefit analysis, for many parameters and in particular for combinations of parameters which make up the environmental outcomes of a proposed action, this is neither theoretically nor practically possible. It is this lack of predictability of many of the inputs (especially environmental) which urges the need to deal explicitly with uncertainty in the decision framework.

## 2.3   THEORETICAL ISSUES BEHIND COST–BENEFIT ANALYSIS

The basis of what to include in cost–benefit analysis is bound up with the assumptions made by neo-classical economics, in relation to the maximization of a social welfare function. The underlying basis of CBA is that it is used to select projects which will increase social welfare. The notion of welfare is based on a distinct conception of economic value which defines economic value in terms of utility, that is value arises if someone is made to feel better off in terms of their wants and desires. Positive economic value therefore arises when people feel better off, while negative economic value arises when people feel worse off. The utilities to be maximized depend, however, on the consumption levels of both marketed and non marketed goods. Thus what are considered positive impacts are either increases in the quantity or quality of goods that generate positive utility, or reductions in the price at which they are supplied. Costs include any decreases in the quality or quantity of goods that generate positive utility, increases in the price at which they are supplied, or opportunity costs which will be incurred as a result of the project (Hanley and Spash, 1993). The importance of valuing both marketed and non-marketed benefits and costs of a particular decision lies in the recognition that an effect on the utility of at least one individual is recorded.

An important assumption made by welfare theory is that preferences are substitutable. If the quantity of one element of an individual's bundle is reduced then it is possible to increase the quantity of some other element, so as to leave the individual no worse off after the change (Freeman, 1993). Substitutability is at the core of the economic concept of value, in that it is from the implied trade-offs that information is revealed about the values which people place on these goods. In order to carry out such substitutions individuals are assumed to rank the alternative bundles according to their preferences. The preference orderings can be represented by an unobservable continuous ordinal preference or utility function. Any policy that changes the consumption bundle so that utility increases, is measured by consumer surplus. This can be expressed either in terms of willingness to pay (WTP) or willingness to accept compensation (WTA). The use of a money metric measure of utility based on consumer surplus allows some expression of the intensity of preference to be exhibited by the individual.

An important issue that must be raised, is that of what the estimates of consumer surplus or willingness to pay are actually measuring, in relation to environmental services or functions and in particular where environmental goods are only substitutable up to a point. This issue can best be explained diagramatically. Figure 2.1 shows conventional supply (marginal cost) and demand (marginal benefit) curves for a marketed good or service. The area *PBQC* is the value that would show up in gross national product (market price times quantity). The cost of the production is the area under the supply curve, *CBQ*. The producer surplus or net rent of the resource is the area between the market price and the supply curve, *PBC*. The consumer surplus, the amount of welfare the consumer receives over and above the price paid in the market, is the area *ABP*. The total economic value of the resource is the sum of the producer and consumer surplus, or the area *ABC* (Costanza *et al.*, 1997b).

Because, as was highlighted earlier, many ecosystem services or functions are only substitutable up to a point, their demand curves in reality may look more like Figure 2.2. In such cases, as the quantity available approaches zero,

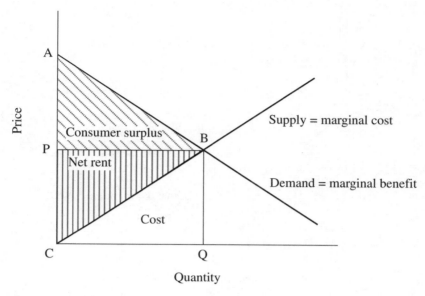

*Source*:   Costanza *et al.*, 1997b

*Figure 2.1   Conventional supply and demand curves for marketed goods*

demand and therefore consumer surplus (as well as total economic value) approaches infinity. A number of uncertainties exist due to substantial practical difficulties in estimating demand curves (Costanza *et al.*, 1997b). Furthermore supply curves of ecosystem services which cannot be increased or decreased by actions of the economy are more nearly vertical as shown in Figure 2.2. Difficulties in estimation therefore result in the likelihood that the estimates gained will be lower bound valuations of the 'true' value of a particular ecosystem. This is highlighted by the fact that the valuation assumes that there are no thresholds, discontinuities or irreversibilities in the ecosystem response functions, when in reality there is a large degree of uncertainty surrounding the presence and impacts of disequilibrium effects. As a result in practice valuation methods assume that the demand and supply curves will look something like Figure 2.1, whereas in reality supply curves for ecosystems are more nearly inelastic, approaching infinity as the quantity of the environmental resource goes to zero. In such cases the consumer and producer surplus and thereby the total value of ecosystem services would also approach infinity (Costanza *et al.*, 1997b).

Uncertainty surrounding the supply of ecosystem services and functions and the presence of possible thresholds could therefore have serious implica-

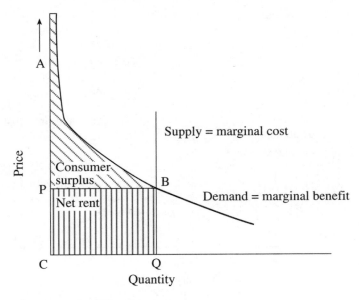

*Source*:   Costanza *et al.*, 1997b

*Figure 2.2   Supply and demand curves for ecosystem services*

tions for the reliability of valuation estimations gained. Moreover, while
ideally the unit value of an ecosystem would be calculated from the sum of
consumer and producer surplus, often the net rent or producer surplus and/or
price times quantity is used as a measure when the first measure is not
available. Given that the demand curve for ecosystem services looks more
like Figure 2.2 than Figure 2.1, then the estimate of area *PBQC* is a conservative estimate of *ABC*. All these factors point us towards the reality that
valuation estimates will be lower bound estimates of the total economic value
of an ecosystem, with the potential size of the error increasing in relation to
the degree of uncertainty surrounding a particular ecosystem.

### 2.3.1   Commensurability and Consumer Sovereignty in Decision Making

A fundamental basis of the measurement of economic value is the assumption of commensurability. Commensurability implies that it is possible to
equate environmental value expressed through monetary preferences with
ordinary goods and services. Implicit in the use of environmental valuation
and cost–benefit analysis is therefore the assumption that individuals regard

features and uses of the natural environment as consumption commodities on an equal footing with ordinary commodities purchased in markets. This is the equivalent of saying that an individual is best able to decide between a preference for, say, improved air quality over that for a new car. This property of substitutability is at the core of the economic concept of value in that it is from the trade-off ratios implied by the substitution of goods that information is revealed about the values that people place on these goods.

There are a number of issues relating to the assumption of commensurability that merit further attention. The first is that individuals may be unwilling to trade off increases/decreases in the quantity of an environmental good against losses/gains in income. For example individuals may refuse to trade off the loss of particular species against a measure of income, that is they exhibit lexicographic preferences (Spash and Hanley, 1995). Lexicographic preferences are such that WTA would be infinite and WTP would equal the entire budget, and imply that an approach built around the Kaldor–Hicks potential compensation test becomes inoperable once the compensatory amounts become infinite (Spash and Hanley, 1995).

A second issue that is very important in relation to the problem of uncertainty is that many individuals may not sufficiently understand a complex issue such as biodiversity loss and hence may not be able to make the trade-off decisions required. Furthermore, even when consumers are sufficiently informed, a high degree of uncertainty surrounding the particular benefits, for example, of biodiversity restricts their ability to make such choices. Environmental goods such as biodiversity often have characteristics which are unclear, and the relationship that biodiversity has in terms of the individual's welfare or utility is often vague and removed from everyday experiences of life. As a result many consumers may not understand all of the attributes of the ecosystem that are necessary to support the ability of the natural system to produce those services from which they benefit directly or indirectly (Bingham *et al.*, 1995).

Consequently, while for certain well defined environmental goods it would be fair to argue that they can be seen as commensurable with marketed goods, for other less tangible services, provided by ecosystems, this may be more problematic. Furthermore the assumption of commensurability, if applied directly to the use of CBA as a decision-making criterion (based on NPV) would imply that all resources are substitutable, breaking any constraints imposed by a definition of sustainability which implies non-declining natural capital. As Russell (1995) argues, the acceptance of physically characterized constraints as part of the definition of sustainability, for example in the identification of a non-substitutable element of natural capital, may not be able to be characterized in the language of individual preferences. Consequently, the use of cost–benefit analysis as a strict decision criterion, especially in relation to crucial life-supporting functions that are not substitutable, would appear problematic.

## Consumer sovereignty

Closely linked to the assumption of commensurability is the notion of consumer sovereignty, which implies that the individual is best able to make choices with respect to preferences between marketed and non-marketed goods that are consistent with his/her own welfare. However, in relation to environmental goods particularly, where a high degree of uncertainty is faced, questions are raised over the extent to which consumers should be given sovereignty over alternative states of nature by making choices based on the assumption of commensurability (Common, 1995). Questions are frequently raised from disciplines outside economics, such as ecology, over whether economic valuation alone can adequately capture all that decision makers need to know to confront irreversible ecosystem modifications that could have long-term economic and social repercussions. It would appear that as yet we do not have 'anything like a full picture of the mutually exclusive set of motivations underlying individual preferences for environmental goods' (Barbier *et al.*, 1995: p. 836).

Even if one believes that the assumption of commensurability does hold, objections to consumer sovereignty can be made on an ethical basis (Blamey and Common, 1994). One major division, highlighted by Sagoff (1988), is in the distinction between individual and citizen preferences. Thus, for example, it is argued that an individual will distinguish between acting as a consumer and a citizen. It is important to recognize that people may play different roles when valuing goods, for example as a decision maker or as a private agent (Bingham *et al.*, 1995).

The different economic and ecological scales at work pose further problems over the reliability of using economic preferences as a basis for welfare measurement in that the broader ecological effects of environmental change often go beyond the traditional calculation and aggregation of welfare measures. Problems therefore remain regarding the extent to which focusing on the individual level of welfare is indeed compatible with valuing the whole ecosystem (Norton, 1995). This argument can be extended to situations of environmental uncertainty in that it could be argued that the way in which an individual adjusts his/her preferences in the face of uncertainty is very different to that of a citizen acting on behalf of society. If this is the case, then this poses a number of largely unanswered problems for the valuation of public goods such as biodiversity conservation.

While Sagoff (1988) may overstate his case by denying that many decisions are made on an economic basis, he does highlight some of the limitations and uncertainties that will still be present when dealing with valuation estimates from complex ecosystems. Although it is important not to disregard individual preferences, it should be also recognized, as Common (1995) argues, that individual preferences are in a large way socially determined. Consequently those preferences alone cannot be used as independent criteria (as implied by the use of an additive social welfare function in CBA) for social ranking arrangements. Again these arguments would suggest that cost–benefit analysis should be interpreted more as a framework for decision making rather than as a strict decision-making rule.

### 2.3.2  Using an Additive Welfare Function

An important issue that will be briefly noted is that net present value is used as an additive value function, where the different dimensions are aggregated using a simple linear weighting rule. The assumption of commensurability implies that the attributes of the utility function, which is maximized by the individual, exhibit the property of preference independence in that the substitutability or trade-off ratios implied between two attributes are independent of the values of the other attributes (Munda, 1996). This implies the ability to separate values, and the use of the additive value function permits the assessment of the marginal contribution of each attribute separately. The marginal value of each attribute can then be added together to yield a total value.

In relation to many environmental attributes this approach would not be consistent with the dynamics of ecosystems which are often non linear. Thus, for example, the combined costs of the loss of a particular mix of species, essential in relation to the resilience of an ecosystem, are likely to be more than the marginal cost of the loss of one particular species. Because there is a large degree of uncertainty surrounding the interaction and mixing of species as well as the exact nature of the biological and chemical flows in an ecosystem, problems are posed for the use of a linear additive function, in that it may underestimate the overall consequences of a particular impact. To illustrate, it is likely that the cumulative effect of species loss in relation to the effect on ecosystem services and functions is greater in value terms than the addition of the individual value of particular species.

The assumption of perfect substitutability inherent in the notion of commensurability would therefore seem to be at odds with the dynamics of complex ecosystems in that one-for-one substitutions between environmental attributes and marketed goods may not be valid when the cumulative impact of losses in environmental attributes is taken into account. Alternatively as was pointed out in Chapter 1, the substitution between key ecosystem components and human capital may simply not be technically possible or desirable. The use of CBA as a decision criterion based on NPV would therefore be faced with additional theoretical problems, which would again point to its interpretation as a more general decision framework.

### 2.3.3 Discounting

The use of discounting in cost–benefit analysis takes into account two under-lying assumptions, first that individuals exhibit a time preference for present rather than future consumption, and second that there is a positive rate of return on capital (which is normally taken as the rate of interest) (Munasinghe, 1993a). Discounting is used by economics in order to compare the total stock of capital over time and thus assess values measured at different time inter-vals. Although the use of discounting raises a number of contentious issues such as its effect on inter-generational equity, the main concern here is that from a theoretical perspective, the choice of discount rate would appear to have major implications with respect to uncertainty. A high discount rate will in effect banish uncertainty regarding future outcomes from detailed consid-eration. In this sense a high rate of discount may in fact screen away many of the long-term uncertainties of a project. However, as will be highlighted in the following chapter, it is often the long-term results of the cumulative effects of a project that are potentially the most catastrophic. The problem of discounting from an ecological perspective is that species with a growth rate of less than the mortality rate will be optimally driven to extinction unless the growth rate of the value of the species sufficiently compensates for this difference, or their extraction is regulated (Barbier *et al.*, 1995). However, such theoretical problems are countered by the practical issue of choosing an alternative 'correct' discount rate, which inevitably implies the making of value judgements. This again weakens arguments that favour the use of CBA as a decision rule and points to the realization that concerns over the uncer-tainties present in any project will have to be accounted for in the context of a more general framework and model of decision making under uncertainty.

## 2.4 INTRODUCTION TO ENVIRONMENTAL VALUATION

Chapter 1 noted that there are a number of critical environmental services or functions which have a significant impact in terms of human welfare, but which are external to the market. The non-existence of well functioning markets for biological resources means that there is no ready index of value and that the true value of the environment to society is often not represented adequately through market signals or more specifically prices (Pearce and Turner, 1990). This issue poses a problem for standard cost–benefit analysis in that, for the criterion of efficiency to be met, all the relevant dimensions underlying the costs and benefits must be identified (Munda, 1996). So long as the environmental impacts of a project or policy cause an increase or decrease in the level of welfare of at least one person in the relevant population, or change the level or quality of some positively valued commodity, then they must be included in the analysis (Hanley and Spash, 1993). It is in response to the need to gain estimates of the social value of environmental services and functions that the field of environmental valuation has been developed.

In a more general sense the need to value the environment stems from the perception that the allocation of biological resources on the basis of current market signals is inefficient and inequitable and leads to losses in social welfare (Barbier *et al.*, 1995). The valuation exercise therefore aims to confront resource users with the full social cost of their behaviour and enables those who invest in conservation to appropriate the benefits (Barbier *et al.*, 1995). The debate surrounding the theory and practice of environmental valuation, however, is without doubt the most controversial aspect of environmental economics. Although this book side-steps the extensive literature surrounding this debate, it is argued that all decisions concerning the allocation of environmental resources will necessarily imply some form of valuation. Thus the use of money as a unit of valuation is merely a device of convenience, rather than an implicit statement that money is all that matters (Hanley and Spash, 1993). The choice comes down to one of whether or not such valuations should be made explicit. Thus: 'we can do them with an explicit acknowledgement of the huge uncertainties involved or not; but as long as we are forced to make choices about the use of resources we are valuing those resources' (Costanza *et al.*, 1997b: p. xxi).

The use of valuation does, where reliable, improve the amount and quality of the information to the decision maker. As such, both environmental and non-environmental values are relied upon by most models of decision making under uncertainty, and indeed as has been pointed out, are utilized in the application of the Shackle model to the case study in Belize. The purpose of this section is not to provide an in depth review of the many theoretical and methodological problems faced in environmental valuation, but instead to provide a basis on which the notion of valuation uncertainty can be developed in the next chapter. The debate on valuation as well as evaluations of the particular methods employed is left to the extensive literature on the topic.

### 2.4.1 Defining Value

Value can be seen to have two major components which can then be further subdivided depending on the particular resource. The first type of value is intrinsic value, which is value that exists independent of the valuer, that is, an environmental resource or attribute has a value in its own right. The second type of value is anthropocentric value. This does not mean, however, that all ecosystem values derive from direct human use, nor that there is no intrinsic value in the environment, only that it is impossible to measure non-anthropocentric value. As Chapter 1 highlighted, many of the most important functions are in fact related to the underlying life-supporting services that are provided. Therefore it is very important to gather sufficient information about ecosystem values that include production functions. These functions are broadly enough defined to include structures and processes that transform matter and energy inputs into ecosystem services that are either directly valued by people or are important in supporting the underlying features of the ecological system that is valued (Bingham *et al.*, 1995). However, the value of ecological services, for example those encapsulated by biodiversity, will depend on many other things besides ecological significance. Value will vary from one place to another and with different cultures. Consequently the value given for example to biodiversity will not only determine its worth in any given society, but also how it is used or abused (Barbier *et al.*, 1995).

### 2.4.2    A Typology of Value

Biological resources can be seen to be of value either directly (they are used directly in consumption or production) or indirectly (they support measures which have direct value). In addition ecological resources also have non-use or passive use value, which is motivated by ethical considerations. If we take the example of a forest, direct use value (DUV) is derived from the extraction of timber and other goods from the forest, and indirect use value (IUV) would relate to the employment and/or recreation that is created from primary use. Two other components of use value have been identified by environmental economists, namely option value (OV) and quasi option value (QOV). Option value relates to the value of retaining an option for making use of a resource in the future, where losses would be irreversible (Weisbrod, 1964; Bishop, 1982; Kristrom, 1990). Quasi option value is defined as the value of the future information protected by preserving a resource (Arrow and Fisher, 1974; Fisher and Hanemann, 1987). Option value and quasi option values have been cited as means of 'dealing' with uncertainty within the valuation process, and will be critically assessed in Chapter 4.

Environmental economists have extended utilitarian use value by including the notion of non-use values. Non-use value can be subdivided into two further categories, namely bequest value (BV) and existence value (EV) (Brown, 1990; Randall, 1991). Bequest value can be defined as the desire to pass on to the next generation or heirs the ability to use or enjoy an environmental resource, to the same extent as at present. Existence value refers to the worth that an individual places on the preservation of some asset which will never be directly used by future generations. By its very nature, existence value is altruistic, covering for instance the pleasure that is derived from knowing that certain species exist, for example blue whales. It is also evident that many environmental resources will also be attributed with a number of cultural and spiritual values (Young, 1995). Cultural values may encompass use values, through direct use of an environmental resource which may be peculiar to a particular indigenous group and/or non-use values in terms of the spiritual use or attachment of spiritual/cultural feelings towards a particular environmental resource. The problem with estimating these values is that it is often difficult to equate them with monetary value as well as to be sure to what extent they are included by environmental valuation as a component, for example, of existence value (Young, 1995).

These values constitute a broadly accepted taxonomy of values used by environmental economists which, when aggregated, can be termed 'total economic value' (TEV). The components of this are illustrated in Figure 2.3. It is important to point out that TEV does not constitute total value (TV). This latter concept is measured by the anthropocentric value (TEV) and the non-anthropocentric instrumental or primary value (PV). This point underlines the sense that economic valuation of the environment will represent only a partial value.

On a conceptual as well as practical basis, the most difficult values to deal with are those values which are not consumed directly. First these consist of indirect use values, for example the ecological services that play an indirect function in the production of a marketed commodity. The role of mangroves as a nursery for seafood stocks is a good example of this. The second category consists of non-use values, which are not consumed directly or indirectly and are often highly intangible. Underlying all this full range of values is what has been termed by Turner (1995) as primary value or insurance value (Barbier *et al.*, 1995). Primary value encapsulates the

$$TEV = f\ (\ \overbrace{DUV, IUV, OV, QO}^{\text{use value}},\ \overbrace{BV,\ EV}^{\text{non-use value}}\ )$$

$$TV = g\ \underbrace{(\ PV,}_{\substack{\text{non-anthropocentric} \\ \text{instrumental value}}}\ \underbrace{TEV\ )}_{\substack{\text{anthropocentric} \\ \text{value}}}$$

*Source*:  Barbier *et al.*, 1995

*Figure 2.3   Total environmental value and total economic value*

prior value of the system or the components that maintain the resilience of the system that is the basis for the flow of other direct and indirect values. In this sense the system has an insurance value in allowing the system to maintain the flow of valued services and functions in the face of change. The notion of primary value is crucial in relation to the problem of uncertainty, in that it is often the primary value of biological resources on which the flow of all other values depends, which is dependent on the complex interactions of species within the ecosystem. Traditionally there has been a lack of mechanisms to incorporate such values into decision making and many have been ignored due to limited appreciation of the importance of the values to ecological sustainability. This emphasizes the point that total economic value only forms a lower band on the social value of biological resources (Barbier *et al.*, 1995).

In practice the range of services provided by ecosystem functions, that is climate moderation and water purification, lies somewhere between primary and secondary values, as although they are tangible they are poorly estimated by environmental scientists and incompletely valued by current valuation methods. It is apparent, however, that the value of these poorly characterized services is potentially quite large (Bingham *et al.*, 1995: p. 79). The existence of complex linkages between the primary value and total economic value of a biological resource results in the problem of valuation uncertainty, which will be dealt with in detail in the next chapter.

## 2.5   COST–BENEFIT ANALYSIS AS AN INTEGRATED DECISION-MAKING FRAMEWORK

In this chapter some of the potential weaknesses and limitations surrounding both the theory and practice of cost–benefit analysis and valuation have been pointed out. The majority of the criticisms of CBA are based on its use as a strict decision criterion based on the NPV rule. It is this strict interpretation of CBA in terms of efficiency and optimality that is most questionable in relation to the problem of environmental uncertainty. As highlighted in Chapter 1, the objective of efficiency is not necessarily compatible with sustainability objectives such as ecosystem resilience, requiring trade-offs to be made. Moreover, while the incorporation of environmental values into cost–benefit analysis aids the attainment of the efficiency criteria, no special treatment of the environment is given (Hanley, 1995). Thus passing the Kaldor–Hicks test is not a sufficient condition for the sustainability of a project or policy, if the sustainability objective is one of non-declining natural capital. Furthermore, the dynamic interdependence of the ecological economic system highlighted in Chapter 1 may imply that strict economic optimizing may actually lead to a decrease in the resilience of ecosystems, contradicting another objective of sustainability (Perrings, 1987; Common and Perrings, 1992).

It is the presence of uncertainty, however, that is crucial in relation to how the use of cost–benefit analysis is interpreted. In the presence of uncertainty, its ability to deal with problems of non-declining natural capital and irreversibility will be limited. Consequently the use of NPV as a single decision criterion in order to find an optimal solution to maximizing social welfare is problematic and at worse nonsensical for situations where the set of project/ policy alternatives considered are not well defined and the alternatives are all mutually exclusive. The reality for many environmental policies or projects is that the necessary conditions which allow CBA to be used as an optimal decision framework are not present, due to uncertainties about both the environmental effects of a particular project or policy and the lack of information about the value of any changes.

However, rather than rejecting the use of cost–benefit analysis outright, a wider interpretation of CBA can be given in which the focus is not so much on its use as an absolute decision criterion, but as a way of organizing and consolidating all the available data on a project (Common, 1995). This is especially the case where multiple sources of market failure are evident and there is no confidence about the use of the NPV criterion as a means of ranking alternative social choices over environmental states. Moreover, even in the unlikely scenario that ecosystem services are perfectly understood and accordingly evaluated in monetary units, it is unlikely that monetary valuation alone would adequately capture all that decision makers need to know to confront irreversible ecosystem modifications that could have serious long-term economic and social repercussions. As a result an important issue in any integrated framework for making decisions is the need to clarify the situations where conventional economic values are sufficient and where broader human values, including non-monetary values, are more appropriate. As a consequence rather than focusing on CBA as a strict efficiency/optimality criterion, a more general framework needs to be adopted to consider projects in relation to socially agreed objectives.

With the emphasis on the use of CBA shifted from that of a simple decision rule to that of a framework which incorporates a set of procedures to help organize available information, many of the theoretical and practical concerns of using traditional cost–benefit analysis are answered. Moreover valuation is given a different role that need not necessarily imply making trade-offs between marketed and non-marketed goods. A further advantage of interpreting CBA simply as a tool for organizing and expressing information about a particular project or policy under consideration is that room is given for more explicit attention to uncertainty, once estimates of the relevant costs and benefits (including environmental costs and benefits) have been obtained.

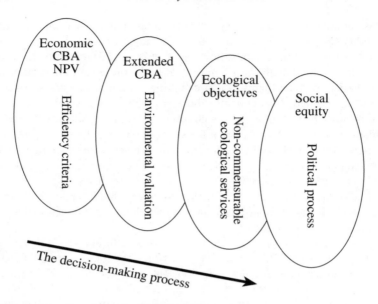

*Figure 2.4    Stages in decision making*

A framework that can therefore be envisaged is one in which a number of stages in the decision-making process can be identified. For example, in the first stage the project could be put through a strict economic analysis where the use of an NPV criterion will be of value. As the number of considerations that CBA focuses on increases, the project will have to be considered in respect of different objectives, so the second stage could be the use of an extended cost–benefit analysis which would incorporate environmental valuation estimates. In this stage the use of the NPV criterion would be of limited use, if at all applicable. Further stages could include consideration of the non-commensurable life-supporting services and social objectives such as equity considerations; a schematic model of such an approach is shown in Figure 2.4.

What any decision-making framework inevitably involves is the equating of often incommensurable units or different objectives. Whatever form the ranking of alternatives takes, it cannot be conducted without the introduction of value judgements. Consequently rather than focusing on the actual decision *per se* which will inevitably involve some form of value judgement, the emphasis turns to an analysis of the decision-making process. This recognition is important in providing a context for explaining the way in which environmental decisions are made, as well as a context in which prescriptions on the way that decisions should be made can be advanced. Within such a decision-making framework the concern in this book is on the way in which uncertainty is evaluated within the decision-making process.[1]

## NOTE

1. Inevitably any decision-making process will deal with personal and political agendas, stakeholder and complex power relationships. A caveat is made here in that while crucial to the decision-making process, this essential political element of the decision making is outside the scope and focus of the book, and will only be dealt with in a cursory manner.

# 3.   Environmental uncertainty

## 3.1   INTRODUCTION

In the previous chapters the nature of the uncertainty problem faced in many environmental issues has been highlighted and the decision-making context in which environmental uncertainty will ultimately dealt with, outlined. A basic premise of this book is that the type of uncertainty faced in many decisions concerning the environment is such that an alternative approach to risk-based models will be required. This assertion is based on the realization that there are a number of different modalities of uncertainty, reflecting the notion that in any given decision the type and level of uncertainty will often vary. This chapter is concerned therefore with developing a more comprehensive theory and definition of uncertainty and in particular environmental uncertainty, which gives a firm basis on which a critique of existing models can be developed.

This chapter is organized into two main sections. The first considers the concept of uncertainty in a general fashion, before developing a framework which will allow the different modalities of uncertainty to be identified. The next stage is to use this framework to highlight some of the different types of uncertainty such as ecological uncertainty and valuation uncertainty, faced in environmental policy making.

## 3.2   CONCEPTUALIZING UNCERTAINTY

The presence of uncertainty in many choices and decisions taken both by individuals and by society would appear irrefutable. Before an attempt can be made to provide explanations or prescriptions of how decision makers do and should account for uncertainty and more specifically environmental uncertainty, a crucial step is to conceptualize uncertainty at an epistemological level. It is only by developing a thorough conceptualization of what is meant by uncertainty and what the different modalities of uncertainty imply for decision makers, that an adequate basis will be provided on which to evaluate the different models attempting to deal with uncertainty.

Most mainstream economic approaches tend, however, to treat the way that uncertainty is conceptualized as a secondary task. While some changes are evident in the environmental-economics literature, too often the tendency is to treat uncertainty as a phenomenon which can be handled within a probability framework, without questioning whether such an approach is suitable or applicable to the particular uncertainty problem in question. More recently a number of contributions from environmental economics and in particular ecological economics have begun to recognize the problem of uncertainty (see for example the important contributions made by: Perrings, 1989, 1997b; Costanza, 1994; Ehrlich, 1994; Vercelli, 1995; Faucheux and Froger, 1995). This implies an increasing readiness to accept that, for particular uncertainty problems, there may be a need to go beyond to the use of probability and accompanying traditional decision-making paradigms. This admission highlights a recurrent theme in the environmental literature, namely that traditional economic modelling approaches are not well equipped to deal with the type of uncertainty often faced in environmental decision making.

Amongst these authors Vercelli (1995) and Faucheux and Froger (1995) are notable in recognizing the need to conceptualize uncertainty and its place in a rational decision-making framework. Perrings (1989, 1997b) and Dalmazzone (1995) have emphasized the need to recognize the problem of uncertainty explicitly and suggest that there is a need to look to alternative frameworks such as Shackle's. Even so, much of the literature in which conceptualizations of uncertainty are found forms part of the wider economic literature relating to expectations and uncertainty. Such work has a long history stretching from Keynes (1921), Knight (1921) and of course Shackle (1949, 1955, 1961) to more recent contributions from Ford (1983, 1987, 1994), Lawson (1988, 1997) and Davidson (1996).

Underlying the different definitions and usages of uncertainty are different conceptualizations of the reality within which an individual operates and on which his or her expectations in the face of uncertainty are formed. It is these different conceptualizations which influence the extent to which uncertainty is tied up with the notion of probability. In essence two main concepts of reality can be identified and these are highlighted by Figure 3.1. The first is that of an *immutable* reality which is not susceptible to change induced by human actions and which can be fully described by unchanging objective conditional probability functions (Davidson, 1996). A distinction is often made between models which assume that the future is known or is at least knowable, and those which accept that in the short run the future is not completely known due to limitations in the ability of humans to process all of the available information. It is this latter type of model which encompasses the dominant literature in economics based on expected utility. Thus in this concept of reality the economic and environmental system is viewed as ergodic, in that the presumption is made of a 'pre-programmed stable, con-

---

A. *Immutable reality*

Type 1.
Rational Expectations school

The future is known or at least knowable in both the short and long run.
Probability as knowledge is an object of external knowledge.
Reality is predetermined.

Type 2.
Subjectivists

In the short run the future is not completely known, even although in the long run reality is predetermined and thus knowable.
Probability is a property of knowledge.

B. *Transmutable reality*

Creative reality. Some aspect of reality will be created by human action or other stimuli today or in the future. The future cannot be corralled by probability.

---

*Source*:  Adapted from Davidson, 1996 and Lawson, 1988

*Figure 3.1   Concepts of economic reality*

servative system where the past, present and future reality are predetermined whether the system is stochastic or not' (Davidson, 1996: p. 481).

This concept of reality lends itself to a solely probabilistic interpretation of uncertainty, in which all future outcomes are captured either by an objective probability distribution or a subjective distribution. The subjective expectations are captured usually, although not always, in the form of Bayesian subjective probabilities. As will be highlighted later, the crucial assumption is that, although in the short run subjective probabilities need not coincide with the presumed immutable objective probabilities, in the long run the objective and subjective probabilities will tend to coincide. Although Knight (1921) is slightly ambiguous on the matter, it would appear that his distinction of risk and uncertainty can be linked to the distinction between the two types of immutable reality concepts. Thus uncertainty comes down to a lack of knowledge about a predetermined external reality. Uncertainty only exists because of the failure of humans to process information which, while not known, is knowable.

The second conceptualization of reality, which Davidson (1996) terms *transmutable* or creative reality, is that in which some aspect of the economic and, by extension, environmental future will be created by human action today or in the future. In Keynes' (1973) view, reality is one in which individuals, groups or societies can permanently change the future. In such a non-ergodic environment, even if agents or decision makers have the capacity to obtain and statistically process information regarding past and current outcomes, this information does not and cannot provide reliable data for forecasting the future. Hicks (1979), for example, concludes that stochastic methods are inapplicable in this situation. If the system is ergodic and the future of such a system is not only uncertain but transmutable then as Keynes wrote: 'There is no scientific basis to form any calculable probability whatever. We simply do not know' (Keynes, 1973: p. 114).

These two different conceptualizations of the nature of reality are mirrored when we look at problems in a ecological context. For instance for Perrings (1997b) uncertainty is derived from measurement error, due to the difficulty of constantly measuring state variables. The presumption is of an immutable reality in which, although the system is too complex to understand fully, the relationship between the key elements of the system is predetermined. The second conceptualization of uncertainty in relation to ecosystems stresses what Shackle would term the uniqueness of reality. This is derived from the evolutionary nature of the ecological system, in that even if the structure of such a system is knowable, the dynamics and interactions of the system, as well as its interaction with the economic system, result in a constantly changing structure. Therefore changes in the system are not predetermined from past changes.

Although tackling the question of uncertainty at a epistemological level is a crucial first step in helping us to handle uncertainty and eventually the problem of environmental uncertainty, practical problems in modelling emerge because there is a tendency to apply only one concept of reality to all parts of the economic–ecological system. Such an approach leads to a position whereby all situations of uncertainty are characterized by the use of a probability distribution, or where the system is so transmutable and fundamentally uncertain that uncertainty can never be reduced to situations of probabilistic risk. A central hypothesis in this book is that in order to deal practically with uncertainty in decision making, any conceptualization of uncertainty must recognize that elements of the environmental–economic system may vary in the type and modality of uncertainty by which they are characterized. Certain variables may indeed be reducible to situations where the use of probability may be relevant. Clearly, however, when combinations of variables or outcomes are considered or even the dynamics of the whole system itself, it is necessary to accept that we are dealing with a future that is not predetermined in the sense that the dynamics of the system itself, combined with the actions and activities of humans, mean that the use of a probability framework is in effect meaningless. An important step in developing a framework for dealing with uncertainty in environmental decision making will therefore be in defining the nature of the uncertainty which is faced in a particular decision problem.

### 3.2.1 Defining Uncertainty

Once the notion of uncertainty has been approached at an epistemological level it becomes more apparent that, while uncertainty is often cited by authors in relation to a particular problem, what they imply by uncertainty is invariably not clarified. Most notably 'risk' and 'uncertainty' are often used interchangeably in the literature. An attempt will be made in this section to disentangle the competing notions of uncertainty and to provide the basis on which a more thorough conceptualization of the different modalities of uncertainty can be provided.

A useful starting point for defining uncertainty is provided by the classical contributions of Knight (1921) and Keynes (1936), who distinguished between a weak version of uncertainty, which they termed '*risk*' and a stronger version which they termed '*uncertainty*'. Unfortunately neo-classical economics, starting with von Neumann and Morgenstern (1944), has constantly blurred this distinction, resulting in the two terms being used interchangeably in the literature, with uncertainty usually referring to Knight–Keynes risk (Williams and Findlay, 1986). This confusion stems from three basic interpretations of risk in relation to uncertainty. The first usage encompasses all modalities of uncertainty (all uncertainty being reducible to risk). In such cases the notion of uncertainty is used interchangeably with that of risk. The second definition of risk is based on situations in which the full set of $j$ outcomes is known and for which a probability distribution can be defined, so uncertainty is defined as a situation where the full range of outcomes is unknown. The third, which is important to note on a more practical level, refers to the possible negative consequences of an uncertain action. According to this last usage any type or modality of uncertainty can therefore imply risk (Vercelli, 1995).

Building on the work of Vercelli (1995), Froger and Zyla (1994), and Faucheux and Froger (1995), to attempt to clarify this situation particularly in relation to the first two definitions, the term *hard uncertainty* (Vercelli, 1995) will be used to define situations where either 1) the set of all possible outcomes or future states is unknown (Dow, 1993) or 2) where the full set of outcomes is known, but the probability distribution of all possible outcomes of the action is unknown or is not fully definable for a lack of reliable information. *Soft uncertainty* or *risk* is used to define situations where 1) the set of all possible outcomes of an action is known and 2) the probability distribution of all possible outcomes is also known. To keep matters clear in the following text, 'risk' will imply the negative consequences of an uncertain action.

It should be noted that the definition of hard uncertainty will encompass both the second type of model based on conceptions of immutable reality and conceptions based on transmutable reality. Whether one believes that, because reality is so complex, decision makers cannot have more than a partial, possibly incorrect, perception or knowledge about relevant behavioural matters of the past and the present, or that the future cannot be known, due to the transmutable nature of reality, a situation of hard uncertainty is still faced.

### 3.2.2 The Different Modalities of Uncertainty

Arguably many of the difficulties both in conceptualizing uncertainty, as well as in the use of particular models of uncertainty is derived from the fact that in reality the type or modality of uncertainty faced in any given choice or decision varies (Faucheux and Froger, 1995). It is the recognition that there are in fact different modalities of uncertainty that will help us to move forward in dealing explicitly with environmental uncertainty. This section provides a framework in which the different modalities of uncertainty can be classified. In the process it is hoped that some of the confusion surrounding definitions of uncertainty will be cleared up.

Based on the above distinction between hard uncertainty and soft uncertainty, a number of different criteria can be used to distinguish between the different modalities faced in any uncertain situation. Figure 3.2 shows diagramatically the different modalities of uncertainty as classified by four different criteria, namely divisibility, seriability, distributionality and additivity. From situations of complete certainty there is a range of situations running through soft uncertainty or risk to hard uncertainty and finally ignorance (Faucheux and Froger, 1995).[1] It is progressively more difficult for the decision maker to come to a decision as one moves from the bottom right hand corner to the upper left corner of the figure.

The characteristics which define the different modalities of uncertainty are summarized as follows.

### Degree of knowledge of future outcomes

The first means of distinguishing between the different modalities of uncertainty is based on the degree of knowledge about the future outcomes of any action. In the case of certainty the possible effects of an action have been reduced to one outcome or variable. In soft uncertainty the complete set of possible outcomes of any action is known. In contrast, in cases of hard uncertainty only an incomplete set of outcomes is hypothesized, with some of the outcomes remaining unanticipated. In the extreme case of uncertainty, all

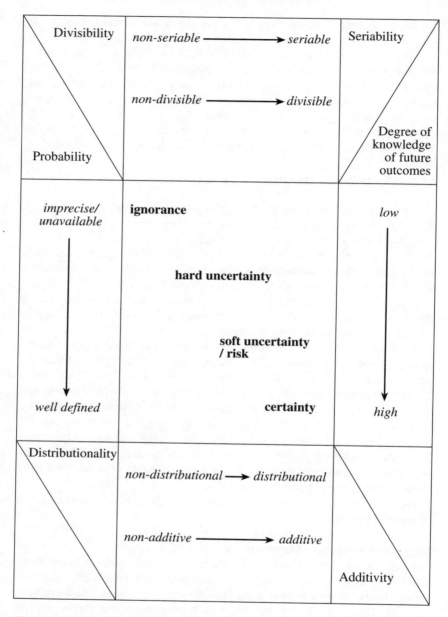

*Figure 3.2    The modalities of uncertainty*

possible outcomes are unanticipated, so that the decision is characterized by ignorance.

## Divisibility

A further modality of uncertainty is based on whether the action is divisible or not. Divisible actions relate to ones that are possible to repeat under the same underlying conditions to produce a range of outcomes. This is based on the notion of relative frequency and is only applicable to roulette-type experiments for which it is possible to generate objective probabilities. It should be pointed out, however, that this type of property is of little use if we want to know what the next outcome will be. This point is particularly true for irreversible actions with respect to the environment, where the notion of relative frequency probability is meaningless, because the action cannot be repeated. Moreover, due to the dynamic nature of economic–environmental interactions, the structure or generating mechanism is not fixed as is the case for roulette-type experiments. This means that however small the change, the action cannot be repeated under exactly the same conditions. A non-divisible action is therefore defined as one which is unprecedented or non-repeatable.

## Seriability

Some events, while non-divisible, can be pooled with other non-divisible experiments. The classic example of this is that of life expectancy, which for any particular individual is necessarily uncertain. However, from the perspective of an insurance company the endowment policy of an individual can be pooled with endowment policies on other people's lives. These are termed seriable actions or experiments. In such situations the uncertainty is effectively redistributed among a class of subjects. Pooling environmental services is often impossible due to their inherent public good nature. For example the effect of biodiversity loss will affect society as a whole rather than just one individual. In addition the uniqueness of many environmental services or functions makes polling impossible.

## Distributionality and additivity

The final criteria on which the different types of uncertainty are based are those of distributionality and additivity. The distributionality condition requires that the complete set of events is known and that the probabilities (subjective or objective) should add up to unity. In the case of an additive event, because the full set of outcomes is known, it is possible to add together the probabilities, which implies that the number of outcomes will affect the probability of each alternative. This is in effect the equivalent of taking a weighted average of all the possible outcomes. In the case of hard uncertainty where the action is non-divisible, Shackle (1961) argues that this approach makes no sense, in that the outcomes are rivals which deny and exclude each other.

**Probability distribution**
The presence of the above characteristics determines whether probability can be applied or not as the appropriate measure. As will be argued, the different modes of uncertainty are fundamental in answering this question. It is suffi-cient to say at this point that in situations characterized by certainty a unique and fully reliable (Faucheux and Froger, 1995) probability distribution is reduced to one variable. In the case of soft uncertainty a unique and reliable probability distribution is available for all the outcomes. In the case of hard uncertainty the use of probability is not applicable. The limiting case of hard uncertainty, that of near ignorance, is seen as '*crucial*' by Shackle (1955, 1961) as there exists no historical precedent for a certain activity. Conse-quently there exists no basis on which to identify all the possible outcomes or to construct a probability distribution of those outcomes.

## 3.3   ENVIRONMENTAL UNCERTAINTY

Now that a framework for defining the different modalities of uncertainty has been developed, it will be possible to go in greater depth into the problem of environmental uncertainty faced in many policy decisions and to demonstrate that often decisions regarding the environment are within the realm of hard uncertainty or ignorance, rather than soft uncertainty. Arguably there are no or very few environmental decisions which are made in the context of cer-tainty. Environmental uncertainty comprises both ecological uncertainty and valuation uncertainty. The former relates to uncertainty about the dynam-ics of the ecological system and the ecological consequences of human induced change. The latter arises as a result of uncertainty over the welfare implications for societies or the value to society of changes to existing ecological systems. Environmental uncertainty is conditioned therefore by the interconnectedness of the ecological–economic system discussed in the first chapter. More particularly uncertainty exists in relation to how changes to the dynamics of one system will affect the other. Although in what will follow, what have been termed ecological and valuation uncertainty will be discussed separately, it should be stressed that both derive from the interconnectedness of the ecological and economic system over different spatial and temporal scales. The interrelation of the two will be demonstrated intuitively in the next section on biodiversity.

### 3.3.1  Biodiversity

One of the main concerns of the sustainable development discourse highlighted in Chapter 1 is that of biodiversity. Decisions which could result in
biodiversity loss are particularly good examples of policy choices which are
characterized by hard uncertainty rather than soft uncertainty or risk. The loss
of a particular species as well as combinations of species that could be vital
in relation to the production of certain ecological functions or services, is a
unique event which cannot be repeated (that is, is not divisible). It is irreversible and only an incomplete set of outcomes for the action can be anticipated.
Such an event would be incorrectly represented by an additive and distributional measure of uncertainty such as probability (subjective or objective).
Moreover, even if on a theoretical basis it was correct to apply the notion of
probability, the lack of information would mean that on a practical basis the
derivation of probabilities would not only be very difficult, but, even if
obtained, unreliable. The decision maker is therefore faced with the situation
that there is hard uncertainty regarding not only the ecological implications
of species loss in the long term, but also the value of those changes to society.
Furthermore, it is conceivable that, although particular functions or services
provided by species or combinations of species may not be seen by society as
vital now, they could be of crucial importance in future evolved states, such
as may be induced by climate change. In this sense, biodiversity loss could
result in unanticipated losses.

Biodiversity problems are characterized by hard uncertainty for a number
of further reasons. Foremost is that as a public good, biodiversity cannot be
characterized as seriable, in that biodiversity loss on a large scale will affect
human welfare at a societal level rather than at the level of the individual. So,
for example, the extinction of a species, which could have held the cures for a
particular disease, affects the whole of society. In evaluating the consequences of biodiversity loss, it is also difficult to draw together a sufficient
number of actions or trials which have similar characteristics as is possible in
the insurance industry. An example of this is that, while the effect of the
introduction of genetically modified crops on biodiversity may be benign in
Northern Europe, due to the presence of different ecosystems and species in
say East Asia, the resulting outcome of the same action is likely to be very
different. Moreover the irreversible and entropic nature of many environmental processes means that the underlying characteristics or structures of the
ecosystem, which respond to a particular action are constantly changing.
Therefore not only are problems which involve biodiversity loss non-seriable
in that the combination of events generating a particular outcome will be
unique, but they are also non-divisible, in the sense that they cannot be
repeated in exactly the same conditions.

### 3.3.2    Ecological Uncertainty

Ecological uncertainty derives from the dynamics of the ecological system, which due to the complex nature of the interactions between its key elements means that the effects of economic activity or natural perturbations are more often than not conditioned by hard uncertainty. In particular, the presence of thresholds, beyond which the resilience of a system is lost, is to a large degree conditioned by hard uncertainty. This is because not only does hard uncertainty exist with respect to the point at which a threshold will be passed and thus with respect to the ability of system to absorb shocks; but is also present in relation to predicting the functioning of an ecosystem after it has flipped and moves to a new equilibrium (or basin of attraction). This is because the way that a particular ecosystem functions may be radically different from the way it operated before the threshold was passed. It is to investigate the role that the resilience of a system and the presence of thresholds plays in the environmental uncertainty problem that the discussion now turns.

#### 3.3.2.1    Ecosystem resilience
An important concept in relation to ecological uncertainty is that of the resilience of the biological and physical systems (Holling, 1973, 1986). For present purposes it will be sufficient to define resilience as the capacity of a system to retain its organizational structure and thus productivity (of all its services and functions) following perturbations. Holling's definition and measure of resilience focuses on the size of the stability domain which is defined as the perturbation that can be absorbed before the system converges on another equilibrium state (Holling, 1973). A closely related interpretation is concerned with the time taken to return to an initial equilibrium (Pimm, 1984). The focus is therefore on the capacity of the system to absorb shocks without losing stability (Dalmazzone and Perrings, 1997). Such a concept, in contrast to that of equilibrium, stresses the dynamic nature of the system in which more than one stable equilibrium state or domain is possible. Moreover, the behaviour of the elements of a system which move from one domain to another is discontinuous, because they become attracted to a different equilibrium condition (Holling, 1986). When perturbation leads to smaller stability domains, then the resilience of the system to shocks is reduced.

If the example of a rain-forest ecosystem is taken, then the perturbation could relate to logging a relatively large part of a particular system, or the removal of certain species or combinations of species. The resilience of the system would therefore refer to the ability of the system to keep functioning in the way that it did prior to the disturbance. So for example in the case of a rain forest, the extent to which nutrient recycling and thus the productive

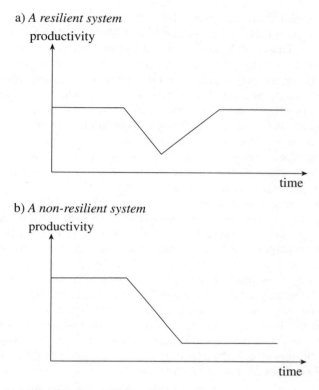

a) *A resilient system*

productivity

time

b) *A non-resilient system*

productivity

time

*Source*:    Adapted from Common, 1995: pp. 52–3

*Figure 3.3    System resilience*

capacity of the system is maintained will depend on the resilience of the system in the face of the disturbance. Figure 3.3 shows in a very simplified manner, the effect of resilience on the productivity of an ecosystem.

In the first diagram (a) the perturbation is within the stability domain of the system, and thus although in the short term the productivity of the system is affected (which in terms of the policy horizon may be of crucial importance), over time the system returns to the local equilibrium and the productivity of the system returns to its original level. In the second diagram (b) where the particular system is not as resilient, the effect of a perturbation is such that the previous local equilibrium is not returned to and instead a new local equilibrium is reached at which productivity is at a much lower level.

In the case of the rain forest, large-scale clearance of the forest for conversion to cattle ranching results in the loss of a number of key functions crucial to maintaining the productivity of the system. The removal of the canopy, which not only is the source of leaf litter but also protects the soil from erosion, can result in the system no longer being able to recycle sufficient nutrients to sustain the system at its previous equilibrium. A new series of features, such as increased nutrient leaching in soils and reduced supply of nutrients from the previous forest litter, mean that, while in the short term productive grasslands are established, after a few years the key elements of the system are attracted to a new basin or equilibrium, which is conditioned by much lower nutrient levels. In the new state only certain species of plants (which are less suitable for cattle rearing) can survive. The difficulty of recreating all the conditions required for the system to converge on the previous equilibrium means that in many cases the process is irreversible without significant intervention.

Holling (1986) characterizes a natural ecosystem in terms of the sequential interaction between four system functions. The first is *'exploitation'*, which is the process responsible for the rapid colonization of disturbed ecosystems. The second is *'conservation'* which is a climax process associated with the accumulation of biomass. The third is *'creative destruction'* caused by an external disturbance which releases energy and matter. The fourth is renewal or reorganization which may involve changes that may or may not involve a new structure. It is this stage that is crucial to the uncertainty problem. If reorganization is based on a new structure (that is, the system moves to a new local equilibrium of stability domain), a whole new set of functional relationships and feedbacks between the different components of the ecosystem are created, implying that previous historic records will no longer be valid in attempting to predict future events. In such cases the system has crossed some threshold and is converging on a different locally stable equilibrium (Dalmazzone and Perrings, 1997).

However, the property of resilience in a system can only be determined *ex post* by observing the behaviour of the system in the face of disturbance (Common, 1995). *Ex ante* it is very difficult to anticipate or predict under what conditions a system will no longer be resilient. For example the effect of incremental degradation of an ecosystem may only become apparent after the effects of a large perturbation. So, for example, while small-scale conversion of wetlands, removal of mangroves and forest clearance may not appear in the short term to be of major consequence, the accumulated effects of these stresses may cause a loss of resilience in the system. As a result, if the system is subject to a large disturbance such as that caused by a hurricane, a threshold is passed and the system flips with possible catastrophic consequences. Predicting the effect of the hurricane is also conditioned by hard uncertainty, because the underlying structure of the system has changed, and thus the effect of the perturbation will also be different from past instances. An example of this is Hurricane Mitch and its devastating effect on Honduras, Nicaragua, Guatemala and El Salvador in November 1998 (The *Guardian*, 1998). Although the region had been subjected to previous hurricanes, the ability of the environment to absorb the perturbation was reduced by the effects of a long period of environmental degradation, and as a result the destruction it caused was of a far higher magnitude than that caused by previous hurricanes.

The reason that it is crucial to deal with hard uncertainty surrounding the resilience of an ecosystem is that resilience is seen as a key property in relation to the sustainability of a system. This is because maintaining resilience helps to sustain the regenerative capacity of the ecological system on which humans depend for a wide range of services and functions (as highlighted in Chapter 1). A reduction in the resilience of a system means that the system, in the face of a shock, is more likely to flip to a different equilibrium level (Dalmazzone and Perrings, 1997). Where the new equilibrium level is associated with lower productivity or a lower range of key services than previously, then this may result in negative consequences for society. Moreover the importance of dealing with hard uncertainty *ex ante* is reinforced by the irreversibility of moving from one locally stable equilibrium to another associated with lower productivity. An example of this is the degradation of rangelands in Northern Africa, where it would appear that the process of desertification is irreversible or only slowly reversible. Reducing the resilience of a system also limits the extent to which that system will be able to adapt or evolve in the face of future unanticipated changes. This is apparent in relation to the effects of climate change. The consequences of shifts in climate patterns will depend on the ability of different ecosystems to absorb those changes. In this manner, reducing the resilience of the ecological system limits the options available to future generations, in that greater resilience implies that the system is more likely to adapt to future change.

There is also a great deal of uncertainty surrounding the key factors which are thought to be crucial in determining the resilience of a system. It is in this context that the concept of biodiversity has been given greater weight. This is because it is generally agreed that there exists some sort of relationship between functional diversity and ecosystem resilience (UNEP, 1995b). It is therefore hypothesized that maintaining the functional diversity of species will help to maintain the resilience of a system in the face of shocks. The question then turns to what level of biodiversity needs to be maintained in order to guarantee the resilience of the ecosystems on which human consumption and production, and in turn human welfare depend (Perrings, 1994). This question, however, is not as clear cut as it sounds. In certain cases a reduction in biodiversity may lead to greater productivity, as has been the case in the agricultural systems of Northern Europe. This though could be due to a greater resilience present in temperate ecosystems as a result of an evolutionary process based on a history of climatic variability and less stability of population sizes of species (Common, 1995). In contrast tropical systems are thought to have a lower resilience generally and thus lower ability to cope with disturbances, such as forest clearance.

The problem that policy makers are faced with is that a great deal of uncertainty exists over how to evaluate the ability of an ecosystem to respond to stresses. For example, although the use of food web structure complexity and density has been suggested, there are considerable uncertainties regarding their relative significance (Bockstael *et al.*, 1995). Indeed often only a few functional relationships have been quantified. What appears to be evident is that the resilience of ecosystems depends on the range of species capable of supporting the critical structuring processes of those systems under different environmental conditions. The problem to consider in terms of the uncertainty arising from human action is that, while in a current state of nature certain species and combinations of species may play a more important role in the functioning and organization of an ecosystem (driver species) than other passenger species (Walker, 1992), this does not imply that all other species are redundant. As Barbier *et al.* (1995) point out: 'The importance of the mix or diversity of species for the resilience of ecosystems lies precisely in the fact that species which are passengers under one state of nature may have a key structuring role to play under other states of nature' (Barbier *et al.*, 1995: p. 833).

As a result species which are not seen as crucial in relation to the resilience of an ecosystem may have unanticipated (and thus uncertain) value in future evolved equilibrium states.

To summarize, the uncertainty problem faced by decision makers is that, although maintaining resilience in the ecological system would appear to be an important policy objective, the whole issue of resilience is conditioned by hard uncertainty. As yet there is insufficient knowledge about the cumulative effects of reducing the resilience of key ecosystems in relation to the functioning of the global system. There is also uncertainty regarding which key indicators and factors determine the resilience of an ecosystem. As a result when considering the results of human actions in terms of their implications for the resilience of the system, there is a large degree of uncertainty surrounding which actions are more likely to cause the lowering of the resilience of an ecosystem to perturbations. Moreover, *ex ante* the consequences of the reduction of resilience are unknown. This is because the question of whether a system can return to its local equilibrium after a shock, as well as the length of time that it will take to reach a local equilibrium, can only be determined in many cases *ex post* due to the uniqueness of the particular system at any one point in time and space. The problem that this poses is that the decision maker is faced with hard uncertainty over the consequences of a particular action, if the system is not resilient enough to return to the local equilibrium state. The shift to a new equilibrium state could have major negative consequences for society, in terms of the value of the services and functions that it is able to provide. Furthermore in this state the ability of the system to evolve to new conditions (economic or environmental) may also be significantly reduced. The key uncertainty issue is the point at which a system in the face of a perturbation will flip out of its current equilibrium state. The issue of thresholds and their implications for environmental decision making is the focus of the next section.

### 3.3.2.2 Ecological thresholds

Lowering the resilience of an ecosystem implies that the system is closer to a particular threshold beyond which the system will flip and move to another local equilibrium. Part of the hard uncertainty surrounding the resilience of an ecosystem to large shocks such as land clearance, mineral exploration, hurricanes or floods, is therefore derived from uncertainty over the ability to observe thresholds in ecosystems (Schulze and Mooney, 1993). Thresholds are important, because passing a system threshold can result in dramatic changes in the organization and structure of the ecosystem. This is because complex ecosystems are usually characterized by strong and non-linear interactions between the constituent parts, the dynamics of which are such that they are discontinuous in the neighbourhood of system thresholds (Perrings and Pearce, 1994).

Thresholds can consist of certain critical values for populations of organisms or biochemical cycles. Threshold values may exist for example for the minimum population size of the different species (species of trees, pollinators and so on) in an ecosystem, that is required for the system to remain resilient to change and to be stable. As it stands, at present it is often not possible for science to specify the minimum viable populations and the minimal habitat sizes for the survival of species (Hohl and Tisdell, 1993), until a threshold or carrying capacity has been exceeded. Consequently at the *ex ante* stage of any decision which could result in the passing of a system threshold, the decision is conditioned by hard uncertainty as the change is irreversible and the evolutionary response of the natural system unpredictable (Barbier *et al.*, 1995). If, however, any one population drops below a critical level then the system may be pushed beyond a particular threshold and the system flips from one locally stable equilibrium (or basin of attraction) to another. This is particularly so when the species in question are driver species, that is determinants of the system of which they are part (Nilsson and Grelsson, 1995). Reductions in the populations of key species, such as for example forest litter invertebrates in rain forests, may result in the self organization of the ecosystem being irreversibly and radically altered (Dalmazzone and Perrings, 1997). Hard uncertainty exists therefore both about the margins regarding the threshold level at which the system may flip (Schindler, 1990; Frost *et al.*, 1994), as well as regards the implication of crossing of thresholds for human welfare.

The possible existence of a threshold relationship between biodiversity and ecosystem functioning is shown by Figure 3.4. When biodiversity is relatively high, the ecosystem is in a stable basin of attraction or equilibrium and the ecosystem process rate which corresponds to the level of production of ecosystem services is high. This is shown by the upper limb of the curve in Figure 3.4. In the face of a modest perturbation the ecosystem will return to the stable state indicated by the solid lines. If biodiversity decreases to level A, then a threshold is passed and the system is perturbed across the break-point shown by the dashed line, it will move to the other stable state, which is characterised by a much lower process rate. To restore the ecosystem to the higher stable state biodiversity will have to be raised above threshold B (Mooney *et al.*, 1995a). The extent to which this could happen would again depend on the irreversibility of the threshold change.

In many cases human action may have unobservable effects on key species or ecosystem functions. For example, although the degradation of sea grass

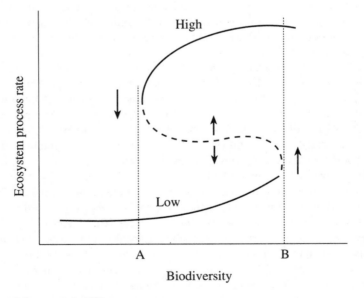

*Source*:   Mooney *et al.*, 1995a

*Figure 3.4    Threshold relationship between an ecosystem process rate and biodiversity*

beds in a maritime ecosystem may not appear at first sight to affect the productivity of a coral reef system such as that present off the coast of Belize, sea grass plays what is thought to be a crucial role in trapping sediment, which can cause damage to the coral system (McField *et al.*, 1995). The problem is that the strength of the relationship between the two is poorly defined, and as a result a large degree of uncertainty exists in relation to the thresholds beyond which sea grass beds can cope with extra sedimentation, from erosion caused by the removal of forest systems in the terrestrial system. Once a phase change occurs as a result of a threshold being passed, then the system structure will often be radically altered. Continuing with our example, degradation of coral past a certain threshold may be impossible (in a human lifetime) to reverse. In this sense any environmental decision which results in altering the characteristics of the ecosystem is in Shackle's words 'unique'. This is because, once the action has been carried out, it is no longer possible to go back and repeat the decision under the same conditions.

The presence of thresholds, as well as significant time and space lags over which the effects of a threshold being passed are felt, means that it becomes very difficult for scientists simply to add up or aggregate small-scale behaviour to arrive at large-scale results. Precisely because it is not possible to observe the underlying structure of the dynamic system (for example population sizes of all critical species and rates of nutrient recycling), the ability of a system to bear stress once a threshold is exceeded is surrounded by uncertainty both in relation to the system dynamics, as well as to the measurement of data (Dalmazzone and Perrings, 1997). Although in an undisturbed system it is possible to observe the stable equilibrium, other equilibria (and their possible implications for human welfare) are not observed. Increased stress, however, will bring the system closer to the boundary of the stability domain, at which there is a greater danger that the system will flip and that irreversible or only slowly reversible change will occur. Nevertheless, because it is not possible to observe how close the system is to a boundary (as for example indicated from observable environmental quality), nor the exact position of the threshold, decisions which may result in a threshold boundary being crossed are conditioned by hard uncertainty. Therefore policy approaches which seek to set limits, in relation to, say, harvesting or emissions are not applicable where the boundaries of a threshold are not observable and thus conditioned by hard uncertainty.

Consequently human action which (intentionally or unintentionally) affects the structure of ecosystems may result in unanticipated movement from one stable domain to another, less stable domain. Often this may be the result of cumulative action such as forest clearance, logging and mining, or combinations of disturbances such as the effect of human actions and a natural disturbance, such as a hurricane. Interestingly Holling (1986) highlights the surprises inherent in ecological systems. This concept has many close parallels to the notion of surprise in Shackle's model. Dalmazzone and Perrings (1997) demonstrate that continuously increasing levels of environmental pressure will inevitably increase the danger of causing a collapse of the natural system by overstepping critical thresholds. Thus, at the margins at which the system is locally stable, it becomes all the more important to take into account the uncertainty surrounding the point at which irreversible change will occur.

Bearing in mind that both economic and ecological systems often exhibit these characteristics when they interact, the lack of predictability becomes increasingly apparent. Precisely because the complex structures and connections of complex ecosystems, such as a wetland system, are not fully understood, there is uncertainty surrounding the precise threshold values of a system combined with the potential for irreversible and unprecedented change. This means that the use of probability-based models to predict the long-range changes in the multiple functions of natural systems arising from human actions, such as the draining of wetland areas, is severely limited (Russell, 1997).

The limitations in our ability to predict the consequence of exceeding a threshold are derived from two main factors. First, in many instances the passing of a particular threshold may not have occurred previously in a similar ecosystem. Consequently there are no previous records from which to infer the consequences of such an action. The extensive clearance and burning of upland vegetation in Great Britain, which resulted in a shift from forest cover (such as the great Caledonian forest) to blanket bogs (Moore, 1982), is an historic example of an action which resulted in a new equilibrium state. The difficulty in pooling often unique or very different ecosystems to derive comparable information on the consequences of a particular action, such as removal of mangrove forests, also means that many of the consequences of passing a particular threshold are non-seriable. Furthermore, if the threshold has never been exceeded before, the likelihood that there will be unanticipated outcomes means that the full range of outcomes will not be known.

The second factor which contributes to the uncertainty problem is derived from the dynamic nature of ecosystems. The key variables and relationships, from which it might be possible to determine the effects of a particular action, such as the effect of fertilizer effluent on sea grass beds, will often radically change after a threshold has passed, and the system moves to another basin of attraction. Once a system has passed a threshold, a new set of key variables and relationships between the ecosystem components will often evolve. Consider for example the changing response of a semi-arid zone, such as the Sahel, to droughts after intensive grazing has taken place together with the irreversible switch to woody vegetation (Holling, 1986). This means that historical records from previous equilibria states will no longer be relevant and, if used to derive probabilities for the consequence of a particular event (such as the consequence of drought on a particular species of grass), may even mislead the decision maker. This is particularly the case where a system is already close to a particular threshold, so that the event or action which is attempted to be predicted may result in the system flipping from one equilibrium to another.

It is increasingly apparent therefore that environmental decisions can often result in the crossing of a particular threshold which cumulatively may lead to the reduction of the resilience of a system to large-scale perturbations. Due to the reasons outlined above, in many decisions the resilience of a particular ecosystem, the point at which a threshold may be passed, and the consequences of the system flipping are conditioned by hard uncertainty and ignorance rather than soft uncertainty or risk. While the consequences of an action which causes the system to move to an alternative equilibrium state may not always be negative (or at least temporarily), in many cases, exemplified by the examples outlined, a move to an alternative equilibrium can result in the loss of key services and functions as well as in reducing the resilience of the system to cope with stress. In many cases it is only after a large shock to the system, such as that caused by flooding or drought, that the full ecological consequences of moving to a new equilibrium state are realized.

### 3.3.3 Valuation Uncertainty

In the last chapter, the development of environmental valuation methods as a response to the absence of a set of market prices for the ecological–economic system, was highlighted. Although the large and extensive debate on the use of such valuation methods has been largely side-stepped, it is important to address the question of the uncertainty which arises. The first type of valuation uncertainty arises as a result of the limitations of current methods in estimating the total value of environmental services or functions. This can include uncertainty derived from methodological issues which question the reliability of the resultant estimates, as well as from uncertainty surrounding future values and preferences. The second type of valuation uncertainty is more fundamental in that, even if theoretical and practical considerations surrounding valuation are overcome, much of the economic–ecological system is unobservable (Perrings, 1997b). An important aspect relating to this difficulty of observing all the elements of the economic–ecological system derive from the problems faced in valuing the primary or prior value of an ecosystem. It is this second type of valuation uncertainty which will be the focus of this section.

A good example of an important attribute which contributes to the primary value of an ecosystem is the mix of species that enables that system both to provide the flow of ecosystem services and to maintain that flow over a range of environmental conditions. Primary value includes the ability of the system to evolve and remain resilient in the face of stress (Marie-Gren *et al.*, 1994). In such a sense, many environmental services, although not directly consumed, are nevertheless necessary for the functioning of ecosystems which in turn produce products or services valued by society. Thus a large component of the value of an ecosystem or biodiversity lies in its role in supporting the productivity of the system from which individual species are extracted or which provide functions that are useful to man. So, for example, forest litter invertebrates may not themselves be seen as a valuable resource, but they are essential to the regeneration of forests from which timber can be extracted. However, the complex nature of links between individual species, ecosystem functions and feedback mechanisms means that the primary value of what are often unappealing species is very difficult to ascertain.

The issues of ecological uncertainty raised in the previous section have a profound effect on our ability to value different ecosystem services. Although a change in the composition of species or the crossing of a threshold that affects the key structuring processes within an ecosystem, may have major implications for the ability of an ecosystem to provide economically valued services, a large degree of hard uncertainty about the link between key species and the critical processes of the ecosystem must be faced. Furthermore, certain species may have unanticipated values (that is *ex ante* the decision maker does not have the full range of outcomes, nor any previous history to base his or her expectations on), in that they can take over certain functions when an ecosystem is perturbed. As a result the implications of exceeding a threshold and the reduction of resilience, in relation to human welfare, are conditioned by hard uncertainty.

A healthy ecosystem will contain a latent reserve of 'keystone species' which are required for system maintenance in the face of stress and shock (Barbier *et al.*, 1995). However, the value of this reserve is fundamentally uncertain, because until the system is put under stress, the species which will play a key role are unknown. As a result, the valuation exercise is faced with hard uncertainty, in that the potential value of the range of species capable of performing particular functions under different environmental conditions is not readily observable. The only way that it is possible to estimate the primary value of the mix of species on which the provision of key ecosystem services and functions depend, is to specify an appropriate production function, taking account of the presence of all interactions, feedbacks and thresholds in the ecological–economic system (Perrings *et al.*, 1993). As a result of uncertainty about specifying the functional form of such relationships, as well as uncertainties which arise in the aggregation from local systems to welfare effects at a societal level, this task is to a large degree impossible at present.

All use and non-use values are therefore contingent on the prior existence of a healthy and evolving ecosystem. As such, there is a prior or primary value which, because it does not constitute a productive output, cannot be measured in conventional economic terms. As a result there will always be a degree of uncertainty surrounding the exact value of environmental change as a result of any policy change, even if all the other corresponding use and non-use values were estimated accurately. Because of this difficulty in observing the value of human action with respect to the organization and structure of an ecosystem, as Perrings (1997b) points out, the distribution of outcomes (and corresponding values) associated with such developments cannot be inferred from history due to the lack of relevant observations. Moreover, the novelty of many human actions in the face of evolving and dynamic ecosystems emphasizes the nature of the hard uncertainty faced.

## 3.4  SUMMARY AND CONCLUSIONS

The central theme of this chapter is that the type of uncertainty or modality faced in a given situation will vary. Accordingly a framework upon which the different modalities of uncertainty can be classified has been proposed. Recognizing that different uncertainty problems will have different underlying characteristics immediately implies that an approach to decision making which does not recognize the full range of the modalities of uncertainty, will be flawed. Building on this, the second part of this chapter highlights that in many decisions regarding the environment we are faced with hard, rather than soft, uncertainty. By demonstrating the nature of the uncertainty faced, it is clear that, when decision makers attempt to determine the environmental consequences of a proposed action and the value of any resulting changes to society, there is a need to deal explicitly with hard uncertainty. This lays the foundations for the next chapter which reviews existing decision models and extends the critique of the applicability of probability based models, such as expected utility, to environmental decisions which are characterized by hard uncertainty.

## NOTE

1.  Froger and Zyla (1994) and Faucheux and Froger (1995) distinguish between ignorance, strong uncertainty, weak uncertainty and certainty, of which the modalities of uncertainty are defined solely in terms of the precision and reliability of probability.

# 4.   Uncertainty and decision making

## 4.1   INTRODUCTION

The previous chapters have outlined the nature of the uncertainty problem and put forward the argument that many environmental problems are conditioned by hard uncertainty. The realization, however, that there are a number of modalities of uncertainty and that in the context of environmental decision making, most decisions are characterized by hard uncertainty or ignorance rather than soft uncertainty, poses a number of problems both in terms of the interpretation and the use of traditional models. In particular, recognizing the presence of hard uncertainty in many environmental decisions requires a different approach to how models of decision making are interpreted and evaluated. This issue is dealt with in Section 4.2. It is argued that in the presence of hard uncertainty the underlying rationality of any decision is necessarily bounded. As such, only the rationality of the decision-making process rather than the decision itself, can be evaluated.

Although the majority of traditional decision-making models rely on the use of probability (either objective or subjective)[1] as a measure of uncertainty, recognizing the different modes of uncertainty implies that the use of one all-encompassing measure will be limited. Although the use of probability may be valid in cases of soft uncertainty or risk, it cannot be applied as a measure of hard uncertainty. The second section therefore aims to further the critique of using a probability framework to deal explicitly with hard uncertainty and to argue that objective and subjective probability can often not be applied to environmental decisions. The third and fourth sections focus on two alternative decision-making mechanisms which utilize probability. The third section specifically focuses on attempts to deal with uncertainty within the valuation stage through the concepts of option value and quasi option value. It is shown that, in addition to their reliance on probability, these approaches have a further number of theoretical and practical difficulties which limit their applicability to decisions characterized by hard uncertainty.

The fourth section forwards a critique of the dominant paradigm of decision making under uncertainty, based on expected utility theory. In particular it is argued that the expected utility approach is not applicable to environmental decisions conditioned by hard uncertainty, because of its reliance on probability, as well as the mechanism by which it weights the uncertain outcome. The lack of applicability of expected utility theory to decisions characterized by hard uncertainty is reinforced by experimental evidence, which questions some of the theoretical constructs on which expected utility theory is based. Moreover, although a number of variations on expected utility theory have been proposed, none provide a suitable mechanism for weighting the outcome and the uncertainty associated with the outcome. The final section of the chapter concludes that an alternative decision-making framework is required for decisions characterized by hard uncertainty.

## 4.2 RATIONALITY AND THE DECISION-MAKING PROCESS

The interpretation of decision-making models in a normative or behavioural/positivist manner is crucial in evaluating the use of such models in the context of hard uncertainty. The distinction defines whether the aim of the model is to explain the way in which decisions are made in the face of uncertainty (that is a behavioural approach) or to prescribe the way in which decisions ought to be made in the face of reality (a normative approach). The latter implies a set of value judgements about an individual or institution, as well as a notion of rationality. In practice, however, in the literature there is a blurring of the distinction between the two, with behavioural models being used either to help construct or alternatively to deconstruct normative models. Therefore the two questions that need to be addressed are first how decisions under environmental uncertainty *should* be made, and second do these models reflect the realities of how decisions *are* made? The second question implies the testing of models or the use of other evidence to assess their applicability. This approach is employed in the case study concerned with the decision to improve an existing road in Southern Belize.

This section aims to deal more with the first question, and in particular how in any normative approach the 'rationality' of a decision should be judged. Again the stance taken here will be that it is not advantageous to separate completely the questions of what should happen from what does happen. Normative approaches, if they are to have any relevance, must recognize the limits of human cognitive ability, as well as the limits and realities inherent in decision-making structures and institutions. They must also be tempered by an understanding of what is the best that the decision-making process can hope to achieve in any given circumstances. This is particularly the case in situations of hard uncertainty where notions of optimality are often meaningless.

Likewise, taking a purely behavioural approach to explaining the way in which decisions are made, limits the usefulness of such models in providing guidance for dealing with uncertainty. These concerns come down to what in effect are *ex post* and *ex ante* approaches to the decision-making problem at hand. Behavioural models are in effect seeking to explain *ex post* the way in which decisions are made, by which time many of the uncertainties facing the decision maker will in fact have been resolved. Only with the benefit of hindsight can the decision itself be judged as 'good' or 'bad'. In the face of uncertainty, whether or not the resultant decision was in fact optimal or not can only be judged *ex post*. This is for the simple reason that the *ex post* set may contain outcomes that are preferable to all those outcomes in the *ex ante* set. *Ex ante*, in situations of hard uncertainty or ignorance, the decision cannot be judged as optimal or not. Notions of optimality therefore only relate to situations of certainty. For example, if we look at decisions which could result in the crossing of a particular ecosystem threshold, *ex ante* the consequences of such an action cannot be predicted. As was argued in the previous chapter such a decision is conditioned by hard uncertainty. As such, this poses serious problems for notions of choosing the optimal policy or course of action.

### 4.2.1   Bounded Rationality and the Procedural Rationality of the Decision-making Process

Following Simon (1964, 1972), a distinction can be drawn between substantive rationality, where rationality refers exclusively to the results of the decision, and procedural rationality where concern is focused on the rationality of the decision-making process itself. Existing decision theories have tended to focus on notions of substantive rationality, based on finding the best solution through the use of a constrained optimization framework (Simon, 1982). The assumption is of course that the individual or collective agents possess perfect information or act as if they do (in the case of Bayesian theory). The realization, however, that *ex ante* in many decisions affecting the environment, the decision maker is constrained by the presence of hard uncertainty, implies that the rationality of any decision will be necessarily bounded. Abbott (1955) and Simon (1957) recognized that limits and lags inherent in the individual learning process about the dynamic environment in which decisions are taken, result in a more limited rationality, normally referred to as 'bounded rationality'. Because the full set of outcomes associated with any action is unknown, it cannot be determined *ex ante* whether or not the decision is optimal. As a result the emphasis in evaluating environmental decisions faced with hard uncertainty will be on procedural rationality. This formally recognizes that the different modalities of any uncertain decision will affect the way in which any model can be evaluated; a point often overlooked in the literature, so that as Faucheux and Froger (1995) argue many authors have denied that any distinction exists between the different types of uncertainty.

Applying the notion of substantive rationality to decision-making models implies a notion of reality which is immutable or predetermined and in which all events are predictable. This position is not valid from two perspectives; first, complexity results in a situation of incomplete knowledge due to lack of information; second, there are inherent indeterminacies in economic–ecological processes, and so the future is to a certain extent transmutable. Using the notion of procedural rationality recognizes these issues and allows the focus to be directed to questions regarding how to improve the basis on which decisions are made. In this vein, Simon emphasizes methods which make satisfactory choices rather than optimal choices. Specifically he stresses that the aim is to provide further insights into the trade-offs inherent in decision making and to make explicit the mechanisms and assumptions on which a decision is made.

It should be noted that for a decision to be made, even on the basis of the limited rationality implied by the use of a procedural rationality framework, a certain amount of information must be available. While the decision is bounded, because the full range of outcomes is unknown, at least a partial set of possible or hypothesized outcomes must be present. Thus, although some authors have highlighted the notion of ignorance in decision-making models and have emphasized the notion of ignorance in Shackle's work (for example, Vickers, 1994; Katzner 1989a, 1989b, 1995), in decisions characterized by complete ignorance no notion of rationality can be attached either to the resultant decision or to the decision-making process itself. Unless the consequences of an action can be at least partially bounded, the future is completely unknown. Defining a conceptual basis on which the rationality of decisions made in complete ignorance can be evaluated is thus very difficult. In such cases, a position of reserved rationality and a precautionary approach may have to be taken (Perrings, 1997b), until such time as enough information is present to reduce the situation to one in which at least a partial set of outcomes can be hypothesized.

### 4.2.2   Individual and Public Decision-making in the face of Uncertainty

The majority of decision-making models under uncertainty, including the Shackle model, focus on individual decision making. However, in developing such models in any normative sense, inevitably there will be an overlap with institutional decision making. Moreover, the nature of many decisions regarding the economic–environmental system, even if made by individuals, will affect society as a whole. In other words, the negative consequences of an uncertain action will be felt by the whole of society and not just the individual in question.

It soon becomes apparent that the number of decisions that are purely personal is very small due to the interconnectedness of society, the economy and the environment. Even so, many decision models typify the situation as one in which the individual makes a series of gambles, in which no one stands to lose from the use of a flawed normative model (Russell, 1997). However, precisely because the use of a flawed normative model may have significant societal consequences, it is crucial that such models be evaluated in relation to whether they deal adequately with hard uncertainty. So the use of an expected value or utility model in the context of an environmental decision conditioned by hard uncertainty may result in severe negative consequences. An example of this could be the large-scale removal of mangroves for tourist development or shrimp farming. This action could have serious repercussions in the face of an uncertain event, such as a severe hurricane. The reduction of the ability of the ecological system to act as a buffer against storm damage would have large societal consequences. As a result, in terms of evaluating *ex ante* the procedural rationality of such decisions, it will be important to place individual decisions taken in the face of uncertainty in a wider context. This recognizes that individual decision makers, especially those agencies with public responsibilities, do not behave as if they are making a private decision.

## 4.3   PROBABILITY AND DECISION MAKING UNDER HARD UNCERTAINTY

Decision-making models which attempt to deal with uncertainty normally rely on two central mechanisms. The first involves a measure of uncertainty, and the second involves a mechanism for evaluating the outcome and its associated measure of uncertainty. Although the latter stage may vary in different models, the use of probability (either in an objective or subjective manner) is by far the dominant measure by which an uncertain event is characterized. This hegemony of probability, in both decision making and other models which attempt to represent the ecological–economic system, is questioned. Consequently, before the applicability of expected utility models is assessed, a fundamental critique of the probability foundations is provided.

The dominance of the probability framework can be partly accounted for by the limited conceptualization of uncertainty in the traditional literature, based on a view of reality as fundamentally indeterminate and immutable. Such an approach does not tend to recognize that the different modalities of uncertainty will affect the way that the problem can be approached and leads to a position where the use of a probability framework is advocated for all cases of uncertainty (Faucheux and Froger, 1995). However, as previously argued, the presence of hard uncertainty in many environmental decisions precludes such an approach. Under conditions of hard uncertainty the use of a probability framework is flawed, in that it does not deal explicitly with uncertainty *per se*. On the basis of the different criteria on which the different modalities of uncertainty were defined in the previous chapter, the next sections will put forward a critique on the basis of using both frequency and subjectivist interpretations of probability in the case of hard uncertainty.

### 4.3.1  Objective Probability

The use of objective probabilities (actual or implicitly assumed) is in essence based on a frequency approach. Based largely on the work of von Mises (1936, 1939), objective probability is usually defined to be the limit of its relative frequency as the number of trials increases without limit (Ford, 1994). The crucial criterion is that the event must be divisible, namely that it can be repeated in constant and unchanging circumstances. The classic example of this is the roulette wheel type of experiment, which, because the generating mechanism remains unchanging, means that an infinite number of trials can be carried out. The generation of objective probabilities therefore relies upon the assumption of a static framework in which there exists a history of repeated trials against nature. In this sense they require a high degree of knowledge rather than being characterized by a lack of knowledge, as Shackle argues:

> Probability as relative frequency is surely a form of knowledge ... By contrast there can be a need to delineate and delimit unknowledge. The decision maker, the chooser of action or of a comprehensive and far reaching policy, is conscious that even the foreground of his field of action in time-to-come is a shifting mist and that all beyond it melts into a void. Choice of course of action is not an experiment which can be repeated under broadly unchanging conditions ... Relative frequency cannot apply to it ... relative frequencies are knowledge because the classes of outcomes they refer to are not rivals. The truth of one, by no means denies the truth of another. (Shackle, 1979: pp. 100–1)

The notion of decisions which can be characterized as a series of infinitely repeatable experiments cannot be applied to all the modalities of uncertainty for a number of reasons. Shackle (1949, 1955) provides a telling critique of such notions, in that for many economic situations, the decision is 'unique'. Many decisions will in essence be unprecedented in that there exists no historical precedent on which objective probabilities can be specified. Shackle's notion of uniqueness in economic decisions can be extended to the ecological–economic system which, because of lack of information due to complexity or fundamental indeterminacies in the system, will not have historical precedents for many actions. Because there exist no historical observations from which the full range of outcomes can be specified, it is not possible to construct a probability distribution for these outcomes. An example of this is the decision to discharge radioactive waste from Sellafield, which has resulted in the unpredictable deposition of radio-nuclides in the Solway Firth salt marshes.

Even if it is possible to assume that the conditions under which an outcome is generated are consistent, and non-changing, then Shackle (1949) is still critical of the probability calculus as a mechanism for handling choice in single decisions (Ford, 1994). This is because, even if the frequency probability of a mutually exclusive set of events is derived, this does not tell us what the probability of the next event will be:

> All concepts of numerical probability are alike in involving the ideas of uniformity in some specified sense in the conditions of the experiments ... Now for many important kinds of decisions which must be taken in human affairs it will be possible to find a sufficient number of past instances which occurred under appropriately similar conditions. This difficulty, however, is a minor one compared with the fact that, even by vicarious experience a probability is established, many kinds of decision are for each individual virtually unique; the die is thrown once and for all ... Is 'probability' in this frequency ratio sense a relevant consideration at all when only one or virtually one 'throw of the die' is going to be allowed to us? It is universally agreed that the numerical probability of a single isolated event has no meaning. (Shackle, 1949: pp. 109–10)

So, for example, although the probability of a hurricane in a particular area may be known (with varying degrees of reliability), this does not tell us when or where the next hurricane will occur, nor the magnitude of its consequences. Predicting the consequences of the hurricane by means of a probability distribution for all the outcomes is not possible due to the complex and ever-changing structures and interconnections between socio-economic and ecological systems. One only has to look at the consequences of Hurricane Mitch in 1998 on Honduras, Nicaragua, Guatemala and El Salvador, to see evidence of this (The *Guardian*, 1998).

Thus a fundamental and far reaching critique of the applicability of frequency probability, in the context of the environmental–economic system, lies in the requirement of a static generating structure from which objective probabilities are derived. While the past may influence the future, the irreversibility of both human actions and movements from one ecosystem state to another means that the structure of the present economic–ecological system, and thus the conditions which generate future outcomes are constantly changing. This is most apparent, where, as highlighted in Chapter 3, a system may flip after passing a particular threshold. Where crossing a threshold involves irreversible change in the structures of the ecological system and its connections with the economic system, due to the entropic nature of such change, the action is not repeatable in identical circumstances. Nevertheless, when a system is in a local equilibrium, it may be possible over time to build up a historical record of the outcomes of economic activity. That is to say, after a sufficient period of time a decision which was previously unprecedented may become more routine, in which case it may gradually change from being a situation characterized by hard uncertainty to one of soft uncertainty. Examples of this would include the use of many pesticides, for which the full consequences of their use in relation to the environment is only now becoming understood, more than 50 years after their widespread application. What must be remembered, however, is that as the system progresses the derivation of probabilities from static historical records may become more unreliable. Alternatively if the system passes a threshold or flips, then the structures may change so radically, that it will not be possible to specify the full set of outcomes from past data. In some instances, the irreversibility and uniqueness of the decision process will mean that objective probabilities cannot be derived. A good example of this would be in the extinction of a particular species, which by definition is unprecedented.

Non-divisible actions, which cannot be repeated, can in certain cases be pooled with other actions to form a number of seriable experiments. However, for an experiment to be seriable, the conditions under which the event occurs should be unchanging. The more that this condition is relaxed, the more unreliable any probability distribution generated becomes. The insurance industry thrives on identifying such poolable events, the classic example being that of life expectancy. In the case of environmental decision making, due to the complex and evolving nature of ecosystems, such a process is fraught with difficulties. This is particularly so when faced with determining the consequences of a particular event such as species loss, rather than defining an actual event, such as the number of species lost. Because the outcomes of a particular action tend to be derived from the combination of different attributes or key variables in the ecological–economic system, the resulting consequences of these combinations are often unique. Thus, for example, pooling the consequences of the loss of individual species is not possible, because of the presence of hard uncertainty surrounding the loss of one species or combinations of species, which is unprecedented. There are no other worlds with which such an 'experiment' can be pooled. In situations of hard uncertainty, therefore, the event is non-seriable.

### 4.3.2  Subjective Probability

In addition to objective probability, the concept of subjective probability, inspired by the work of Ramsey (1926, 1931), de Finetti (1951) and Savage (1954), is the other dominant measure of uncertainty used in literature on decision making.[2] Subjective probability is the means by which individuals specify the degree of belief that they attach to the occurrence of the different possible outcomes of any action. The requirement of objective probability for a divisible decision, with a historic record, is overcome by the use of subjective measure of probability based on belief. The use of subjective probabilities assumes that even if objective probabilities are not available, the individual can subjectively allocate a probability distribution to all the consequences of an action. As such, it does allow room for different individuals to have different degrees of belief in any given hypothesis. In such a framework all forms of uncertainty are reduced to soft uncertainty or risk.

The use of subjective probabilities is consistent with the notion of a predetermined reality, in that even if in the short run subjective probabilities do not coincide with the presumed immutable objective probabilities, in the long run subjective probabilities tend to converge to the assumed (but unknown) underlying objective probability distributions. In the case of Bayesian theory, where initially subjective probabilities differ from objective probabilities, agents learn over time and can revise previous, subjectively formed probabilities. Under Bayesian theory economic actors behave as if they had complete knowledge of the parameters of the real world. The subjectivist view advocated by Shafer (1976) stresses the notion of probability as a property of belief or knowledge, so that, while in the long run subjective probabilities will tend to coincide with objective probabilities, in the short term it is possible for the individual to calculate subjective probabilities that are statistically reliable on the basis of existing information. Accordingly Bayesian theory supposes that agents will make decisions as if they knew the collection of future states of nature or the probabilities of the occurrence for the future states (Faucheux and Froger, 1995).

While the requirement of divisibility is circumvented through this approach, the use of subjective probability in the case of hard uncertainty can be attacked in that, in common with objective probability, subjective probability presupposes that the complete set of outcomes can be hypothesized. Again it was Shackle (1969) who was foremost in voicing concern at this presupposition. On the basis of the different modalities of uncertainty outlined in Chapter 3, it is evident that in cases of hard uncertainty a full set of outcomes cannot be specified and thus cannot be represented by a distributional variable. Even if subjective probability is used the individual is assumed to compile an exhaustive list of all the consequences of any particular action

(Ford, 1994). Whether or not subjective probability is used, an exhaustive list of consequences must be defined. Thus, where applied to environmental decision making the decision maker must be able to specify all the possible states of the world that could occur as a consequence of a particular decision. From the preceding chapters, given the complex and dynamic nature of the ecological–economic system, it is apparent that this will only be the case in a small number of environmental decisions.

Where the full range of outcomes cannot be specified, the situation is characterized by hard uncertainty, or where none of the outcomes are known, ignorance. In the case of soft uncertainty or risk, in contrast, there is no room for what Shackle (1969) terms a 'residual hypothesis' (the possibility that an unspecified outcome might occur), as all possible outcomes are enumerated. In hard uncertainty, in addition to the outcomes which can be hypothesized or imagined, there is the possibility of an unanticipated outcome (a residual hypothesis). Accordingly in this context it does not make sense for the measure of uncertainty (objective or subjective) to be additive and to add to unity. The use of probability in cases of hard uncertainty would in effect ignore the presence of the residual hypothesis, in that because the probabilities are constrained to add to unity, probabilities are only specified for the set of known outcomes. As a result, if applied to cases of hard uncertainty, one flaw in using a subjective or objective probability measure is that it does not deal explicitly with the uncertainty *per se*. Outcomes that are not specified are in effect excluded from the decision process.

The interpretation of probability in a subjectivist manner emphasizes the notion of probability as a property of belief (Lawson, 1988). Stressing the role of the individual in relation to his or her belief in the occurrence of a particular event (as opposed to probability being used to characterize an objective phenomenon) has led to a number of criticisms of the use of subjective probability being advanced. In addition, less fundamental than the issue of knowledge regarding the full set of outcomes and the divisibility of the action, Shackle puts forward further arguments against the use of probability as a measure for uncertainty. The basis of these criticisms rests on whether subjective probability is appropriate as a measure which captures the way that an individual characterizes his or her belief in the occurrence of a set of outcomes. Foremost is the criticism that in a probability framework the degree of belief attached to the occurrence of an event is dependent on the other outcomes. This property of additivity (as a result of which probability is constrained to add to unity) is problematic in that, as Shackle (1969) argues, there is no reason why the probability of one outcome should affect the probability of another outcome in a mutually exclusive set, when the outcomes are rivals. In other words, if one outcome occurs, then the other hypothesized outcomes cannot occur. While Shackle perhaps over-extended the argument of non-rivalness to all cases of uncertainty, a more appropriate application will be to restrict the assumption of non-rivalness to situations characterized by soft uncertainty or risk. Take the case of a repeatable action such as throwing a dice for example, where the outcomes are not in fact rivals, and thus a frequency probability approach is perfectly valid. So, for example, rolling a six on a dice does not preclude rolling another six. In contrast for situations of hard uncertainty, non-rivalness cannot be assumed; accordingly the decision maker 'recognises his knowledge as merely setting bounds to a wide spectrum of mutually exclusive ideas' (Shackle, 1969: p. 92). Because, as is the case in many environmental decisions, non-rivalness cannot be assumed, a further argument against the use of a subjective or objective probability approach is presented.

For many uncertain situations the belief attached to the possibility of the occurrence of a particular outcome need not necessarily be influenced by its rivals. A simple example of this is the inability of probability to deal with an individual belief that three candidates have a 50–50 chance of winning a presidential election (Ford, 1994). The condition that the sum of probabilities must add to unity is also problematic for Shackle (1952, 1969), because even if an individual believes that the occurrence of two outcomes is perfectly possible (and would thus want to assign them a high probability or even both a probability of 1) (s)he is constrained to give the two outcomes a maximum probability of 0.5. The critique therefore follows that the decision maker's belief in the possible occurrence of the outcomes is not adequately reflected in a probability of 0.5. Furthermore, if further hypotheses are added to the individual's list of outcomes, then under a subjective probability framework, the probability of the other outcomes must be lowered (unless a probability of zero is allocated to the new hypothesis), even if with the addition of another possible outcome the individual's belief in the occurrence of the original outcome has not been reduced. This strict condition of subjective probability is often inappropriate for many decisions characterized by hard uncertainty on a practical basis, because, when the decision maker subjectively estimates the possibility of the occurrence of a particular outcome, its relation to the occurrence of the other outcome is often poorly defined.

## 4.4  DECISION MAKING AND EVALUATING UNCERTAIN CONSEQUENCES

Although probability is the dominant measure of uncertainty used in models of decision making there are two main alternative ways of evaluating the values of the outcomes and their associated uncertainty. The first involves attempts to deal with uncertainty within the valuation stage and subsequent cost–benefit analysis by means of estimating option or quasi option values. The second centres on dealing with uncertainty outside the valuation stage. In such approaches any valuations attached to the various outcomes are done first and then a mechanism is adopted which allows the individual to evaluate the competing options. In this latter section particular attention will be given to the dominant model of decision making under uncertainty, namely those based on expected utility (EU). It will be argued that in cases of hard uncertainty, the valuation stage can not adequately deal with the problem because of its reliance on probability. Similarly, even though it may be advantageous to attempt to deal with uncertainty outside the valuation stage, the use of an expected utility approach is not suitable for many environmental decisions conditioned by hard uncertainty.

### 4.4.1 Dealing with Uncertainty within the Valuation Stage

If it were possible to deal with uncertainty within the valuation stage, then the values obtained could then be inserted into a cost–benefit framework directly. The development of this approach has been largely within the environmental economics literature and focuses on the concepts of option and quasi option value. Although there have been a number of interpretations attached to the notion of option value (Ready, 1995), option value or more correctly option price (Cicchetti and Freeman, 1971) addresses the correct measurement of welfare change under uncertainty, with the emphasis on the additional value that is attached to maintaining the future supply of a good or service in the face of uncertainty (Graham-Tomasi, 1995). In contrast quasi option value can be defined as the expected value of future information, which is conditional on delaying an irreversible decision to develop an environmental resource. To a certain extent they also take a different level of analysis in that option value focuses on the individual economic agent, whereas quasi option value focuses attention at the level of the public decision maker evaluating policies or projects. It should be noted immediately that at a conceptual level both the option value and quasi option value debates do not distinguish between different modalities of uncertainty. As a result the assumption is made that they are potentially applicable to all case of uncertainty. The concept of quasi option value does, however, stress the importance of irreversibility.

While the debates on option value and quasi option value have generated an extensive literature, the question to be addressed here is whether or not they provide a suitable framework for dealing with hard uncertainty and thus whether hard uncertainty can be incorporated within the valuation stage at all.

#### 4.4.1.1   Option value

The literature surrounding the notion of option value (OV) is concerned with identifying a welfare measure that logically and consistently estimates the benefits and costs from a policy change, whose impacts are uncertain (Ready, 1995). To answer whether such an approach is viable and will deal adequately with environmental decisions conditioned by hard uncertainty, some of the theoretical issues which have cast doubt on the applicability of option value must be raised. Foremost of these is the issue of whether or not the benefits and costs of a policy under uncertainty are being analysed *ex ante* or *ex post*. From the previous sections it is apparent that the problem for decision makers facing uncertainty is at the *ex ante* stage. Analysis of the optimality of any decision and the resulting welfare implications can only be carried out *ex post*. It is this distinction between *ex ante* and *ex post* analysis that plays a pivotal role in determining the usefulness of the concept of option value.

In particular on closer scrutiny it becomes apparent that what option value represents is simply the difference between an *ex ante* measure of welfare and the expected value of an *ex post* measure. Thus the option price (OP) is the maximum that an individual would *ex ante* be willing to pay to keep open the option of using a particular service or good and can be defined by:

$$\sum_{i=1}^{M} \pi_k \mathbf{V}(\mathbf{Y} - \mathbf{OP}, \delta_1, \mathbf{s}_k) = \sum_{i=1}^{M} \pi_k \mathbf{V}(\mathbf{Y}, \delta_0, \mathbf{s}_k) \qquad (4.1)$$

where $\delta$ = policy vector (e.g. $\delta_0$ = develop the resource and $\delta_1$ = conserve the resource), $\mathbf{s}$ = state of the world vector (e.g. $\mathbf{s}_0$ = does not need to use the resource in future and $\mathbf{s}_1$ = does want to use resource in future), $\pi_k$ = *ex ante* probability of state k where $\Sigma \pi_k = 1$ and it is assumed that $\pi_k$ is not a function of $\delta$. Finally $\mathbf{Y}$ = income.

In contrast expected consumer surplus (E(CS)) is the expected value of the *ex post* welfare benefits of the use of the particular resource. Thus, if consumer surplus is defined as:

$$\mathbf{V}(\mathbf{Y} - \mathbf{CS}_k, \delta_1, \mathbf{s}_k) = \mathbf{V}(\mathbf{Y}, \delta_0, \mathbf{s}_k) \qquad (4.2)$$

where $\mathbf{V}(\mathbf{Y}, \delta, \mathbf{s})$ represents an *ex post* indirect utility function, then expected consumer surplus is defined by:

$$\mathbf{E}(\mathbf{CS}) = \sum_{i=1}^{M} \pi_k \mathbf{CS}_k \qquad (4.3)$$

What Cicchetti and Freeman (1971) realized was that the two alternative welfare measures need not be equal, or that more formally:

$$OV = OP - E(CS) \qquad (4.4)$$

It is immediately apparent from the above, that option value is purely the algebraic difference between consumer surplus and the state independent option price, and cannot be measured as a separate component of value.

If, as was stated, the primary concern is with the *ex ante* evaluation of uncertainty, then the corresponding compensation test should also be *ex ante* (Ulph, 1982; Ready, 1995, Freeman, 1986, Bishop, 1982). Thus, option price rather than expected consumer surplus is the relevant welfare measure. The problem is that on a practical basis OP is difficult to measure due to a lack of observable behaviour. The debate in the literature therefore turns to one of whether E(CS) could be used as a proxy for OP. This of course will depend on the size and the sign of the option value. However, as Schmalensee (1972) argued for demand side uncertainties and Freeman (1985, 1993) showed for supply side uncertainties, it is not possible to determine the sign or magnitude of any option value. This problem poses a severe obstacle to applying the concept of option prices in any meaningful way.

Moreover, whether the concept of option value is any use in relation to dealing with hard uncertainty rests on whether a probability framework is accepted. From both equations 4.1 and 4.3 it is apparent that the assumption is made that all possible states of the world are known and that these are captured by a reliable probability distribution. Thus, even if it was possible to use E(CS) as a proxy for OP, both concepts rely on the use of probability, which, as has been argued, is not applicable in cases of hard uncertainty. An interesting attempt by Graham (1981), who focused on the concept of the willingness to pay (WTP) locus to overcome the difficulties faced by using option value, also relies on the specification of probabilities for the known states of nature. The practical use of the WTP locus as means of measuring welfare changes under uncertainty is further weakened by the argument that state dependent compensation payments must also be observed (Ready, 1995), if aggregate willingness to pay for an uncertain policy change is not to be overestimated. Thus, although the notion of option value appears intuitively attractive, it offers little as a practical means for dealing with the welfare consequences of uncertainty, and even on a theoretical basis would only be applicable to cases of soft uncertainty or risk. As such, as a means of dealing with the kind of hard uncertainty commonly experienced in environmental decision making, its usefulness would appear limited.

### 4.4.1.2 Quasi option value

A different approach to that of option value, is the notion of quasi option value, developed by Arrow and Fisher (1974). What these authors demonstrated was that relative to a situation in which the decision maker ignores opportunities for learning, an extra value is attached to the preservation, when it is realized that it is possible to learn the true benefits of preservation. This is termed quasi option value (QOV). Like option value the concept is intuitively appealing, and in the context of irreversible change and uncertainty about the consequences of that change, advocates a precautionary approach. QOV is then the value of the extra information gained by postponing the development of a resource. It does not deal therefore with uncertainty *per se*, but aims to highlight the potential value of information gained from not irreversibly developing a resource. An example could be the quasi option value derived from the decision to preserve a species, where time allows knowledge about the true value of the species to be obtained. Although further research could result in knowledge that a particular species is not especially valuable, the mere prospect of improved research on the value of a particular species or ecosystem should lead to greater conservation. Thus, in a sense the application of QOV (if positive) acts as a buffer against irreversible decisions, until the point at which the uncertainty surrounding the decision is considerably reduced. It should be emphasized that quasi option value does not measure the net benefit of preservation (Fisher and Hanemann, 1987).

Arrow and Fisher (1974) showed that, as quasi option value is not dependent on risk aversion, it can be present when the decision maker makes choices on the basis of the expected monetary values of benefits and costs. However, the discussion of uncertainty in the context of quasi option value is based on a narrow conceptualization of uncertainty which implies that all situations are reducible to risk or soft uncertainty. As such in the model the probability of the net benefits of the different options in the second time period is assumed to be known and can be specified. Although quasi option value does introduce a dynamic aspect to the decision-making process, in that the decision maker can update the probabilities using Bayesian rules (Graham-Tomasi, 1995), it is still constrained within a probability framework, in which the full set of outcomes is known. As such, given the preceding arguments, it is not applicable to situations of hard uncertainty.

Moreover, as an *ex ante* decision framework for dealing with hard uncertainty it would appear of limited use. As Freeman (1993) has argued, quasi option value is not a separate component of an individual's utility function (if known) and as such cannot be estimated separately and added into cost–benefit analysis calculations. What quasi option value attempts to measure is the benefit of adopting better decision procedures. As such its magnitude can only be revealed *ex post* by comparing two strategies, where one involves optimal sequential decision making, to take advantage of the information obtained by delaying irreversible resource commitments. Even then such *ex post* analysis is restricted by notions of optimality which require the specification of probabilities, and so is inappropriate for environmental decisions conditioned by hard uncertainty. As an *ex ante* decision framework for dealing with hard uncertainty it is clearly redundant, because it does not help to assess the uncertainties surrounding the consequences of an irreversible decision.

## 4.5 EXPECTED UTILITY APPROACHES TO DECISION MAKING UNDER UNCERTAINTY

The second approach in decision-making models is to value the outcomes first (with no explicit attention given to uncertainty) and then to account for the uncertainty surrounding the occurrence of that outcome separately. The majority of decision-making models under uncertainty come into this category and rely on a separate mechanism under which the value of the outcomes and some measure of uncertainty associated with the specific outcomes are specified and some form of weighting procedure carried out in order to rank the different outcomes. Although the Shackle model also deals with uncertainty by means of a weighting mechanism outside the valuation process, because of its significant differences from the traditional framework it will be introduced in greater detail in Chapter 5. Instead, because of the relative hegemony that expected value and expected utility approaches have achieved in the literature, this section will be devoted to a critique of their applicability in environmental decision making, and in particular to decisions conditioned by hard uncertainty.

The immediate assumption that both expected value and utility approaches make is that of the applicability of probability. The conceptualization of uncertainty is such that for any action or policy an exhaustive list of possible outcomes or consequences can be specified, each with an associated probability, with the constraint that the probabilities will sum to unity. In the case of expected value the decision regarding the prospect[3] is evaluated in terms of the expected value ($\bar{x}$) of a gamble offering payoffs (outcomes) $(x_1, \ldots, x_n)$ with probabilities $(p_1, \ldots, p_n)$ using the formula:

$$\bar{x} = \sum_{i=1}^{n} x_i p_i \qquad (4.5)$$

Setting aside for the moment the issue of probability, the expected value approach has been criticized in the mainstream literature in relation to its inadequacy as a measure of the attractiveness of a monetary prospect. This is because expected value infers that the decision maker and his/her constituents are in fact risk-neutral.

Accordingly an alternative formulation can be based on the assumption that a risky prospect is evaluated by reference to not only the mathematical expectation of an outcome but also the level of the individual's subjective utility (at given levels of wealth) from that outcome. Consequently the expected utility of an outcome (EU) is calculated by the expression:

$$EU = \sum_{i=1}^{n} U(x_i)p_i \qquad (4.6)$$

where $U(\cdot)$ is termed a von Neumann–Morgenstern utility function after the work carried out by von Neumann and Morgenstern (1947).[4] The choices of the individual are then analysed by assuming that he maximize his preferences which are represented by a von Neumann–Morgenstern utility function.

The von Neumann–Morgenstern utility function differs from the ordinal utility function of standard consumer theory in that the only transformations possible are positive linear ones. Thus, only transformations which do not change the shape of the functions are possible. A concave function represents risk aversion, a linear function represents risk neutrality and a convex utility function represents a risk-loving individual. The von Neumann–Morgenstern function assumes that preferences between prospects are transitive, continuous and independent. These three properties are embodied in the following axioms:

1. *Complete ordering axiom*   For two alternatives A and B one of the following must be true: the consumer either prefers A to B, prefers B to A, or is indifferent between them. The consumer's evaluation of alternatives is transitive if, preferring A to B and B to C, they also prefer A to C.
2. *Continuity axiom*   Let A be preferred to B and B to C. The axiom asserts that there exists some probability p, ( 0 < p < 1 ), such that the consumer is indifferent between outcome B with certainty and a lottery (p, A,C)
3. *Independence axiom*   Let A be preferred to B and C be any outcome whatever. If one lottery $L_1$, offers outcomes A and C with probabilities p and 1 – p respectively, and another $L_2$ offers the outcomes B and C with the same probabilities p and 1 – p, then the consumer will prefer $L_1$. This is the equivalent of saying that that preferences (utilities) over outcomes are independent of the probabilities of those outcomes.

In the subjective utility model advanced by Savage (1954), who developed the work of de Finetti and Ramsey in the early 1930s, the use of an objective probability is substituted for the use of subjective probability. This step introduces the possibility of learning following Bayesian decision rules. The utility framework and its underlying axioms remain, however. In both expected utility and subjective utility approaches, the basis of the underlying axioms of utility provides a framework under which the rationality of the resulting decision is judged. The emphasis is very much on the substantive rationality of the decision itself. So that in order to act rationally (or optimally) an agent should maximize his or her utility value associated with the outcome from the particular scheme.

### 4.5.1  A Critique of Expected Utility Models of Decision Making in Relation to Hard Uncertainty

Expected utility (EU) theories and their variants can be critically evaluated in relation to three basic factors: first on the basis of their use of objective or subjective probabilities; second on whether the axioms used to represent the utility of the individual accurately reflect reality; and third on how the probability and utility function are combined in order to weight the different outcomes. The first factor, that of the applicability of both objective and subjective forms of probability for situations of hard uncertainty was dealt with in Section 4.3. From the preceding arguments it is evident that in decisions characterized by hard uncertainty as is present in many environmental problems, the reliance on probability within expected utility models appears problematic to say the least. The second and third arguments against the adoption of EU models of decision making have not yet been addressed however, and are therefore tackled in the two following sections. Again, the discussion will inevitably involve an overlap between a normative or prescriptive position of how individuals ought to behave and a behavioural approach reflecting how individuals actually make choices under uncertainty. In the second section the question that will need to be addressed is whether or not they are suitable mechanisms in relation to the procedural rationality of the decision process. The focus in this context will be on whether or not they capture the nature of the trade-off between uncertainty and the costs and benefits of a decision.

### 4.5.1.1  Expected utility theory and experimental evidence relating to its applicability

In addition to the critique of the applicability of expected utility approaches to cases of hard uncertainty, due to their reliance on a probability framework, further criticisms of expected utility have been made on the basis of experimental evidence. What the empirical evidence suggests is that many of the fundamental assumptions or axioms embodied in expected utility theory do not reflect the reality of how individuals make decisions in the face of uncertainty (Dalmazzone, 1995). The emphasis is therefore often on testing the behavioural predictions of the model. Interestingly much of the evidence has been collected from artificial or simulated choices in laboratory conditions. Very few 'real world' decision examples have been applied. Many of the results of the evidence point to the weakness at an empirical level of EU and subjective EU in dealing with all the modalities of uncertainty. However, instead of recognizing the effect that the different types of uncertainty may have on the applicability of EU theory, the tendency in the literature is to label such situations as ambiguous (Camerer and Weber, 1992). Thus, rather than using the experimental evidence as a reason to question the limited conceptualization of uncertainty, or to move completely outside the EU framework (see Ford and Ghose, 1995a, for a notable exception), alternatives tend to work on the relaxation of the assumption in question. Some of these variants will be briefly discussed in the next section.

The classic experimental evidence relating to 'ambiguity' is that of the Ellsberg paradox. In his experiment Ellsberg (1961) found that most of the actions of his subjects were inconsistent with the predictions of EU theory. Of most importance was the observation that people prefer to bet on states that they know more about, even if they have the same subjective probability. Some authors have interpreted this as second degree uncertainty or lack of confidence in one's first degree judgements. An alternative interpretation could be that subjective probability did not capture or best describe the type of uncertainty faced in such a decision (Ford and Ghose, 1995a). Thus rather than there being ambiguity about the probability, the use of probability and the expected utility mechanism for evaluating such outcomes may simply not have been used by the individuals to deal with the type of uncertainty faced in the experiment.

What some of the evidence does point to, in addition to the weaknesses of the assumption of the use of probability for all situations of uncertainty, is weaknesses in the way that EU theory characterizes 'rational' behaviour, and in particular behaviour in relation to the outcome (or value) of an uncertain action. One of the first critiques levelled by Friedman and Savage (1948) was that individual attitudes to risk are highly sensitive to levels of income. Thus, people of low incomes tend to be 'risk' averse (they are averse to the negative consequences of an uncertain action) while high income individuals tend to be 'risk' seekers. Whether this is the case for hard uncertainty remains to be seen. Are, for example, low income countries more averse to the uncertain consequences of biodiversity loss than high income countries?

Another important result is that empirical research has shown that people may in fact have asymmetric attitudes to gains and losses. Prospect theory (Kahneman and Tversky, 1979) suggests that outcomes are actually interpreted by agents with reference to their current asset position. This is because the consequence of a loss may influence individuals more than any increase in utility of the same amount. This may be particularly important in the context of environmental decisions, because it would suggest that individuals would assign a greater weight to the loss of an environmental service relative to the current state of nature than they would to a gain in environmental quality. The majority of experiments seeking to test the validity of EU theory, however, are only based on gain lotteries because of the simple problem that it is more difficult to organize laboratory experiments where the participants are subject to actual financial losses. This would again point to the need for more 'real world 'experiments to be carried out.

The famous Allais paradox (Allais, 1953) also poses difficulties for the expected utility approach in that it suggests that attitudes to different prospects may not in fact be independent. So for example, in the case where there are only two prospects with equal probability, the more that one prospect will leave an individual better off, the more risk averse they become about the other. This effect, also commonly known as 'common consequence effect' clearly breaks the independence axiom at the heart of EU theory (see for example Kahneman and Tversky, 1979 and Ford, 1994).

A final and more practical problem, and one particularly relevant in the context of environmental decision making, is that the power of the expected utility hypothesis tends to decline as the probabilities of the outcomes tend to unity or zero. One reason for this is that people facing a very unlikely event tend either to overestimate its likelihood of occurrence or alternatively assume that it is zero. This would also appear to break the assumption that the utility associated with an outcome is independent of the probability attached to the outcome. When low probability events are combined with possible catastrophic events, then expected utility has even more difficulty in dealing with the choices of individuals. In such cases it can be argued that expected utility does not account for behaviour, which seeks to avoid the consequences of a catastrophe, even when the probability attached to such a consequence is particularly low. This echoes one of Shackle's (1969) concerns that expected utility does not handle unique and irreversible decisions characterized by hard uncertainty very well. The notion of the focus value approach utilized in Shackle's model will be introduced in the next chapter as a possible means of dealing with this type of situation.

### 4.5.1.2 Evaluating an uncertain outcome: difficulties with the weighting mechanism in expected utility models and other averaging-based models

While much of the empirical research carried out on expected utility tests whether EU theory is a good descriptive theory, there is very little analysis devoted to whether it is normatively adequate. This is even although, as Camerer and Weber (1992) point out, most of the alternatives are meant to be normative improvements too. As a result unclear standards exist by which the proposed models are evaluated. With the aim of improving the procedural rationality of decision making, a normative improvement will be equated with the explicit recognition of uncertainty. Accordingly, this section will be limited to reviewing the central mechanism by which the models evaluate uncertain outcomes, rather than the different models themselves or the experimental evidence that led to their development (see Ford and Ghose, 1998, and Camerer and Weber, 1992). Instead the objective will be to provide a critique of the way that the outcome value and its respective measure of uncertainty (probability in the case of EU theory) is weighted.

The problems inherent in the underlying axioms of probability and the expected utility approach have led to the relaxation of some of the assumptions which form the basis of EU theory, as well as the subsequent development of a number of variants. While the different approaches are often ingenious attempts to overcome the difficulties of EU theory, as Ford and Ghose (1998) correctly point out, none move fully outside the paradigm of expected utility. Following Ford and Ghose (1998) it is possible to tabulate the functional forms of EU theory and some of the main suggested alternatives within what can be grouped collectively as averaging-based utility theories which are presented in Table 4.1.

The following notation applies to the table. First the $n$ outcomes (which are taken to be monetary) in any uncertain choice are represented by $x_i$, while $p_i$ denotes probability, $U(\cdot)$ denotes utility and $\pi$ denotes a non-linear probability function. In Hey's (1984) theory $g(\cdot)$ denotes a probability transformation function. In respect of Regret Theory let the two lotteries be A and B and the objective functional be $V(.)$, then there will be $i = 1, \ldots, n$ states of the world and the utility from an outcome, $x_{ij}$, will be $u(x_{ij})$, where j = A, B. The objective functional is a modified form of expected utility and is written as $V_A^B$ where it represents the choice of lottery A over that of lottery B, and vice versa. $M(\cdot)$ denotes the modified utility function which balances the attainment of one outcome against the regret of not having the other outcome.

The equations in Table 4.1 define the preference functional or action-choice index of each theory, and as such are the central mechanisms for evaluating the outcome of an uncertain action. What is common to all these models is that, as Ford and Ghose (1998) point out, the underlying mechanisms take a weighted average of the set of hypothesized outcomes. The important issue to consider when interpreting such models in a normative sense in the context of hard uncertainty is the way in which the different outcomes and their corresponding uncertainty measures (probabilities in the above) are weighted by a decision maker. Because of the limits imposed by hard uncertainty, the emphasis in this judgement will be on the procedural rather than substantive rationality of the evaluation mechanism. In other

*Table 4.1    Expected utility theories and other averaging-based alternatives*

| Theory | Functional: Authors |
|---|---|
| Expected Utility Theory | $\sum U(x_i)p_i$ <br><br> von Neumann and Morgenstern (1947) |
| Separable Prospect Theories | $\sum U(x_i)\pi p_i$ <br><br> Edwards (1955); Kahneman and Tversky (1979); Viscusi (1989) <br><br> $$\frac{\sum U(x_i)\pi(p_i)}{\sum \pi(p_i)}$$ <br><br> Karmarkar (1978) <br><br> $$\frac{\sum U(x_i)p_i}{\sum \tau(p_i)p_i}$$ <br><br> Chew (1983); Fishburn (1983) <br><br> $\sum U(x_i)g(p_i; x_1, x_2, x_3, \ldots, x_n)$ <br><br> Hey (1984) |
| Cumulative Prospect Theory | $\sum U(x_i)\left[g(p_1 + p_2 + \ldots + p_i) - g(p_1 + p_2 + \ldots + p_{i-1})\right]$ <br><br> Quiggin (1982); Yaari (1987); Green (1988); Segal (1989); Luce (1991); Luce and Fishburn (1991); Tversky and Kahneman (1992) |
| Machina's Theory | $\sum U(x_i)p_i + \left[\sum \tau(x_i)p_i\right]^2$ <br><br> Machina (1982) |
| Regret Theory | $V_A^B = \sum p_i M(u(x_{Ai}), u(x_{Bi}))$ <br><br> Bell (1982); Loomes and Sudgen (1982) |

*Source*:   Ford and Ghose, 1998

words, do the weighting functions explicitly deal with both the outcome of a particular action, and the uncertainty surrounding the occurrence of the outcome? What is common to EU theory and its variants in Table 4.1 is that they all employ a weighted average to arrive at an evaluation of the outcomes. They also make the crucial assumption that the weight or utility associated with a particular outcome is independent of the degree of uncertainty associated with that outcome. None weight or attach a utility to both the outcome value and its measure of uncertainty (probability in all the above cases). As such it is doubtful if they will make explicit any adjustment that is made in the mind of the decision maker between different outcomes with correspondingly different values, and the differing degrees of uncertainty attached to those outcomes. For an approach where the weighting attached to an action depends both on the outcome and measure of uncertainty, we will turn in the next chapter to the focus value approach advocated by Shackle.

### 4.5.2 Expected Utility Approaches and their Applicability to Environmental Decision Making

The argument has been made that different types of decisions are characterized by different underlying modalities of uncertainty and that for many environmental decisions the dominant mode is characterized by hard uncertainty. Drawing together our critiques of expected utility, it becomes apparent that expected utility models will have limited scope in relation to their application to environmental decisions. Part of the problem with expected utility theory has been its application to all types of decisions regardless of the mode of uncertainty encountered in the particular decision. This lack of attention paid by many exponents of EU to sufficiently exploring the different dimensions of uncertainty and thus recognizing the limitations of its application is surprising given that Savage (1954: p. 15) stressed that expected utility theory, because of the complete ordering axiom presumes that a finite set of outcomes can be specified by the individual. In this sense EU is not a general theory of decision making, because it does not explicitly deal with uncertainty *per se* (Davidson, 1996). Savage admits therefore that his 'look before you leap' analysis may not be applicable in all cases of uncertainty because 'a person may not know all the consequences of the acts open to him in each state of the world' (Savage, 1954: p. 15).

Savage (1954: pp. 15–16) accordingly concedes that there is a practical necessity to confine the use of EU and subjective EU to relatively simple situations. Not only will expected utility theory be limited in explaining behaviour in situations not characterized by soft uncertainty or risk, but it may also give flawed prescriptions of how decision makers should act. As a result, as in the case of hard uncertainty, the full range of outcomes cannot be specified, and there exists insufficient *a priori* information on which to assign subjective or objective probabilities.

If expected utility models are used in decisions characterized by hard uncertainty, then as Perrings and Opschoor (1994) argue, this may lead to unacceptable outcomes. For example the use of an expected utility framework may result in an 'optimal' decision when evaluated in terms of its substantive rationality, even if for example, such an action results in the loss of resilience to an ecosystem. Such a scenario could occur because the decision maker incorrectly assumed that all the consequences of a particular action or policy were known sufficiently well to define accurate probability distributions for their occurrence. If the probabilities attached to the decision are unreliable, then the resulting expected utility associated with any action will be necessarily misleading. It may be that because of the difficulty of observing system thresholds, the possibility of exceeding such a threshold and of the system flipping has not been anticipated (an exhaustive set of outcomes was incorrectly assumed) or only a very low probability has been allocated. In such cases both the assumption that it is possible to define an accurate probability distribution, as well as the (substantive) rationality on which the decision is judged are fundamentally flawed. Moreover, if it is known that an action may cause profound and irreversible damage which permanently reduces the welfare of future generations, but the objective probability of such damage is not known, then it is as Perrings (1997b: p. 160) states 'inequitable to act as if the probability is known'. Thus the assumption made in subjective expected utility theory that the decision maker can assume that subjective probabilities will accurately represent objective probabilities may result in very serious consequences for society.

In addition to the problem of the reliance of EU and subjective EU on probability, further doubts have been raised about the assumptions that expected utility theory makes. While the evidence collected is not specific to environmental decisions, many of the results would appear even more valid in the context of environmental decisions. In contrast to expected utility theory it would seem intuitive that environmental losses will be treated differently to environmental gains. Some of the evidence also points out some of the problems that EU theory has in dealing with events about which little is known (an all too common situation in complex environmental decisions). These behavioural limitations of the theory overlap with its normative limitations. In the last section the fact that EU weights the outcome and the measure of uncertainty associated with the outcome separately was highlighted. It is evident that this does not allow the decision maker to pay explicit attention to uncertainty, because the decision maker cannot adjust the overall weighting correspondingly. Moreover, rather than attaching importance to the weighted average of the outcomes, the decision maker may be drawn to a specific outcome. So, for example, even although an outcome with a very large negative consequence may be given the minimum utility possible, if a very small probability has been allocated that outcome will play a very limited role in the evaluation of the particular action or policy. This will be the case even if the decision maker believes that the negative consequence of the outcome outweighs the low probability associated with that outcome. This type of behaviour, where the decision maker focuses on a particular outcome, could be envisaged in decisions relating to building nuclear power stations after the Chernobyl disaster.

The significant problems that expected utility models face in terms of their application to environmental decisions conditioned by hard uncertainty suggest that it will not be sufficient simply to relax certain assumptions or to modify the model slightly. Instead, an alternative model to those encompassed by the expected utility umbrella will be needed. Foremost in such an alternative model of environmental decision making will be the requirement that it does not rely either on objective probability or subjective probability as a measure of uncertainty. Second, its assumptions and axioms will need to reflect the behaviour of decision makers more accurately when faced with hard uncertainty and finally the model will need to be based on an alternative mechanism for weighting both the outcome and its associated measure of uncertainty.

## 4.6   CONCLUSIONS

This chapter has argued that the problem of hard uncertainty implies that concepts of rationality must necessarily be bounded. Because the full set of outcomes cannot be specified, it is not possible to evaluate *ex ante* the optimality of a decision. As a result, because of the presence of hard uncertainty in many environmental decisions, the focus needs to be on the procedural rationality rather than substantive rationality of the decision-making process. This distinction between *ex ante* and *ex post* evaluation is crucial and highlights in many senses some of the confusion apparent both in the approaches taken to decision making under uncertainty and in whether or not a normative or purely behavioural framework is adopted. While explaining the way that decisions are made *ex post* is undoubtedly a useful exercise, if decision-making models are to contribute in any meaningful sense to the making of *ex ante* decisions conditioned by hard uncertainty, then they will need to be interpreted or adapted in a normative or prescriptive sense as well.

Building on the previous chapter the use of both objective probability and subjective probability has been criticized as inappropriate. The most important factors in this critique are that of the non-divisibility, or uniqueness of environmental decision conditioned by hard uncertainty, as well as the argument that in many such cases it is not possible to specify the full set of outcomes of an action. Consequently, it has been shown that dealing with hard uncertainty within the valuation process is not possible, because of the reliance on a probability framework, as well as problems relating to the estimation of separate option and quasi option values.

The dominant paradigm in decision making under uncertainty, based on expected utility and its subjective form, is also flawed in the context of modelling decisions under hard uncertainty, in that once again it relies on the use of probabilities. The lack of recognition in such models of the different modalities of uncertainty can be seen as a major factor in their failure; a point echoed by the experimental evidence which would seem to suggest that many of the fundamental axioms or assumptions of EU theory do not in fact reflect reality. A more limited critique can be put forward, in that both the underlying mode of rationality and other assumptions, while perhaps applicable in the case of soft uncertainty or risk, cannot be extended to situations of hard uncertainty. A final point was made regarding the extent to which the evaluation mechanisms used by EU theory and its variants provide explicit attention to weighting both the value of an action and the uncertainty surrounding its occurrence. This critique of the dominant decision-making paradigm as a means of dealing with hard uncertainty in environmental decision making leads us to a review of an alternative approach, based on the work of George Shackle, in the next chapter.

## NOTES

1. The distinction between objective and subjective probability is defined in Sections 4.3.1 and 4.3.2.
2. Two other measures of probability exist, one based on the work of Keynes (1921), Jeffreys (1939, 1948) and Carnap (1945) and the other based on the propensity interpretation expounded by Popper (1959–60, 1972, 1990). However, due to their limited use in decision-making models, they are not reviewed in this chapter.
3. A prospect is defined in the expected utility literature as a vector of probabilities that given states of the world will occur, with the corresponding vector of outcomes associated with such states of the world (Dalmazzone, 1995).
4. The underlying approach was that of Bernouilli (1738, 1954).

# 5. The Shackle model

## 5.1 INTRODUCTION

The thesis argued so far is that the application of decision-making models such as expected utility (EU), which rely on a probability framework and which are based on the notion of substantive rationality, will be limited to decisions characterized by soft uncertainty or risk. Where the decision is characterized by hard uncertainty, as is the case in many environmental decisions, the need for an alternative approach becomes apparent. In this chapter an alternative model, based on the work of Shackle, is introduced and critically assessed in relation to its applicability to environmental decision making.

Shackle's theory is attractive in the context of environmental decision making, because it is one of the few models that steps completely outside the expected utility and probability frameworks. This is because Shackle's model not only rejects the use of the probability calculus and suggest its replacement with an alternative measure of uncertainty, but it also puts forward an alternative mechanism for evaluating the outcomes associated with an action and their corresponding measures of uncertainty. This mechanism, which can be interpreted as a focus value approach (Ford, 1994; Ford and Ghose, 1998), is markedly different from the weighted average models utilized by expected utility and its variants.

The application of the Shackle model can be demonstrated in two contexts. The first is its use as a descriptive tool for explaining the way that environmental decisions characterized by hard uncertainty are made. This hypothesis is tested by the use of a case study involving a road building project in Belize. The second, which builds on the arguments made in the preceding chapters, is that the application of Shackle's ideas in a normative sense can be used as a basis for the development of an improved framework which can help to improve the procedural rationality of the decision-making process. As such it holds a number of advantages over its rivals. Before these hypotheses can be put to the test, it will be necessary to provide a detailed theoretical exposition of Shackle's model of decision making under uncertainty. This chapter therefore has two main purposes: first, to outline the main tenents of Shackle's approach; and second critically to assess the model in relation to providing a suitable operational framework for analysing decision making in the context of hard uncertainty. It does not offer a comprehensive review of Shackle's theory and its critiques *per se* but an interpretation of Shackle's model of decision making under uncertainty.[1]

### 5.1.1 Interpreting Shackle's Theory of Decision Making under Uncertainty: An Alternative Approach

In the preceding chapters some of the main critiques that Shackle forwarded against the probability and expected utility framework have been outlined. While Shackle's main concerns were restricted to more economic concerns such as the making of investment decisions, many of his arguments can be fruitfully extended to the environmental–economic system. Shackle's ideas are particularly applicable to irreversible environmental decisions characterized by hard uncertainty, in which the decision moment can be characterized as unique and embedded in the unidirectional flow of time (Vickers, 1986). This problem of historical time exists where there are no historical precedents for the constituent actions, or where the boundary conditions change as a result of the activity. The passing of an ecological threshold is a prime example of such a decision.

In addition to the uniqueness and time dependence of the external conditions that a decision maker faces, the entire epistemological baggage and status of the individual is characterized by Shackle as unique. This is because in the flow of time, knowledge, a unique series of information and experiences, is acquired by the decision maker and cannot be unlearned. Decisions are therefore seen by Shackle as 'self-destructive' (Shackle, 1961) in that the taking of them forever changes both the possible structure of future decision environments and the knowledge status of the decision maker himself. As such, therefore, in Shackle's framework the notion that identical decision conditions are 'never to be repeated' (Shackle, 1955: p. 7) is a key element in his theory. The future is transmutable precisely because it is created by crucial choice decisions.

Although Shackle did allow for the notion of some decisions becoming routine, in the sense that they are repeated in more or less unchanging circumstances, he did not accept that in such cases it might be possible to represent the decision within the confines of a probability framework, such as that adopted by EUT. At the same time, traditional economics has stubbornly refused to characterize uncertainty by anything other than probability. Arguably, part of the reason for Shackle's failure to persuade his peers, was that he regarded all decisions as unique and as such there was no room for any alternative theories, particularly those based on the probability calculus. Thus no explicit attention was given in the debate to consider more fully the question (first posed by Knight, 1921) over whether there may in fact be a distinction between different situations of uncertainty. While traditional economics has been reluctant to move away from the idea that all forms of uncertainty could be captured by the probability concept (Ford, 1994), Shackle (1949, 1961) as well as Katzner (1995) and Vickers (1994) appear equally to stress that Shackle's theory should be applied to all modes of uncertainty. There is a degree, therefore, to which the two sides of the debate have been in some instances talking past each other, while ignoring questions surrounding the different underlying modalities of uncertainty that are faced in any given decision.

The recognition that there are a number of different modalities of uncertainty, with a particular distinction being drawn between situations characterized by soft uncertainty and hard uncertainty, implies the need for decision-making models to reflect the different underlying modalities of uncertainty. Thus, while Shackle's conceptualization of uncertainty is very persuasive, particularly where a decision maker is drawn to focus on one particular outcome (Dalmazzone, 1995), it is conceded that for certain situations, characterized by soft uncertainty or risk, the use of a probability framework is possible. In contrast, where a decision is to be taken in the context of hard uncertainty, as was demonstrated in the last chapter, the use of a probability based approach, such as expected utility, is clearly not applicable. By taking a position which does not advocate the use of one all-encompassing decision model it may help to re-focus the debate. Indeed more recent signs from economics, environmental economics and ecological economics show there is a greater willingness to consider alternative conceptualizations of uncertainty. Combined with the redefinition of Shackle's theory in relation to hard uncertainty employed here this suggests that Shackle's theory can play a fruitful role within the discourse.

## 5.2   SHACKLE'S MODEL OF DECISION MAKING UNDER UNCERTAINTY

Shackle's theory, when it was published in the 1940s constituted one of the most original approaches to decision making under uncertainty, and a powerful alternative to the application of expected utility theory to cases of hard uncertainty. While Shackle's theory has been largely ignored by mainstream economics, a number of authors have been notable in developing and applying his ideas. Most notably Ford (1994) has provided an excellent review of Shackle's work, which along with his other major contributions (1983, 1987) have arguably provided a clarity to Shackle's theory, often missing in much of the literature. Vickers (1994) and Katzner (1995) have also published extensively on Shackle, and have made attempts to develop variations on the original model. Earl (1983) has absorbed the theory into the framework of behavioural economics. The literature and development of Shackle's theory in the context of environmental–economic decisions is more limited however. Although Dalmazzone (1995) has highlighted the possibility of applying the Shackle model in the context of environmental uncertainty and Perrings (1989) introduced the model in the context of environmental bonds, an in-depth analysis and application of Shackle's theory in the context of environmental uncertainty has not been carried out.

Shackle's model of decision making under uncertainty is based on three main pillars. The first is the replacement of probability as a measure of uncertainty by an alternative, degree of surprise. This indicates the individual's degree of uncertainty regarding the hypothesized outcomes resulting from a particular action, with gains and losses being considered separately. The second is the decision or action choice index, which is the mechanism by which the different outcomes and their corresponding degree of surprise are evaluated. This is the procedure by which the decision maker simplifies and edits the expectational elements of any strategy and focuses on two outcomes, one the focus gain and the other the focus loss. The third element is the gambler's preference map, which is put forward as a means of comparing two different policies or actions. In the gambler's preference map, each prospect would in effect be represented by a focus gain and focus loss. The purpose of the gambler's preference map is therefore to allow the balancing of the worst and best that can happen with any action, with an alternative course of action. Before a more detailed exposition and critique of these separate elements in relation to their operationalization is undertaken, a brief synopsis of how these elements function together in Shackle's model will be provided.

The first element of Shackle's model is his replacement of probability as a measure of uncertainty, with what he terms 'potential surprise'. Potential surprise indicates the individual's degree of uncertainty as to the hypothetical outcomes of any action scheme; with gains (positive returns) and losses (negative returns) being considered separately. To illustrate the concept of degree of surprise, which Shackle invariably denotes by the symbol $y$, imagine that a decision maker is confronted by a particular choice or action which has a range of outcomes $x_i$ ($i = 1, ..., n$). In most of Shackle's examples $x$ is taken to be a monetary amount, such as the gross value of an outcome. The value assigned to the degree of surprise, which reflects the individual's degree of belief in a given outcome, can range from zero to some subjective maximum value, normally indicated by $\bar{y}$ (Shackle also uses the notation $\hat{y}$). On the basis of this, a potential surprise function can be assigned over all outcomes:

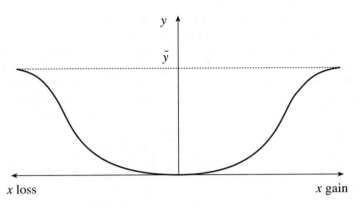

*Figure 5.1    The potential surprise function*

$$y = y(x) \tag{5.1}$$

Because outcomes are separated by gains and losses, there are effectively two branches of the potential surprise function, namely one for positive outcomes $g_i$ ($i = 1, \ldots, n$) and one for the negative outcomes $l_i$ ($i = 1, \ldots, n$). The potential surprise function can in principle assume any form over either the gain or loss branch, and can be continuous or discontinuous over gains and losses depending on the expectations of the individual. This function is often drawn by Shackle in the form of an inverted bell (see Figure 5.1) although it can in theory take any shape. It is because Shackle often drew the potential surprise function in this way that some authors mistakenly took potential surprise as merely representing the inverse of probability, although this is not in fact the case (Ford, 1994).

The next stage in Shackle's model is the specification of the ascendancy function, which is the means by which both the outcome and corresponding degree of surprise are weighted by the individual. The ascendancy function indicates the weight that any outcome/degree of surprise pair or element ($x$, $y$) is given, or in Shackle's terminology the power of any pair to arrest the attention of the individual. The individual's ascendancy function is therefore denoted by:

$$\phi = \phi(x, y) \tag{5.2}$$

Where $x$ again denotes either a positive (gain) outcome ($g$) or a negative (loss) outcome ($l$). The properties of the ascendancy function are such that the partial derivative of $\phi(\cdot)$ is positive with respect to $x$ and negative with respect to $y$:

$$\frac{\partial \phi}{\partial x} > 0; \quad \frac{\partial \phi}{\partial y} < 0 \tag{5.3}$$

where, if $x$ happens to be denoted by a loss, it is measured by the absolute magnitude of the loss. As is the case for potential surprise equation (5.2), it need not be defined the same over gains and losses. As a result, all things being equal, the higher the gain in any investment, the higher will its power be to attract the attention of the decision maker, or the higher will be the weight attached to the outcome; equally the larger the loss, the larger will be its ascendancy or weight in the mind of the decision maker. If everything else remains constant, as the potential surprise attached to a gain or loss increases, then that outcome will increasingly lose its ascendancy or weighting in the mind of the decision maker.

The process by which the individual is hypothesized to use the ascendancy function to edit the set of outcomes and to focus on one gain and one loss outcome (the focus values) is best explained diagramatically (see Figure 5.2). If the assumption is made that the ascendancy function is continuous then we can derive for each possible level of $\phi$ an indifference curve which traces out for us the combinations of $(g, y)$ or $(l, y)$ consistent with a given level of $\phi$. The resultant indifference curves will have positive slopes in their respective gain and loss quadrants. These are represented in Figure 5.2 by the dashed lines, and in the positive orthant of the diagram the level of $\phi$ increases as we move to the right, and in the negative orthant the level of $\phi$ increases as we move to the left. The shape of the indifference curves will be determined by the second order conditions, which are assumed by Shackle to be such that we can construct the $\phi$ indifference curves as portrayed in Figure 5.2.

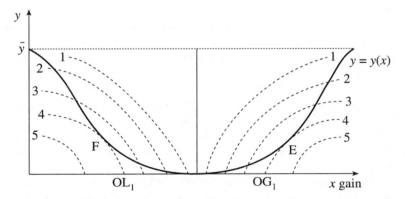

*Figure 5.2   The ascendancy indifference curves and potential surprise function*

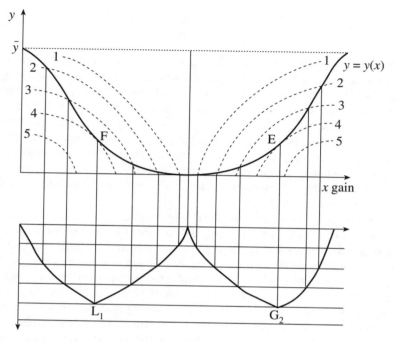

*Note:*    1, 2, ..., 5 are levels of φ, with 5 corresponding to the highest level.

*Figure 5.3    The ascendancy function and focus values*

Based on the existence of the different levels of φ represented by the indifference curves, the individual is assumed to maximize φ subject to the constraint placed on it by the potential surprise function, which represents the degree of uncertainty attached to the outcomes associated with any action; this is represented by the solid line drawn in Figure 5.1. So for example at point E the individual has maximized the level of φ subject to the constraint of the potential surprise function. The ascendancy function is therefore defined by the points at which the potential surprise function (based on the range of outcomes) is tangential to, or intersects the ascendancy indifference curves. The derivation of the ascendancy function in this manner is usually represented by Shackle (for example 1961: p. 159) in the manner reproduced in Figure 5.3.

The ascendancy function is therefore defined by the constraints imposed by the potential surprise function as well as the underlying shape of the ascendancy indifference curves. Thus, the diagram which lies in the bottom half of Figure 5.3 epitomises the properties of φ(·), when the function has been specified solely in terms of the outcome, $x$, and where the potential surprise value is effectively replaced, by means of the potential surprise function $y = y(x)$, by the value of $x$ to which $y$ is assigned.

By this process, the ascendancy function is the means by which the decision maker is envisaged to focus or edit the different outcome/uncertainty pairs and to focus on two outcomes (one from the gain branch and one from the loss branch) which maximize the ascendancy function and arrive at two focus values, namely the focus gain $G_1$ and the focus loss $L_1$, which are collectively termed the primary focus values. These values represent the best to be hoped for and the worst to be feared, in any prospect, where a prospect is defined as a possible course of action with at least a partial set of hypothesized outcomes.

The next and final step in the decision or action choice stage of the model is the calculation of the standardized focus values. This is achieved by removing the potential surprise argument from the primary focus values, the purpose of which is as Shackle contends, to allow the decision maker to compare the gains and losses from competing investments or projects on an equal footing (Shackle, 1949). The emphasis at this stage is to allow comparison of competing projects or investments. Equivalence measures for the focus gain and focus loss values, which remove the potential surprise element, are obtained by locating that gain or loss value with attached zero degree of surprise. This is identical to the focus gain/loss, in that it produces the same level of $\phi$ (that is, it is on the same ascendancy indifference curve) as the focus gain or loss value. This is shown by $OG_1$ (the standardized focus gain and $OL_1$ (standardized focus loss) in Figure 5.2. This places the best and the worst hypothesized outcome in any competing action on comparable monetary values, one gain and one loss, sometimes referred to as the 'certainty equivalents' (Shackle, 1955).

The final pillar or stage of Shackle's model is the process by which, for competing actions or investments, the different standardized focus gain and focus loss values are compared. This ranking of the different focus pairs of any one project against those of another is achieved by the introduction of the gambler's preference map, which epitomizes the balancing of the best against the worst that can happen as the result of any action. The gambler's preference map can be represented by Figure 5.4 and consists of a series of gambler-preference indifference curves, which are ranked in ascending order from south west to north west. The indifference curves implicitly represent different levels of preferences for combinations of gain/loss pairs and can be regarded as an indicator of utility or some other index (Ford, 1994). The standardized focus gain/loss pair that lies on the highest curve will determine the investment which is chosen. The gambler's preference indifference curves represent an extra opportunity in Shackle's model for the individual to express

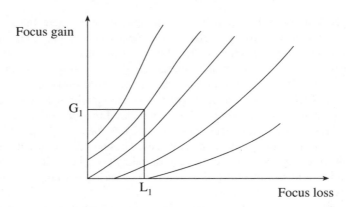

*Figure 5.4    The gambler preference map*

his or her preference or aversion to losses or what Shackle terms as risk preference (Shackle, 1949).

Shackle (1949) argues that no one indifference curve is forced to be uniquely related to any other, and as such they are free to depict the individual's varying attitude to 'risk'. In this sense he does not specify the existence of a gambler's preference function (Ford, 1994; Ford and Ghose, 1998). Shackle does however point out that the indifference curves may exhibit thresholds, for example the maximum loss that can be tolerated relative to the individual's wealth or the maximum losses that could be experienced (Shackle, 1969).

## 5.3   OPERATIONALIZING SHACKLE'S THEORY IN THE CONTEXT OF HARD UNCERTAINTY

Shackle's theory of decision making has been interpreted in a number of different manners. As was stated at the start of the chapter, Shackle's theory is best applied to the context of hard uncertainty rather than to the other modes of uncertainty. Limiting the application of Shackle's theory to hard uncertainty is important in relation to operationalizing his model of decision-making under uncertainty in that it allows some of the main criticisms that Shackle's theory faces to be tackled head on. Moreover, because Shackle's model is to be operationalized in the context of hard uncertainty as opposed to ignorance, soft uncertainty or certainty, then this implies a different discourse to that employed by the dominant language of probability and which recognizes the fundamentally different modality on which hard uncertainty is based. Consequently the evaluation of the model can only take place within the bounds of a limited rationality. This is because in hard uncertainty only an incomplete set of outcomes is known, and only a non-exhaustive set of hypothesized outcomes, which may result from any action or policy, can be specified.

In the context of hard uncertainty there can be no meaning attached to the difference between making an optimal decision between, say, policy A and policy B. Precisely because an exhaustive set of outcomes cannot be specified, there may always be at least one outcome which is more optimal than the outcomes specified in action A or B. Thus, as has been argued previously in the context of hard uncertainty, the discussion is limited in relation to evaluating Shackle's model purely in terms of the procedural rationality of the decision-making process. Therefore the emphasis will be on the decision model in relation to the evaluation of the different outcomes of a single action or policy rather than its evaluation of alternative actions or policies (such as A or B). Similarly, where the outcomes that are to be considered are what Shackle (1952) would term rival outcomes, it makes no sense to 'choose' between rival outcomes, because only one will occur.

Operationalizing the model in the context of the hard uncertainty surrounding environmental problems, again raises the question of the interpretation of the model in a behavioural or normative sense. Operationality implies in both interpretations that the model should be demonstrably relevant to the real world and thus relate to real world phenomena (Katzner, 1995). If the model is to be operationalized in a behavioural sense then the aim is to shed light on actual behaviour. As such, therefore, to be operational, a theory should be capable of being empirically tested or its propositions evaluated subjectively. It is important to recognize as Katzner (1995) points out, that it is not possible to submit behavioural models to an absolute test which will determine whether the propositions of the model are true or false nor is it possible to deduce that a model is the single correct analysis of the phenomena in question. All that can be deduced is that under certain criteria and particular sets of data, the propositions that the model makes are verified or falsified under these conditions.

Shackle argues that there are three main ways that theories of uncertainty can be tested empirically. The first is by conducting experiments, the second is by analysing time series data and the third is by case studies compiled by watching decision takers making real world decisions (Ford, 1994). Shackle also cautions against any conclusions made with respect to results from experiments testing theories, particularly due to the problems of avoiding framing or context factors, as well as the reward structures and the fact that experimental tests will never truly mirror real world decisions (Ford, 1994). The majority of commentators have focused on Shackle's model in a behavioural sense and have criticized the constructs and axioms on which it is built, from a theoretical viewpoint, in relation to how they explain decision making under uncertainty. In a few notable cases (Hey, 1985; Ford and Ghose, 1994a, 1994b, 1995a, 1995b, 1995c) successful attempts have been made to test empirically the predictions that Shackle's model makes; the majority of these have been carried out in laboratory experiments. The focus of these studies has been in uncovering evidence of the use of Shackle's constructs and attempts to distinguish between whether choices between lotteries conform with Shackle's theory or to expected utility and its variants (see Ford and Ghose, 1998). In general, however, there has been a lack of studies directed towards case studies of real decisions and none directed to environmental decisions.

The operationalization of Shackle's model of decision making under uncertainty in a normative sense has received much less attention. Indeed a number of authors (for example Earl, 1983; Ford, 1994) have emphasized the application of Shackle's theory in a behavioural rather than a normative sense. Although it is doubtful whether Shackle's theory can be interpreted in a normative context in relation to providing optimizing decision criteria (based on a notion of substantive rationality), it is argued that in the context of procedural rationality it is possible to apply it in a normative sense. The normative interpretation of the model of decision making under hard uncertainty is based on the extent that the model establishes propositions indicating how the uncertainty present in a decision should be evaluated. In this sense the model will be normatively operational if it can generate rules of thumb which will guide what ought to be done in relation to the procedural rationality of the decision making process itself. It is argued that, although less frequently discussed, Shackle's model of decision making under uncertainty can make an important contribution when applied in this sense.

While the positive predictions of a model can be to a certain degree tested empirically, this information is only of use in a normative sense in that it will indicate if a model or the particular features of a model will lend itself to being practically implemented. Normatively operational criteria may or may not be positively operational. As Katzner (1995) argues however: 'The only way to discover if an individual is actually using a normatively operational criterion to guide his behaviour is to ask him' (Katzner, 1995: p. 239).

While this type of questioning is not sufficient to verify completely whether a model is positively operational, it does give an indication of what an individual thinks that (s)he is doing. Moreover if the individual is aware of what (s)he is doing then they are aware that they are following some criterion in a normative sense. These issues will be raised again in Chapter 7. It is sufficient to say at the present that operationalizing a model normatively may imply a different relationship between theory and reality than does positive operationality (Katzner, 1995). It is with a view to operationalizing Shackle's model of decision making under uncertainty (positively and normatively), that the following section reviews the different elements of the model before a variation of Shackle's original model is developed.

## 5.4 THE KEY ELEMENTS OF THE SHACKLE MODEL OF DECISION MAKING UNDER UNCERTAINTY

Now that the context in which the Shackle model will be interpreted has been outlined, attention is focused on the main elements of Shackle's model. It should be emphasized that this section does not attempt to review all the critiques of Shackle's theory (see Ford, 1994 for a comprehensive review) but is limited to those elements which can be operationalized and applied in the context of hard uncertainty in both a behavioural and normative manner. As such it will draw not only on the work of Shackle but also the contributions made by Ford (1983, 1987, 1994) as well as Katzner (1995) and Vickers (1994) in suggesting variations of Shackle's original model as outlined previously. The possible adaptation of the model will remain, however, within the interpretative framework outlined above and also contrasts in the form taken to those variations proposed by Ford (1983), Katzner (1995) and Vickers (1994).

In terms of the evaluation of the Shackle model in relation to hard uncertainty, there are two underlying features of the model which intuitively appear attractive. First, the model replaces probability as a measure of uncertainty with an alternative measure based on degree of surprise. The concept of degree of surprise will be evaluated in this section. Second, the model proposes an alternative mechanism for evaluating outcomes and their corresponding uncertainty. Shackle's original formulation relies on two components, namely the use of an ascendancy function which weights both the outcome and its related degree of surprise and second the gambler's preference map. It is to review these individual elements that this thesis now turns.

### 5.4.1 An Alternative Measure of Uncertainty: Potential Surprise

Potential surprise as a measure of uncertainty is conceived on a cardinal scale such as degrees Celsius (Ford, 1994) and is used with upper and lower bounds (Shackle, 1961). Thus the occurrence of the alternatives is conceived as ranging from the perfectly possible at one end of the scale through to the impossible. The degrees of potential surprise assigned by the decision maker in Shackle's schema are meant to be direct reflections of the degree of possibility the decision maker thinks resides in the realization of the alternative outcomes which can result in any outcome. As Shackle argues:

A man cannot, in general, tell what will happen, but his conception of the nature of things, the nature of men and their institutions and affairs of the non-human world enables him to form a judgement as to whether any suggested thing can happen. In telling himself that such and such a thing can happen, he means that its occurrence would not surprise him; for we are surprised at the occurrence of what we had supposed to be against nature ... If a man feels that ... the occurrence of a given thing would not surprise him in the slightest degree ... that thing is perfectly possible. We are taking the certainty of the wrongness of a proposition to be a state of mind familiar to everyone and needing no definition ... This state of mind ... is a judgement that the thing in question is impossible ... (it has) an absolute maximum degree of surprise ... If surprise corresponds to possibility, then we can say that there are degrees of possibility ... Surprise provides us with a means of knowing how strongly we doubted the possibility of a given happening or a given outcome of some act of our own. (Shackle, 1961: pp. 67–8)

The construction of degree of surprise as an alternative measure of uncertainty is based on Shackle's critique of probability. Unlike the notion of probability, potential surprise is applicable to unique or crucial events. As a subjective concept in the mind of the decision maker, its derivation does not rely on the replication of a series of trials under unchanging conditions (that is it is non-divisible). Because degree of surprise has an independent existence, as a notion of belief, it is applicable to unique events (Venn, 1888).[2] More fundamental in its critique of both objective and subjective probability is that an appropriate measure of uncertainty should not require that the complete set of outcomes is known and can be specified. Shackle therefore constructed potential surprise as a non-distributional variable, where because of the nature of the uncertainty, the decision maker is only able to draw up a necessarily incomplete list of outcomes. As a non-distributional variable then it possesses meaning, unlike probability, in hard uncertainty. This is because Shackle (1949, 1961) allows room for the notion of a 'residual hypothesis' which allows for a conception of reality in which unanticipated events may occur. The future is not corralled by the complete set of outcomes required for the use of probability, so the assumption is not made that the universe is fully known. As such potential surprise is not constrained to add up to unity.

The importance of potential surprise being a non-distributional variable is reflected in the fact that Shackle also defines it as non-additive. Because only an incomplete set of outcomes is known it makes no sense for them to be added together. Furthermore, where the incomplete set of outcomes are in effect mutually exclusive, no meaning can be attached to permitting the alternative outcomes, which are in effect rivals, to have a share in the evaluation of a specific action. As a result, degree of surprise is constructed as a non-additive variable and is not constrained to add up to unity. The degree of surprise attached to the occurrence of one outcome is not conditional on the

degree of surprise attached to other outcomes. The decision maker therefore
is unrestricted in allotting degrees of surprise to the competing outcomes. As
Ford (1994) points out, situations can be imagined in which the degrees of
potential surprise allotted to an outcome may change as the number of rivals
changes. The crucial difference between Shackle's concept and that of probability, however, is that, because it is non-additive, the individual is not
forced to make adjustments to the degrees of potential surprise accorded to
the different outcomes. Moreover, as a non-additive measure, no meaning can
be attached to its multiplication with any outcome as the basis for a decision
index, as is found in the weighted averaging mechanism utilized in expected
utility models.

### 5.4.1.1 Shackle's axioms for potential surprise

Underlying the intuitive rationale for the use of potential surprise as an
alternative measure of uncertainty, Shackle (1949, 1952, 1961) detailed a
number of other features of the variable in his formal axiom system. It is the
axioms of potential surprise that give a strictly distinct meaning to probability, and which mean that it can in no way be taken as the inverse of probability
(see Ford, 1994; Katzner, 1986). These axioms are presented as follows, with
the majority taken from Shackle (1952: pp. 130–1) except axiom 7 which
comes from Shackle (1949) and Shackle (1961: p. 83). This is arguably the
clearest version of Shackle's axioms (Ford, 1994).

1.  An individual's degree of belief in a hypothesis can be thought of as
    consisting in a degree of potential surprise associated with the hypoth-
    esis, and in another degree associated with its contradictory.
2.  Degrees of potential surprise can be zero or greater than zero. No mean-
    ing is assigned to a degree of potential surprise less than zero. Degrees of
    potential surprise are bounded by that degree $\hat{y}$, called the absolute maxi-
    mum of potential surprise, which signifies the absolute rejection of the
    hypothesis to which it is assigned, absolute disbelief in the truth of the
    suggested answer to a question or the possibility of the suggested out-
    come of an 'experiment'.
3.  Equality between the respective degrees of belief felt by an individual in
    two hypotheses will then require, for its expression in terms of potential
    surprise, two statements, namely that some given degree of potential
    surprise is attached to both hypotheses, and that some given degree is
    attached to the contradictories of both.
4.  The degree of potential surprise associated with any hypothesis will be
    the least degree amongst all those appropriate to different mutually
    exclusive sets of hypotheses (each set considered as a whole) whose
    truth appears to the individual to imply the truth of this hypothesis.

5. All the members of an exhaustive set of rival hypotheses can carry zero degrees of potential surprise.
6. When H is any hypothesis, the degree of potential surprise attached to the contradictory of H is equal to the smallest degree attached to any rival of H.
7. The degree of surprise assigned to the joint (simultaneous) truth of two hypotheses is equal to the greater of the respective degrees assigned to the separate hypotheses.

or expressed alternatively:

7. Given the degree of potential surprise $y^a$ assigned to a hypothesis A, and the degree $y_0^b$ which would be assigned to a hypothesis B if $y^a$ were zero, the degree in fact assigned to B will be the greater of $y^a$, $y_0^b$.
8. Any hypothesis and its contradictory together constitute an exhaustive set of rival hypotheses.
9. At least one member of an exhaustive set of rival hypotheses must carry zero potential surprise.

The interpretation and the verification of the axioms will depend in part on whether they are being evaluated in terms of their ability to explain or predict the behaviour of individuals, or whether in a normative sense they adequately capture the nature of hard uncertainty and as such whether potential surprise is an appropriate measure of hard uncertainty. A number of problems are present in respect of Shackle's original axioms, which Ford (1994) argues do not appear sufficiently precise for this purpose. Axiom 7 in particular has been subject to critical discussion from Levi (1966) (see Ford, 1994 for a comprehensive review). Katzner (1986) notably attempted a formalization of Shackle's axioms systems. However a number of problems exist in his exposition (Ford, 1994), because the mirroring of Shackle's original axioms attempted does not allow for the valid critiques in Shackle's original exposition of potential surprise.

The important feature of potential surprise as far as hard uncertainty is concerned is that it is a non-distributional, non-additive variable. Given therefore that potential surprise, when applied to situations of hard uncertainty, is constructed as a measure of the degree of surprise that an individual would feel at the occurrence of an incomplete set of outcomes, then there are a number of key features or axioms that can be stated:

A1. Degree of potential surprise is dependent on the extent that an individual believes that a particular outcome is possible. Zero degree of surprise indicates that the individual believes that it is perfectly possible that the outcome will occur, while the absolute maximum degree of surprise $\bar{y}$ indicates that the individual believes the occurrence of the outcome to be impossible.

A2. At least one member of an exhaustive set of rival hypotheses must carry zero degree of potential surprise.

A3. Every member of an exhaustive set of rival hypotheses can be assigned a zero degree of potential surprise.

A4. The potential surprise of either outcome $x_1$ or outcome $x_2$ is equal to the minimum potential surprise of $y(x_1)$ or $y(x_2)$.

A5. The degree of surprise assigned to any outcome need not depend on the degree of surprise attached to the occurrence of its rivals.

The first axiom defines potential surprise as a measure of the uncertainty associated with the occurrence of an incomplete set of outcomes. The emphasis is therefore placed on potential surprise as a measure of uncertainty, which is consistent with the features of hard uncertainty, rather than a direct measure of the belief of the occurrence of a particular hypothesis. Much of the original criticism (see for example Carter, 1953 and Dorfman, 1955) directed at Shackle's original concept of potential surprise focused on its replacement of probability as a measure of belief. While it may be correct to emphasize the role of belief in probability (as a measure of knowledge), arguably the notion of belief is not so crucial when we are dealing with hard uncertainty defined by a lack of knowledge. Part of Shackle's original concern was that any measure of uncertainty cannot include a certainty of rightness, because the complete set of outcomes is not fully known. This concern is reflected in the above axioms in that, although there is a measure of certainty of wrongness which is expressed by assigning the maximum degree of potential surprise, there is no indicator for certainty of rightness because more than one outcome can be assigned zero degrees of surprise. It should also be noted that while potential surprise is envisaged as a measure of uncertainty, it is defined in terms of the subjective expectations of the individual. As such therefore it does not measure the absolute level of uncertainty *per se*. This is done at the start of the decision-making process when the level and mode of uncertainty encountered in any decision are subjectively evaluated by the decision maker.

Recognizing that probability and potential surprise are measures which correspond to fundamentally different modes of uncertainty implies that the basis of the measures (such as belief, possibility, credibility) of the different modes of uncertainty can also be expected to vary accordingly. Moreover given the subjective nature of the way that the hard uncertainty surrounding the occurrence of an outcome is evaluated, it is perhaps unrealistic to expect that individuals will consistently apply the same interpretation to any measure of uncertainty. On a practical note it is also difficult to determine in a positive manner on what the alternative measures of uncertainty are actually based (see Ford and Ghose, 1994b). The emphasis will therefore be on testing the positive operationality of potential surprise as a measure of hard uncertainty, as well as indicating the normative constructs on which a measure of hard uncertainty should be based.

The second axiom (Ford and Ghose, 1994a), A2, directly corresponds to the ninth axiom in Shackle's list and emphasizes the point that in an exhaustive set of outcomes at least one must be regarded as perfectly possible. Of course, in situations of hard uncertainty defined by a non-exhaustive set, by definition this requirement is not necessary. Axiom A3 corresponds to Shackle's fifth axiom. This axiom is important in defining a partial ordering only and is also important in defining potential surprise as a non-distributional variable. Axioms A4 and A5 epitomize a central notion in Shackle's model, namely that the measure of uncertainty should be non-additive and non-distributional. Although in some cases hard uncertainty will be dealing with policies defined by sets of mutually exclusive outcomes, there may also be situations in which there may be weak interdependence between two possible actions, or the nature of the connection between any two outcomes may itself be uncertain. Axiom A5 leaves sufficient room for such situations, in that the only constraint is the necessity to adjust the degrees of potential surprises attached to the other outcomes, because the potential surprise of one of the outcomes changes. Because potential surprise is not constrained to add to unity then it is a non-distributional variable.

### 5.4.1.2 Operationalizing potential surprise as a measure of hard uncertainty

Although potential surprise as a measure of hard uncertainty resides in the mind of the decision maker it is possible to elicit a potential surprise function for an individual and so test the extent to which individuals correspond to the axioms that have been set out. The emphasis, as Katzner (1995) points out, is that for the concept of potential surprise to be operational in some positive sense, all that is required is that some implied or assumed aspects of potential surprise be testable against observed behaviour in principle. The case study discussed later in this book aims to extend this to testing observed behaviour in practice. Operationalizing potential surprise normatively involves evaluating its suitability as a measure which captures the nature of hard uncertainty. The crucial issue is whether or not it reflects the various characteristics of uncertainty that hard uncertainty encompasses. The key here is in relation to interpreting the axioms as giving guidance or rules of thumb to assigning degrees of surprise to the different outcomes. The clear advantage that potential surprise has over probability as a measure of hard uncertainty is that it explicitly deals with uncertainty, in that it allows for the presence of a residual hypothesis, namely that the complete set of hypothesized outcomes is not assumed. As a non-additive, non-distributional subjective variable, applicable to unique decisions, potential surprise would appear logically consistent with the underlying characteristics of hard uncertainty.

## 5.5 THE EVALUATION MECHANISM

The second main difference in Shackle's model of uncertainty to that utilized by expected utility models and variants is in relation to the mechanism by which the outcome and corresponding measure of uncertainty are evaluated. To recap, in Shackle's model there are two main stages, first the specification of the ascendancy function as a means of editing the different outcomes and second the use of the gambler's preference map. Like the concept of potential surprise, these elements are often criticized by the literature. This section therefore goes into more detail about the construction of these different elements, as well as evaluating their applicability to the problem of hard uncertainty (and thus the environmental problems on which this thesis is focusing). A critical view will then be taken as regards which elements of these two pillars of Shackle's model should be carried forward.

### 5.5.1 The Separation of Gains and Losses

The ascendancy function is the means by which, for any decision, the incomplete set of outcomes and their corresponding measure of uncertainty are evaluated. Because both the potential surprise function and the ascendancy indifference curves are separated by gains and losses, this process immediately differs from that of expected utility. This allows the individual to have a different potential surprise function for gains and losses and allows differing degrees of uncertainty aversion to be exhibited by the decision maker in relation to the construction of the different elements, where an element is defined as an outcome and its corresponding degree of potential surprise. The main insight that Shackle provided here is psychological (Ford, 1994), in that individuals being safety first will consider gains and losses separately.

### 5.5.2 Uncertainty Aversion: Ascendancy Indifference Curves

The most important point about the separation of gains and losses is that by combining the potential surprise function with the ascendancy indifference curves by means of the ascendancy function, different degrees of uncertainty aversion or preference can be shown over gains and losses. It would appear intuitive that decision makers making public decisions may show a greater aversion to uncertainty surrounding large losses than to uncertainty over gains, and thus weight them higher or give them greater ascendancy. Even if decision makers showed uniform preference or aversion over gains and losses under hard uncertainty, the ascendancy function does give the opportunity for variations to be exhibited. This important feature plays an integral part in the other crucial element of the ascendancy function, in that it provides a mechanism for evaluating both the gain/loss outcome and the corresponding measure of uncertainty.[3]

This is in contrast to the expected utility model and variants highlighted in the previous chapter, which only weight the outcome, or in some cases the outcome and the probability separately.[4] The crucial property is that the ascendancy function encapsulates the subjective trade-off in the mind of the decision maker between the extent to which an outcome on one hand and the measure of uncertainty (potential surprise) on the other, contribute to the overall weighting of the outcome.

This property of the ascendancy function is defined from the ascendancy indifference curves from which it is derived. Each indifference curve, where $\phi(x, y) =$ constant $> 0$, implicitly associates a degree of potential surprise with each specific outcome, $x$. As this degree of surprise is defined differently to the potential surprise function, $y = y(x)$, based on the set of actual hypothesized outcomes (although it remains on the same scale and is thus drawn on the same axis in Figure 5.2 and 5.3) it will be labelled $y' = y'(x)$. Thus each indifference curve can be defined as:

$$\phi\{x, y'(x)\} \equiv \text{constant} \tag{5.4}$$

Differentiating the above we get:

$$d\phi \equiv 0 \equiv \frac{\partial \phi}{\partial x} dx + \frac{\partial \phi}{\partial y'} dy' \tag{5.5}$$

so that everywhere on such a contour line the slope or the curve which represents the trade-off between potential surprise and the outcomes, $x$, is defined by:

$$\frac{dy'}{dx} = -\frac{\partial \phi}{\partial x} \bigg/ \frac{\partial \phi}{\partial y'} \tag{5.6}$$

Thus as indicated in Figures 5.2 and 5.3, when $x > 0$ and $\partial \phi / \partial x > 0$ and $\partial \phi / \partial y' < 0$, then $dy' / dx$ will everywhere be positive and the contour line will slope upwards. For losses, where $x < 0$ (rather than the absolute value of $x$ defined within the ascendancy function), similarly the indifference or contour line will slope upwards towards the left. The actual form of the indifference curves is indicated by the second derivative of the above relations, and is drawn in Figures 5.2 and 5.3, which indicate increasing uncertainty aversion, that is at successively higher values of potential surprise, progressively larger increments in outcomes are required to maintain a given level of $\phi$. This can be defined by;

$$\frac{d^2 y'}{dx^2} < 0 \qquad (5.7)$$

This in effect reflects what is portrayed in Figure 5.2 as increasing uncertainty aversion on both the gain side and loss side. As the degree of potential surprise increases, it exerts an increasing negative effect on the weight or ascendancy attached to the particular $(x, y)$ element. So while for low potential surprise values, increasing magnitudes of the outcomes will tend to increase the weighting allocated to a particular element, as the degree of surprise becomes higher, it will begin to outweigh the magnitude of the outcome in determining the ascendancy of the element. It is by the making of these subjective adjustments between the power of the outcome and its degree of surprise in determining the overall weight given to the element in the decision process, that explicit attention is given to hard uncertainty.

Shackle (1952) allows room for differing forms of the uncertainty/outcome trade-off to be exhibited by the individual. However, it is important to emphasize that, because any given weighting or level of ascendancy corresponds to combinations of both the outcome and the degree of surprise (as a measure of uncertainty), changing the level of $\phi$ captures the nature of the trade-off between the two factors. It will be emphasized, as will soon be made evident, however, that the ascendancy indifference curves are not a stand-alone element in Shackle's theory, but just a demonstration in a formal analytical manner of the rationale which underlies the derivation of an ascendancy function, which will be considered now.

### 5.5.3 The Specification of the Ascendancy Function

To recap, the ascendancy function $\phi = (x, y)$ is the process by which the individual is envisaged to consider the different gain and loss $(x, y)$ elements in order to arrive at a subjective evaluation of the range of uncertain outcomes, which could occur as a result of a particular action or policy. This ranking procedure then allows the decision maker to arrive at a focus gain value and a focus loss value. These points represent the gain and loss scenarios to which the decision maker attaches most weight when considering the merits of a particular course of action. The ascendancy function is derived theoretically from all the points on the different ascendancy indifference curves which lie tangential to or intersect the potential surprise function, $y =$

$y(x)$ (see Figure 5.3). The decision maker therefore weights the different outcomes and their corresponding degree of surprise, assigning the greatest weight to that element (the set of which is constrained or limited to those elements previously defined by the potential surprise function), which lies on the maximum $\phi$ indifference curve (see Figure 5.3).

Although the notion of the ascendancy indifference curves is useful in an analytical sense, as Shackle concedes (1952), it is unlikely that an individual would go through the process of defining a series of ascendancy indifference curves before specifying his or her ascendancy function. Moreover, although the ascendancy function is derived from the concept of a series of indifference curves, the actual process by which the different hypothesized outcomes of any action are edited, to allow the decision maker to focus on the 'worst to be feared' and the 'best to be hoped for', is sufficiently captured by the ascendancy function. Although, therefore, the ascendancy indifference curves are a useful analytical tool and provide a formal presentation of the process envisaged in Shackle's model, they are superseded in an operational sense by the specification of the ascendancy function.[5] It is the ascendancy function that will therefore take centre stage in the variation of Shackle's model developed in this thesis.

It should be noted that the interpretation of ascendancy taken here does not in any sense relate to the notion of a utility function. It is the interpretation of the ascendancy function by some authors as a representation of a kind of utility function (Mars, 1950a, 1950b), as well as its conflation with the gambler's preference map (which would appear to be evident in Vickers' (1994) model),[6] which has resulted in some of the confusion surrounding Shackle's model. The maximization of the ascendancy function to arrive at the focus values does not represent the gain and loss elements with the highest utility. Instead they represent those elements on which the decision maker's attention is focused (Shackle, 1949) or what can be interpreted as those elements that are given the highest weight in the decision maker's mind. The ascendancy function does not, therefore, rank the gain and loss elements according to the highest utility (based on the trade-off relationship between uncertainty and the monetary outcome). This type of process is limited to the choice between actions or policies (rather than the evaluation of the incomplete set of outcomes and the uncertainty attached to their occurrence).

Although it is possible to choose between different actions or policies, it is not possible to determine or choose between the possible occurrence of the outcomes associated with an action. Which outcome occurs will depend on the resulting state of nature, which is by definition not known in situations of hard uncertainty. The ascendancy function as interpreted in this research is therefore limited to the evaluation of the set of outcomes and their associated uncertainty which could occur as the result of a particular action, rather than some form of ranking method to guide choices between policies. In Shackle's schema, the notion of utility is limited to making decisions between policies or different prospects, and is therefore captured in the notion of the gambler's preference map. In Katzner's (1993) model the outcomes which form part of the argument in the ascendancy function are replaced by a value which corresponds to the utility of that outcome. The ascendancy function, which is given a similar interpretation to that which is incorporated in Shackle's original model, is then maximized, and the focus values derived in the usual manner. Katzner then formulates a decision index similar to Vickers (1994) which is in essence a linear form of the gambler's preference map, the difference being that any asymmetrical weighting of the outcomes and losses is captured in the utility function over the outcomes. Although this is an interesting approach, from an operational perspective the specification of a utility function over the outcomes adds a further degree of complication to the process. Moreover, as has been argued, the validity of attaching a utility to situations where the outcomes are rivals is also questionable.

### 5.5.4 Specifying the Ascendancy Function

The ascendancy or weighting function as defined by equation (5.2) and with the properties denoted by equation (5.3) can be seen operationally as the process by which the different elements of any action are weighted. In Shackle's terminology this weighting will correspond to the power of any outcome/surprise element to arrest the attention of the individual (Shackle, 1952). The element on the gain side with the highest weighting will therefore correspond to the focus gain (the best to be hoped for) and the element on the loss branch with the highest weighting, the focus loss (the worst to be feared). The properties of the ascendancy function can be defined further by assuming the following functional form:[7]

$$\phi = ax^{0.5} - by^2 \qquad (5.8)$$

where $a$ and $b$ are the coefficients with respect to the outcome $x$ and the degree of potential surprise $y$ and where $x$ is defined as the absolute value of the outcome (for example monetary value). Although the ascendancy function can be defined separately over gains and losses, for ease of exposition it is assumed to take the same form over gains and losses. The proposition that the ascendancy function will increase with respect to increasing outcome magnitudes (that is higher outcome values will be assigned a higher weighting) and decrease with respect to increasing levels of potential surprise is shown by the first order partial derivatives:

$$\frac{\partial \phi}{\partial x} = 0.5ax^{-0.5} > 0; \quad \frac{\partial \phi}{\partial y} = -2by < 0 \tag{5.9}$$

The second order partial derivatives of $\phi(\cdot)$ will indicate the underlying shape of the indifference curves (which are not observable), and thus the following propositions can be constructed. First the proposition that when $y$ remains constant, the effect of larger outcome magnitudes, although increasing the level of $\phi$ will do so at a decreasing rate, is shown by:

$$\frac{\partial^2 \phi}{\partial x^2} = -0.25ax^{-1.5} < 0 \tag{5.10}$$

Second the proposition that while $x$ remains constant, as the degree of potential surprise increases it will decrease the level of $\phi$ but do so at an increasing rate, is shown by:

$$\frac{\partial^2 \phi}{\partial y^2} = -2b > 0 \tag{5.11}$$

In addition the extent to which the outcome magnitudes and potential surprise contribute to the overall weighting, and so the specification of the focus gain and focus loss, will be defined by the sizes of the respective coefficients. As such these propositions are positively operational and testable and can be defined normatively to derive appropriate rules of thumb. In terms of the normative properties of the ascendancy function, the key statements which will need to be evaluated are the extent to which the ascendancy function allows varying degrees of uncertainty aversion to be shown. Because Shackle's theory is separated by gains and losses, this allows aversion or preference for uncertainty also to vary in terms of gains and losses. Moreover, as a mechanism which considers both the outcome and degree of surprise jointly, the decision maker can balance or make trade-offs in allocating weights to the prospective outcomes. Therefore, the uncertainty associated with the hypothesized outcomes is considered explicitly and the decision maker can adjust for this uncertainty in weighting the possible outcomes associated with a policy before deciding whether to proceed or not. This process is normatively consistent with the aim of improving the procedural rationality of decision making.

### 5.5.5   The Ascendancy Function as a Focusing Device

The ascendancy function offers a completely different means of evaluating or weighting the different possible hypothesized outcomes of any action to that proposed by the weighted averaging mechanism used in the expected utility model and its variants. Shackle was very critical of using any form of averaging mechanism over rival outcomes and as such the ascendancy function is the mechanism by which the individual sifts through the different outcomes to arrive at only two values, namely the focus gain and focus loss values. This non-averaging mechanism is derived in part from the definition of potential surprise as a non-additive measure of uncertainty, which is itself an argument in the ascendancy function. Shackle's proposition that, when considering a range of hypothesized outcomes which could occur as a result of an action or policy, the decision maker will focus on one gain and one loss outcome is a proposition that is positively operational, as will be shown in the case study. It can be tested whether individuals, when faced with a range of outcomes, do indeed edit the range of outcomes and focus on just two values.

On a normative basis the use of a focusing device would seem to have some merit in relation to improving the way that decisions are made, in that there is a need to make a particular decision manageable. It is unlikely that any decision maker will be able to evaluate comprehensively every possible outcome, but will find it necessary to have some mechanism for ranking or simplifying the different prospects of a decision. For example, a decision maker may feel so surprised at the possibility of an outcome occurring that they want to exclude that outcome from consideration. By editing the range of outcomes associated with any policy, the decision maker provides a basis by which s/he can summarize the best and worst of any project and do so by considering explicitly the uncertainty associated with the outcomes.

### 5.5.6   The Standardized Focus Values

Once the focus gain and focus loss values have been derived by means of the ascendancy function, the next step in Shackle's model is to remove the potential surprise element from the focus values by the process described previously. The aim of this step is to allow comparison of different policies on a different footing (Shackle, 1949). However, in the variation of the model developed here this step will be dispensed with, as is the case with a number of variations on Shackle's model (for example Ford, 1983, 1987; Vickers 1994). There are a number of reasons for doing this. First, as stated the purpose of standardizing the focus elements is to allow comparisons between actions or policies to be made. However, the interpretation of the variation on Shackle's model developed here is in relation to explaining the way that the uncertainty in any decision conditioned by hard uncertainty is evaluated and a decision is taken to proceed or to reject a particular policy. The interpretation of the model put forward here does not attempt to explain choices between policies, but only to test whether the model helps to explain the basis on which environmental policies conditioned by hard uncertainty are made, that is it is limited in relation to the procedural rationality of the model.

By limiting the development of the model to the decision-making process, rather than to the decisions themselves, the model is not being used to compare choices between policies. Consequently the need to standardize the focus elements is removed. Even if we were to use Shackle's model in relation to making choices between policies or actions under uncertainty, as Ford (1994) forcefully argues, it is unlikely that the standardized equivalents will in any case remove the uncertainty. By using an equivalent element in terms of the level of ascendancy, the decision maker would appear to be acting in defiance of their expectations, because such an element has not been hypothesized as a possible scenario of the policy. To regard the potential surprise of the standardized focus gain, and so attempt to remove the uncertainty which is of vital consideration when choosing between policies (as well as evaluating the range of prospects associated with a policy), would appear logically inconsistent.

Further arguments for dropping the standardized focus values derive from concerns over the operationality of the concept. From a normative perspective, if the aim is to deal explicitly with the uncertainty when evaluating a given decision, it would appear illogical to advance a procedure which attempts to remove the uncertainty. On a practical level the derivation of a rule of thumb to guide how decision makers should do this would also appear difficult. The concept also has a number of drawbacks in relation to how it can be positively operationalized. The process of defining the standardized focus values is, as will be recalled, derived from the ascendancy indifference curves, which are in themselves difficult to operationalize. Although they may be assumed to exist from an analytical perspective, for the purpose of operationalizing the model, we have bypassed their construction and proceeded directly with the specification of the ascendancy function.

### 5.5.7  Stochastic Dominance

A large part of the critique directed at the use of the ascendancy function in Shackle's model is directed at the role of the ascendancy function in arriving at the focus values. In particular it is argued that as a means of ranking the different prospects or elements of any action in relation to the attention or weight accorded to them, the ascendancy function by focusing on only one gain and one loss value ignores the full range of information associated with a policy that is captured by the potential surprise function. This critique (Graaff and Baumol, 1949: p. 339) is directed once again at the role of the ascendancy function in arriving at the focus values, which by means of the gambler's preference map, allows the focus values of different policies or

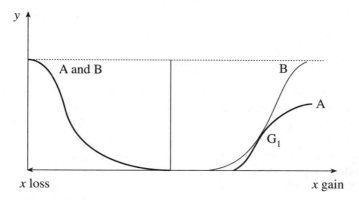

*Source*:   Adapted from Ford, 1994: p. 101

*Figure 5.5    Stochastic dominance*

actions to be compared. The problem that this poses for Shackle's model is termed stochastic dominance and is best explained by the use of Figure 5.5. What Figure 5.5 shows is the potential surprise curves of two actions or policies A and B. While on the loss side they are identical, on the gain side all of the possible outcomes for A offer equal or higher gains at lower or equal degrees of potential surprise. In this sense project A stochastically dominates project B. However, if point G is defined as the focus gain, that is it is defined by the ascendancy function as the maximal element, then when the policies are compared by means of the gambler's preference map, the decision maker will be indifferent to the outcomes. Alternative scenarios could be hypothesized where all the outcomes of a policy are seen as having a lower weighting than any other policy except one which is given the greatest weight. In this sense one strategy can dominate another when their potential surprise functions are compared, yet when interpreted in this way the model can produce an identical value of the $\phi$ function.

Although it is possible that Shackle's model could be envisaged as being applied to many states of the world the problem of stochastic dominance remains pertinent both in the original model as well as the variations introduced by Katzner (1995), and Vickers (1994). As such this reinforces the interpretation of the Shackle model taken here in relation to hard uncertainty, as a means of evaluating the outcomes and their corresponding uncertainty which may occur as the result of an action or policy, rather than as a model of the choices made between different policies or actions. The emphasis is again on the development of the model in relation to the decision-making process, rather than as a model that seeks to explain the decisions itself. If the model is restricted in this sense, then the problem of stochastic dominance is circumvented.

### 5.5.8 The Gambler's Preference Map

From what was said in the previous section it is apparent that the final step in Shackle's theory, encapsulated by the use of the gambler's preference map, will also be redundant. Although some form of the gambler's preference map, which would make use of the focus values rather than the standardized focus values appears intuitively appealing, the gambler's preference map is only relevant to models where the aim is to compare choices between policies or actions with uncertain outcomes. In such a framework it does have the advantage of incorporating a measure of utility over the different polices or prospects, although again it faces operational problems as well as the problem of stochastic dominance. In our more limited interpretation and development of the Shackle model in relation to hard uncertainty, the gambler's preference map is of no use in relation to evaluating the different outcomes of any policy. Arguably that role, together with the ability to incorporate the differing effects of gains and losses as well as uncertainty aversion, is captured sufficiently by the use of the ascendancy function.

## 5.6 SUMMARY OF THE VARIATION OF THE SHACKLE MODEL FORWARDED

The model that has been developed above differs in its interpretation of Shackle's original model, due to the removal of some of the stages included in the original version. The model has also been given a more limited interpretation in relation to its application to situations characterized by hard uncertainty. As such, the model that has been developed has two interpretations. In a behavioural or positivist sense, it can be used to explain the way that the uncertainty associated with a particular policy or action (in this thesis restricted to environmental policies) is evaluated by the decision maker, in assessing the overall merits or drawbacks of a particular action. It is hypothesized that this process will result in the decision maker being left to balance what is in effect the best to be hoped for, against the worst to be feared. The development of the model is not applied as a means of explaining decisions between policies conditioned by uncertainty. This is not to say that Shackle's theory has nothing to say in respect of this issue, nor that such investigation is not a worthwhile endeavour, but that the interpretation of the model in such a light creates a number of difficulties (although not as many as is sometimes suggested) that have yet to be resolved. This issue will be returned to in the discussion chapter. What is achieved by a more limited development of Shackle's model is a firmer basis on which it can be operationalized. This is the task in the following chapters.

The interpretation of the Shackle model in a normative sense is perhaps clearer. Because of the presence of hard uncertainty, we are limited to evaluating the procedural rationality of the model. The variation of the model that has been developed in this chapter is therefore designed in relation to deriving key features of the decision-making process that will improve the way that it deals with hard uncertainty. The focus is therefore on the model in a normative sense, in relation to its possible use as an evaluation tool, rather than as a means of making the decision for the decision maker, or resulting in some absolute decision criteria. This interpretation is consistent with the decision-making framework outlined in Chapter 2.

The main features of the modified Shackle model that has been developed, are as follows. First, the level and mode of uncertainty that is faced in a particular decision is evaluated. If the decision surrounding a particular policy is conditioned by hard uncertainty then in the second stage, the individual is expected to assign to the incomplete set of outcomes associated with a policy or action a degree of potential surprise, by means of the potential surprise function. Potential surprise is defined as a non-additive, non-distributional variable. As is followed for the rest of the model, gains and losses are defined separately. The next stage is the weighting of the various $(x, y)$ elements or prospects of the action, by means of the ascendancy function, which edits the range of possible outcomes to arrive at the focus gain value and the focus loss value. It is these focus values which can then be considered by the decision maker and which summarize his or her concerns surrounding the uncertainty of a policy. The question of how the focus values can be incorporated into a more general decision-making framework will be returned to in Chapter 9.

### 5.6.1 Operationalizing Shackle's Model in the Context of Environmental Uncertainty

The realization that many environmental decisions are conditioned by hard uncertainty is evident from the arguments made in the previous chapters. What is now also clearer, is that in contrast to expected utility-based models, the Shackle model would appear to be a more appropriate framework in which to tackle the problem of environmental uncertainty. Indeed it is apparent that many of Shackle's concerns over the nature of decision making and uncertainty, as well as his critique of probability-based frameworks, can be fruitfully extended to environmental decision making. The interpretation of the model in relation to hard uncertainty has also brought us to the stage where it will be possible to assess in more detail the operationalization of Shackle's theory in relation to environmental decision making.

In terms of the positive operationality of the model, the modification that has been developed in this chapter provides a number of testable propositions that can be used to assess the extent to which the model actually explains behaviour. As such by focusing on those aspects of Shackle's original theory which can be operationalized, it is possible to put his theory under a greater degree of scrutiny than has been possible previously. The operationalization of the theory in a normative sense in relation to environmental decision making leads to a consideration of the key features of the model that have been developed, and whether or not they are consistent with the aim of improving the procedural rationality of the decision-making process by dealing explicitly with hard uncertainty. The second issue relates to whether normative rules of thumb or decision-making procedures can be derived from the model that has been developed in this chapter. This will be considered in Chapter 9.

Returning briefly to consider at this stage some of the key features of the modified Shackle model will allow us to link some of the main issues raised by the presence of hard uncertainty in environmental decision making. In particular it is apparent that as a measure which reflects the underlying modalities of hard uncertainty, potential surprise holds a number of advantages over probability. Most importantly as a non-distributional, non-additive variable, it does not require a previous history of repeated trials, nor does it require that the full range of outcomes is known. Moreover, the argument that in many environmental decisions, such as those regarding biodiversity loss, we are dealing with actions which are associated with the occurrence of mutually exclusive outcomes, is reflected in the underlying design of potential surprise.

Another feature of the model, which would appear to make it amenable to the sort of environmental decisions that are the focus of this book, is that by separating gains and losses the model embodies what is effectively a safety first feature or a form of precaution. The basis of this assumption would appear to be tenable in relation to the evaluation of a project to build a nuclear power station for example. Although the probabilities (which in this case are not likely to be reliable) may be very low in relation to a catastrophic event, such as occurred at Chernobyl, the outcome and the resulting losses may be weighted higher in the mind of the individual than any possible gains. On a practical note, the fact that in cost–benefit analysis, the costs and benefits are calculated separately means that many decision makers familiar with this technique will be comfortable in separating gains and losses in the decision-making process.

The nuclear power example also encapsulates another key feature of the model in relation to environmental uncertainty, in that the ascendancy function weights both the outcome magnitude and the degree of surprise associated with the occurrence of that outcome jointly. By this process explicit attention is given to hard uncertainty in the evaluation process of any policy. Moreover the ascendancy function captures the trade-off between the magnitude of the outcome and its degree of surprise in relation to the final weighting that the decision maker gives that prospect in his or her overall evaluation of the project. As such the model allows room for various degrees of uncertainty aversion to be exhibited by the decision maker.

This chapter has served to demonstrate the theoretical power of the Shackle model and its applicability in real world cases. Now that the key features of the positive and normative operationality of the model of decision making under hard uncertainty have been highlighted, and a firm basis on which to interpret the model found, we can move to the application of Shackle's theory to environmental decision making by means of a case study, based on the evaluation of a road project in Southern Belize. The case study will enable us to test further the operationality of the variation on the Shackle model developed.

## NOTES

1. An excellent and comprehensive review of Shackle's theory can be found instead in Ford (1994).
2. The notion of surprise introduced by John Venn, the founder of frequency probability, can perhaps be seen as the parent of the concept of potential surprise later introduced by Shackle (Carter, 1950; Ford, 1994).
3. Ford's (1987) perspective theory as well as Hey's (1994) theory are more recent variations which utilize the same procedure but remain within the probability framework. As such while they are not applicable to situations of hard uncertainty, they may indeed be applicable to decisions characterized by risk or soft uncertainty.
4. Katzner's (1995) variation of Shackle's theory weights the outcome (by a form of utility function) and then weights both the weighted outcome and the potential surprise by means of the ascendancy or what he terms the attractiveness index.
5. The difficulty of positively operationalizing indifference curves will be returned to in Chapter 7.
6. In Vickers' (1994) model the ascendancy function is replaced by an attractiveness function. Although Vickers recognizes that Shackle's ascendancy function is in no way related to the notion of a utility function, his interpretation of his attractiveness function and what he terms iso-attractiveness contours would appear to be one which incorporates elements of a utility function, for example larger negative values of $x$ will decrease the value of the attractiveness function. The decision index is then in essence a linear version of the gambler's preference map.
7. The choice of, and assumptions behind the functional form in equation 5.8 will be described in more detail in Chapter 8.

# 6. Case study: The Belize Southern Highway

## 6.1 INTRODUCTION

In order to test the operationality of the variation of the Shackle model that has been developed in the previous chapter, a suitable case study was chosen. This chapter is devoted to a brief explanation of the environmental background behind the case study of a road project in Belize, the Southern Highway project, and the decision process to which the Shackle model has been applied.

## 6.2 INTRODUCTION TO BELIZE AND ITS ENVIRONMENT

Belize is located in the north-east of Central America and has an area of approximately 22,963 km$^2$ or 5.4 million acres (World Bank, 1996) (see Figure 6.1). Belize is high in biodiversity with over 4000 native flowering plant species, 504 species of birds, 121 mammal species, 107 species of reptiles and 26 species of amphibians. However, because of the lack of natural barriers, species endemism is limited. Forest mammals include howler monkeys, brocket deer, otters, jaguars, ocelots, margay cats, jaguarondis, pumas and tapirs. Approximately 60 per cent of Belize is closed forest, of which 47 per cent is broadleafed cover and the majority of the rest needle leaf. In Southern Belize (the area affected by the road) about 70 per cent is under dense cover, particularly in the inner areas of the Mayan foothills. The coastal waters of Belize (50 per cent of its national territory) are also rich in species partly due to the presence of the largest barrier reef in the Western Hemisphere and the second largest in the world. The coastal and marine ecosystems also include extensive mangroves, coastal lagoons and sea grass beds (World Bank, 1996). Many endangered species exist in the coastal zone, such as the West Indian manatee, American crocodile, sea turtles and threatened bird species.

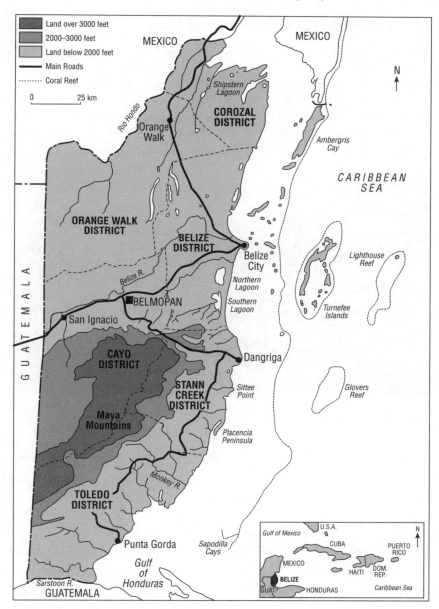

*Figure 6.1   Map of Belize*

### 6.2.1 Case Study: The Southern Highway Project

The Southern Highway project involves the upgrade of 64 km of the original Southern Highway, a dirt road, to one of a paved standard, as well as to rehabilitate about 176 km of connecting rural feeder roads. The road extends from the intersection with the Stann Creek Valley Road near Dangriga to Belize's most southern town Punta Gorda (see Figure 6.1). The existing road was loosely gravelled and dusty in dry weather, while in the wet season the southern section was often severely flooded (see Figure 6.2).

*Figure 6.2    Flooding of the Southern Highway*

The proposed construction of the road itself was split into five sections, from south to north (see Figure 6.3):

| | |
|---|---|
| Section 1: | Punta Gorda to Rice Mill, 30.1 km |
| Section 2: | Rice Mill to Bladen Bridge, 38.9 km |
| Section 3: | Bladen Bridge to Big Creek Port, 41.5 km |
| Sections 4 and 5: | Mango Creek Junction to Stann Creek Valley Rd, 63.4 km (IDB, 1997a) |

There were a number of different parties involved in the financing of the different sections, although analysis of the decision-making process was restricted to the Government of Belize (GoBl), The Inter-American Development Bank (IDB) and the DFID (Department for Foreign and International Development, previously the ODA).

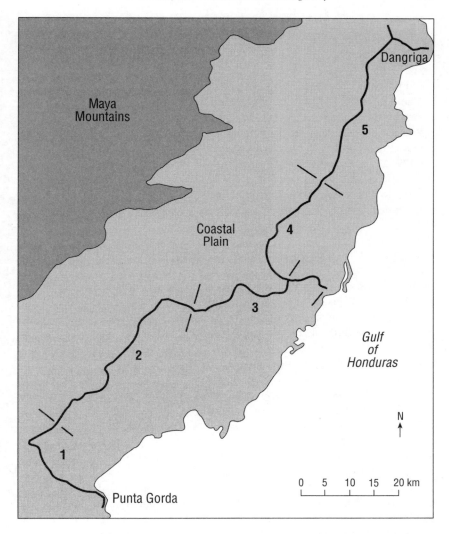

*Figure 6.3    Map of the different sections of the Southern Highway*

Although initially the focus was solely on the physical construction works, in terms of the reports commissioned by the GoBl, the IDB and the ODA, by 1995 emphasis had shifted to putting into place mitigative measures to prevent possible negative environmental and social consequences of the road.[1] The environmental and social concerns expressed about the road project resulted in the setting up of the Environmental and Social Technical Assist-

ance Programme (ESTAP). ESTAP was designed specifically to help to mitigate any possible negative social and environmental impacts of the road and
specifically to prepare a Regional Development Plan which would form the
basis of the response to the social and environmental transformations that
could possibly occur as a result of upgrading the highway.

The aim of ESTAP was to ensure that the transformation process associated with the road project would be consistent with the optimal allocation of
resources, social equity, environmental protection and long-term sustainable
development (IDB, 1997a). Public consultation was to be a key element of
the ESTAP programme. It was therefore in the period from 1994 until the
road project was finally agreed in 1998 that the project was evaluated in
relation to its possible environmental effects. Consequently it is for this period
that the decision process associated with the road project has been analysed.

## 6.3   THE ENVIRONMENTAL CONTEXT

In this section a summary of the main ecological systems present in Belize
will be given. This is important as it highlights the key services that the
environmental system provides as well as the complexity of the linkages
between the ecological and economic system in Belize.

### 6.3.1   Rain Forest and Moist Forest

Southern Belize has extensive areas of rain forest and moist forest (classified
on the basis of the Holdridge System, NARMAP, 1996), which are some of the
most diverse and productive systems in Belize. Their productivity is dependent
on the rapid recycling of nutrients between soil and plants and most of the
nutrient material is stored in the plants. As such, if forest cover is removed, soil
erosion can be rapid and normal nutrient and hydraulic cycling impeded
(Costanza *et al.*, 1997b; Henrot and Robertson, 1994). The extent to which
change to such forests is reversible depends on the extent of the damage, and
although secondary forest may re-colonize deforested areas if the soil is not too
degraded, succession to a composition and structure approximating the original
forest may take hundreds of years (ODA, 1996). The forests of Southern Belize
therefore play a critical role in moderating the impacts of heavy rainfall in the
area, not only in reducing erosion and consequent siltation, but in providing
pathways for water retention, reducing the effects of peak flooding events
common in Southern Belize. On a more general level the forests act as a
protective buffer by diminishing tropical storm intensities.

Information on the species composition of the rain and moist forest is
being gradually built up, especially for reserves such as the Columbia Forest,

which is the focus of a study by the Forest Planning and Management Project, Ministry of Natural Resources. However, in other areas, such as the Sittee River forest reserve (see Figure 6.4), no ecological studies have been carried out. In terms of understanding the dynamics of the forest ecosystem, most of the research is at a preliminary stage, This is shown by a study of the Bladen Nature Reserve, which identified three species of plants new to science (Iremonger and Sayre, 1993), as well as two species of frogs in the Columbia forest reserve (Campbell *et al.*, 1994). As a result, while information on the composition of species is being built up, there is little information on key processes, such as the breeding mechanisms of tree flora (Bird, 1997). Consequently, key ecological processes such as the importance of different pollination and seed dispersal agents is 'largely a matter of conjecture' (Bird, 1997: p. 2). The rain and tropical moist forests in Southern Belize are also subject to natural disturbances, which have a fundamental effect on the dynamics of the ecosystem. In addition to regular tropical storms which can uproot unstable trees, hurricanes such as Hurricane Hattie in 1961 can cause catastrophic damage.

### 6.3.2　Pine Forests and Savannahs

The pine ridge and pine ridge savannahs are important in terms of the biodiversity of Belize due to the relatively high levels of endemics (NARMAP, 1996). These areas are therefore a significant source of genetic resources in Belize. The pine forests, as well as transitional areas, are also important in acting as storm buffers, as well as regulating water run-off. Because of the poor quality of soils upon which they are often found (commonly leached and gleyed), they are also important in preventing further nutrient leaching and erosion. This is because evidence would appear to suggest that savannah trees and shrubs may preferentially enrich the soil around them, resulting in the gradual accumulation of nutrients (Kellman, 1979). Moreover, as the savannahs and pine savannahs tend to occur on very infertile soils, then this function is particularly important (Kellman and Sanmugadas, 1985). The structure of the needle forests is heavily influenced by the pattern of the disturbance regime, with fire in particular playing an important role in stimulating a progression from pine forests and savannah back to pinelands (Iremonger and Brokaw, 1996). Savannahs are important locally in terms of climate regulation due to vegetation cover and transpiration. They are also important in acting as a water regulator by reducing run-off. As such, along with the other main ecosystems in the area they are crucial in providing a water management function. Other functions include controlling erosion and facilitating soil formation (UNEP, 1995).

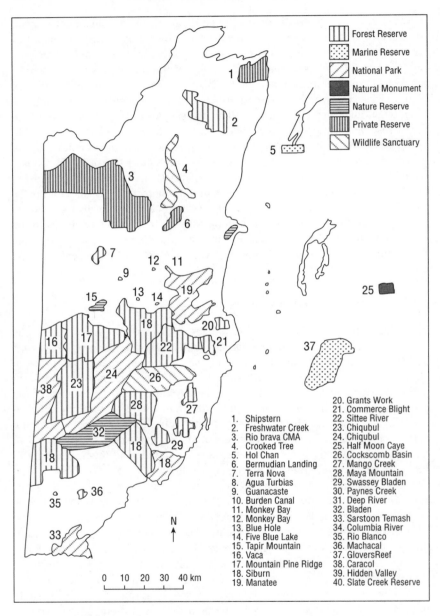

Legend:
- Forest Reserve
- Marine Reserve
- National Park
- Natural Monument
- Nature Reserve
- Private Reserve
- Wildlife Sanctuary

1. Shipstern
2. Freshwater Creek
3. Rio brava CMA
4. Crooked Tree
5. Hol Chan
6. Bermudian Landing
7. Terra Nova
8. Agua Turbias
9. Guanacaste
10. Burden Canal
11. Monkey Bay
12. Monkey Bay
13. Blue Hole
14. Five Blue Lake
15. Tapir Mountain
16. Vaca
17. Mountain Pine Ridge
18. Siburn
19. Manatee
20. Grants Work
21. Commerce Blight
22. Sittee River
23. Chiqubul
24. Chiqubul
25. Half Moon Caye
26. Cockscomb Basin
27. Mango Creek
28. Maya Mountain
29. Swassey Bladen
30. Paynes Creek
31. Deep River
32. Bladen
33. Sarstoon Temash
34. Columbia River
35. Rio Blanco
36. Machacal
37. GloversReef
38. Caracol
39. Hidden Valley
40. Slate Creek Reserve

0 10 20 30 40 km

*Source*: Based on map produced by the Belize Center of Environmental Studies, 1995, in Zisman, 1996

*Figure 6.4 Map of reserves in Southern Belize*

### 6.3.3   Wetlands and Swamps

The fresh water wetlands and swamps of Southern Belize are key ecosystems, both in terms of area and the ecological functions that they provide. Like the rain forests they accommodate great biological diversity and are highly productive and dynamic, due both to abiotic factors and food web structures (Costanza *et al.*, 1997b). They also play a key role in Southern Belize in terms of flood control, water protection, storm protection, nutrient and waste recycling. These functions in turn play an important part in limiting the effects of a disturbance caused by tropical storms on other ecosystems. The waste recycling function may be particularly important with respect to use of fertilizers and pesticides on citrus and banana crop ecosystems. Wetlands are also important in terms of acting as a habitat and refuge for wildlife, acting for example as a nursery for important fish and crustaceans, as well as resting and feeding areas for migratory birds (Costanza *et al.*, 1997b). Many of the important wetland areas, such as in Sarstoon Temash and Paynes Creek (see Figure 6.4), have had little or no ecological study carried out on them (Zisman, 1996). These would give a greater understanding of the particular dynamics of the diverse wetland communities present in Southern Belize.

### 6.3.4   Mangroves

Mangroves are widespread along the Belize coast and cover approximately 296 miles or 3.4 per cent of the land area (Zisman, in McField *et al.*, 1995). At present the ecological integrity of the mangrove systems is thought to be good and, in comparison with neighbouring countries, Belize has a relatively high proportion of intact mangroves. Mangroves are important as a protection against storm damage, floods and beach erosion. They are also important in acting as a natural purification system, binding fine silts as well as industrial, agrochemical and human wastes (McField *et al.*, 1995). As such, they act as an important buffer zone, protecting terrestrial systems from increased storm damage, as well as reducing the effects of pollution and sedimentation on sea grass areas and outlying coral reef. Mangroves in Belize also provide a service to the fisheries sector by creating a habitat for juvenile snapper, grouper and for larval recruitment of lobster (McField *et al.*, 1995). They are also important for subsistence fishing, as well as for providing a habitat for endangered species such as manatee and crocodiles.

Mangroves have been mapped and their importance highlighted in a number of reports (for example McField *et al.*, 1995; Zisman, 1992), although relatively few studies provide detailed accounts of the dynamics of mangrove systems (Zisman, 1992). A key colonizing species is the red mangrove, which first becomes established in sheltered areas, as its roots help to suspend organic matter, absorb wave energy and stabilize coastal sediments. To enable breathing in permanently saturated substrates, it has developed arching aerial prop roots. The black mangrove has a higher salinity tolerance, although it is more susceptible to wind throw because of shallow rooting. It is insect pollinated and produces floating seeds. Black mangroves are highly intolerant to changes in hydrological patterns such as drought or flooding (Zisman, 1992). White mangrove is found over a similar range of conditions, but develops best in low to moderate saline conditions. Pollination is again by insects which visit its flowers. In optimal conditions mangroves will grow to approximately 30 m, as in the Temash river area, although over half of Belize's mangroves are dwarf (Zisman, 1992).

### 6.3.5   Sea Grass

Extensive sea grass beds have developed in Belize. However, no detailed scientific studies have been carried out and their full distribution is not known (McField *et al.*, 1995). Generally in Belize sea grass beds are currently thought to be in excellent condition, and although productivity is dependent on a number of factors, they are understood to be a good indicator of the health of the maritime system. Sea grass beds are a highly productive habitat based on the trapping of sediments which contain organic matter, so they are important in the recycling of nutrients that would otherwise be lost. As such, sea grass beds act as an important trophic link between the coral and mangroves, preventing sediment accumulating on the coral (McField *et al.*, 1995). They are also important breeding grounds for commercially valuable species such as lobster, conch and many fish, as well as having a high conservation value, providing for example a habitat for turtles and manatees. Sea grasses require, however, good water quality and particular turbidity, as well as certain temperature and salinity limits. Thresholds for sediment limits may occur and sea grasses may be particular susceptible to increased agrochemical run-off from herbicides (McField *et al.*, 1995).

### 6.3.6   Coral Reefs

Belize's coral reefs are generally thought to be in good condition, although more recently some reef degradation has occurred. Since 1993 a monitoring programme has been conducted by the Coastal Zone Management Unit, which will increase the amount of available information. As such no broad scale assessment of the current status of Belize's coral reef system has been conducted and no long-term data are available from which to infer the dynamics of the reef systems. Due to a lack of baseline data and ecological studies, it is difficult to establish and quantify any clear cause and effect relationships, involving possible negative influences on the coral (McField *et al.*, 1995). Nevertheless a number of factors are thought to influence their development. One is the growth of algae, which can overgrow corals and is in part caused by nutrient enrichment of rivers. Another key factor is the amount of sediment dissolved in the water. Coral is also susceptible to water quality changes, with diseases such as black band disease thought to be induced by ecosystem stress and pollution. In terms of natural disturbances, the major threat is from hurricanes (McField *et al.*, 1995). The coral reef is of vital importance to Belize in environmental and economic terms. It provides an important habitat for commercial fishing species, as well as conservation species. It is also of crucial importance in terms of tourism, which is one of the mainstays of the Belizean economy.

## 6.4  UNCERTAINTY AND THE BELIZE SOUTHERN HIGHWAY PROJECT

Now that the environmental context surrounding the upgrading of the Southern Highway project has been explained, the main uncertainties faced by the decision makers when evaluating the project can be highlighted. Because an existing road, built in 1958 (DHV, 1994a), was already present in Southern Belize, albeit of a rudimentary nature, the majority of direct impacts of the road fall within the realms of soft uncertainty or risk. This is reinforced by the previous upgrading of the Northern, Western and Hummingbird Highways since the 1980s. In contrast, however, it is the indirect impacts of upgrading the Southern Highway that are to a large degree conditioned by hard uncertainty, and which form the focus of this investigation.

Although there is a past history in the upgrading of other roads in Belize, which arguably can be drawn on to predict the direct effects of the road, it is difficult to draw on this to assess the indirect impacts of the road project, because of the different social, economic and environmental conditions present in Southern Belize, as well as differences due to significant time lags between the upgrading of the other highways and the Southern Highway. It is because of the significant differences in the conditions that collectively determine the consequences of the project that hard uncertainty surrounding the possible outcomes of the road exists. The next section will therefore identify a number of these uncertainties, which will in turn influence the nature of the environmental uncertainties faced by the decision makers.

### 6.4.1   Key Uncertainties Associated with the Indirect Effects of the Rehabilitation of the Southern Highway

Many of the possible indirect environmental impacts of the road project are themselves related to a number of socio-economic uncertainties which provide the context for assessing the impact of upgrading the Southern Highway. By reviewing these it is apparent that a major problem for decision makers is that, in evaluating the possible indirect effects of the road, it is only possible to consider an incomplete set of future outcomes. In the following discussion, key uncertainties are identified from the reports available to decision makers. In some cases the impacts of more recent events will be used to demonstrate that decisions of the kind embodied in evaluating the Southern Highway Project are often characterized by hard uncertainty. The Environmental Impact Assessment (EIA) carried out by DHV consultants (1994a) recognized, 'That as a result of the road, accelerated development is expected for the southern districts which in turn will have secondary environmental impacts' (DHV, 1994a: p. 2). The nature and extent of such impacts (over and above the base case of the existing road) will depend on the occurrence of a combination of a number of uncertain factors. As the IDB environmental summary (1997a) points out:

> there is considerable uncertainty with regard to the magnitude of indirect impacts associated with the rehabilitation of the Southern Highway. Problems in assessing these indirect effects are compounded by the fact that incomplete data exist on land use trends. In addition, reliable projections of how rehabilitation will affect land use in the southern region are not available. (IDB, 1997a: p. 34)

Other factors which contribute to the uncertainty surrounding the consequences of the road rehabilitation identified in the project's evaluation reports are:

1.   The degree to which the road will result in increased migration internally from other areas of Belize, as well as from other Latin American Countries, notably El Salvador and Guatemala. In particular increased populations could lead to increased deforestation, due to the expansion of cultivated land and illegal squatting (Kocks Consult, 1993; DHV, 1994a; Harrison *et al.*, 1995; IDB, 1997a).
2.   The success of environmental mitigation measures (DHV, 1994a), in particular the ESTAP programme (IDB, 1997a), and the commitment to ESTAP for the duration of the project (until 2015).[2]
3.   The extent to which increased commercial agricultural expansion (Kocks Consult, 1993) (citrus, bananas and rice) will result in a reduction of natural habitat, biodiversity and forest cover, both as a result of increases

in the area of direct use, as well as from increased cultivation by the labourers brought in to work on the plantations (Kocks Consult, 1993; DHV, 1994a; Harrison *et al.*, 1995; IDB, 1997a).

4.  The indirect effects of the highway rehabilitation on the traditional Milpa systems, including whether the area of Milpa farming significantly increases or is no longer sustainable, due to reductions in the fallow period or shifts to other forms of agriculture (IDB, 1997a).

5.  The extent to which increased agricultural expansion will result in erosion, especially from uncontrolled agriculture on steep slopes and the highly erodable surface soils of the flood plain (DHV, 1994a; BECCA, 1995).

6.  The degree to which land clearance and deforestation lead to increased sedimentation in the drainage system, which will eventually feed into the marine system (DHV, 1994a; BECCA, 1995; IDB, 1997a) with unknown effects on coral and sea grass systems (IDB, 1997a).

7.  The impact of increased human settlements in the area on losses in wildlife (DHV, 1994a).

8.  The possible increase in aquaculture caused by better economic returns (DHV, 1994b) resulting from improved transportation and the possibility of increased erosion, consequential siltation and sedimentation and nutrient enrichment (DHV, 1994a).

9.  Difficulties in enforcing the existence of the protected areas, due to lack of personnel caused by the stretching of resources to cope with increased pressures in the affected areas (Kocks Consult, 1993; DHV, 1994a; IDB, 1997a).

10. The results of increased run-off from agrochemicals such as fertilizers, insecticides and herbicides associated with the expansion of commercial citrus and banana production, particularly in relation to coastal water quality (DHV, 1994a; IDB, 1997a).

11. The negative impact of increased tourism in the area and the resulting development, especially on the transitional areas, such as mangroves and fragile shorelines (DHV, 1994a; IDB, 1997a).

12. The extent of land tenure conflicts and uncertainty surrounding land tenure, especially in relation to the Mayan reserves (DHV, 1994a; Harrison *et al.*, 1995; IDB, 1997a).

13. The indirect effects of highway rehabilitation on logging activities which may either be increased through improved access or better controlled as a result of more effective enforcement and prevention of illegal logging (DHV, 1994a, IDB, 1997a).

14. Changes in preferential agreements for banana export to the European Union and the subsequent quota (DHV, 1994a; Harrison *et al.*, 1995), as a result of world trade talks.

15. The general economic situation in Belize, which is heavily dependent on changes in US policy and more specifically commodity prices (Kocks Consult, 1993).
16. The availability of future government funds for additional social services associated with rapid development, particularly in health and education (IDB, 1997a).

These preceding factors mean that the Southern Highway project is characterized by hard uncertainty on a number of grounds. First, although previous experience in improving the road network in Belize does provide an indication of possible consequences, the underlying conditions and factors which will determine the outcome of this project are fundamentally different. It is not therefore a seriable decision. The decision is in this sense unique, which is reinforced by the fact that it is not repeatable. Moreover, many of the outcomes from the rehabilitation of the Southern Highway are irreversible and the decision is non-divisible. When these factors are considered in relation to the environmental impacts of the road, only an incomplete set of possible future states is also available for evaluation. Therefore, any measure of the uncertainty surrounding the occurrence of the environmental impact will require to be non-additive as well as non-distributional. The presence of ecological uncertainty and valuation uncertainty merely compounds this situation. It is the combination of these factors connected with environmental uncertainty which will now be discussed.

### 6.4.2 Environmental Uncertainty and the Belize Southern Highway Project

Although the majority of this section will deal with the uncertainty surrounding the possible indirect impacts of the road, there are some important aspects connected with the direct impacts of the road project, for which there is a large degree of uncertainty. One of these is in relation to the ability of the road construction to cope with flooding. This is a problem, because very few reliable records exist on water levels and flows for the river and in designing the specifications of the road, assumptions such as the run-off coefficient have had to be made. Hard uncertainty over whether the assumed value is a sufficient basis for designing the road will depend on whether the indirect impacts of the roads result in an increased run-off (DHV, 1994a).

However, in relation to the indirect impacts of the rehabilitation of the Southern Highway, the most important factors facing decision makers are characterized by hard uncertainty. Given the complex nature of the terrestrial and marine ecosystems that exist in the affected area, a large degree of ecological uncertainty exists surrounding the effects of any changes caused by the road (themselves surrounded by uncertainty) on key ecosystem functions. For example, a major uncertainty is connected with the effect that deforestation may have in terms of flood control, as well as in terms of acting as a buffer against damage caused by hurricanes. Not only is the future occurrence and magnitude of hurricanes unclear, but also the effects of a hurricane are uncertain and will depend to a large extent on the degree of deforestation that has occurred, as well as other factors such as the indirect effects of the road on other key ecosystems such as mangroves and wetlands which act as a buffer against the worst effects of a hurricane. In the case of hurricane Mitch (The *Guardian*, 1998), which hit Honduras, Nicaragua, Guatemala and El Salvador in 1998 a contributory factor to the scale of the disaster would appear to have been the reduction of the capacity of the natural environment to mitigate the hurricane. Reducing the resilience of key ecosystems in Belize may also mean that their ability to recover after the effects of such a disturbance is also reduced. Again, however, the exact threshold at which the resilience of, say, a mangrove system is lost is characterized by hard uncertainty.

Other ecological uncertainties relate to the effects of human-induced disturbances, due to a lack of information on the key processes in many of Belize's main ecosystems. So, for example, the effect of habitat fragmentation caused by deforestation will depend on the pollination mechanisms employed by the different tree species, which at present are largely a matter of conjecture (Bird, 1997). The extent to which land clearance and deforestation will result in erosion, siltation and sedimentation is also unknown due to 'an enormous gap in present day knowledge' (DHV, 1994a: p. 42). Another issue is the extent to which accelerated deforestation will lead to biodiversity losses. Other uncertainties relate to the interaction of the different ecosystems. Thus the effect of increased sedimentation and nutrient enrichment, which could be caused by increased agricultural development on mangrove, sea grass and coral systems is unknown. What threshold of increased sedimentation will cause sea grass communities to become vulnerable is not understood, nor is the long-term impact of increased run-off of fertilizers or pesticides on such ecosystems. The possible impacts of these factors on the coral reef are also surrounded by hard uncertainty. For example, increased nutrient enrichment can cause the development of previously unknown harmful microbes and toxic algae, which can have a devastating affect on marine life (Warrick, 1997).

A further dimension to the hard uncertainty surrounding the environmental effects of the road relates to the value of possible changes in the environment. It is evident from the dependence of the economy on the natural environment in Southern Belize that the key functions and services that the forests, swamps, mangroves, savannahs, sea grass and coral provide are highly valued and the links to the economic system are very strong. However, the nature of the complex linkages between the economic system and the ecological system is typified by hard uncertainty caused by a lack of information on the functional relationships between the existence of ecosystems and their management. As such, the value of possible environmental changes associated with the road is very difficult to ascertain. To return to the value of both Belize's terrestrial and marine ecosystems as buffers against the effects of a hurricane, it is possible that key thresholds may be passed. In particular the effect of marginal changes in the ecosystem structure (both qualitative and quantitative) is unlikely to be continuous and so the true value of any changes can only be determined *ex post*, after the event has occurred. Thus, while it is evident that a major part of the value of the environment in Belize is in terms of damage avoidance, the true value of this cannot to a large degree be unanticipated.

The loss of biodiversity associated with increased deforestation rates as a result of the upgrading of the road may result in the loss of species that have an unanticipated value in future equilibrium states. For example, increases in rain and moist forest deforestation, with accompanying erosion and degradation of soils, means that certain species may have a specific value in preventing further erosion and allowing over long time periods the accumulation of nutrients (Kellman, 1979) and possible reversion to the previous state. Thus, the endemic species currently found in transitional savannah pine systems (which exist on poor soils) may be crucial in allowing nutrient enrichment and regeneration of degraded areas. As such, it is evident that many species will have a latent or unanticipated value at the time of the project evaluation.

Lack of knowledge of the functioning of the ecosystems present in the area affected by the project means also that, to a large degree, the result of factors such as increased fertilizer run-off on sea grass and coral systems is uncertain and therefore the value of such a change is difficult to ascertain *ex ante*. Moreover, to be able to identify the link between increased fertilizer run-off and the economic consequences of degraded reef systems in terms of tourism would require an understanding of the links between sea grass systems and corals. Even if it is possible to estimate this, it is also evident that the different species possibly affected by the road will have a primary value in maintaining healthy functioning ecosystems, on which the directly valued services described in Section 6.3 are based. Thus, although individual species that could be affected by the road will have a conservation and biodiversity value, the largest component of their true worth will be in relation to maintaining the provision of valued services and functions. As a result, a large degree of uncertainty will surround the valuation of changes which could arise as a consequence of the rehabilitation of the Southern Highway.

## 6.5 THE DECISION CONTEXT

The focus of this research is on the way that environmental uncertainty is dealt with in the decision-making process. The emphasis is therefore not on the decision that is eventually made nor on the politics surrounding such a decision, but on the decision process and in particular the way that a course of action or policy is evaluated in the presence of hard uncertainty. Although the application of the Shackle model that has been developed is in relation to individual decision making, it is important to recognize the part that the wider context plays in the decision-making process. In particular it is important to have a greater understanding of the main actors involved in the decision-making process, as well as the way in which the decision process itself is structured.

There are three main institutions which make up the decision-making context to the case study. The first is the Government of Belize, which plays its part as the initiator and co-ordinator of the project, and as such is both the executing agency as well as co-financier. The GoBl's interaction with the other financing agencies is a also a key element in the analysis of the decision process associated with the road. The other main organizations that will form the focus of the case study are the Inter-American Development Bank (IDB) and the Department for International Development (DFID, formerly the ODA). The IDB, as well as having a specific part in the decision process associated with the Southern Highway, provides a wider context for the investigation, in that it is involved in the evaluation of many similar projects in Latin America involving environmental uncertainty. Due to the fact that for many projects the overall decision context and evaluation framework are very similar, the case study will provide an insight into wider issues associated with project evaluation. The last actor investigated was DFID, although this was limited to accessing reports rather than comprehensive interviews (which were carried out with the GoBl and the IDB). It was these three organizations that were involved in producing the main reports between 1995 and 1998[3] which were the focus of the project evaluation.

## NOTES

1. Personal communication with senior decision maker.
2. Unpublished report
3. Personal communication with senior decision maker.

# 7.  Methodology

## 7.1  INTRODUCTION

The purpose of the case study examined in Chapter 6 is to assess whether Shackle's theory can be operationalized in the context of environmental uncertainty. In designing a methodology to test the applicability of the Shackle model a deductive approach was taken, whereby the focus is on the questions of whether the model is useful in explaining the way that hard uncertainty is evaluated in environmental decisions and whether at an individual level actual behaviour is consistent with the key elements of the model outlined in Chapter 5. However, what cannot be assessed is whether an individual, when faced with hard uncertainty, approaches the decision process in a manner consistent with the Shackle model, as opposed to, for example, the expected utility (or variant) model.[1] This issue has been dealt with earlier at a theoretical level.

Although this section is primarily concerned with the design of a suitable methodology which will enable an evaluation of the behavioural or positive assumptions of the developed model, it is not advantageous completely to separate questions of what should happen from what does happen. Normative approaches, if they are to have any relevance, must recognize the limits of human cognitive ability, as well as the limits and realities inherent in decision-making structures and institutions. They must also be tempered by what is the best that the decision-making process can hope to achieve in given circumstances. This is particularly the case in situations of hard uncertainty where, as was argued in the previous chapters, notions of optimality are often meaningless. Therefore, one eye was kept on assessing whether particular features of the model of decision making under hard uncertainty lend themselves to being operationalized in a normative manner.

## 7.2  THE COLLECTION OF DATA

Two main sources of data were used in the research. The first involved the collection and analysis of relevant documents on the Southern Highway Project while the second involved the interviewing of decision makers involved directly with the evaluation of the project. Additionally interviews were carried out with those involved in a more general way in the decision-making process, and capable of giving insights into how environmental uncertainty was evaluated in the decision-making process.

### 7.2.1 Conducting the Interviews

Although the use of interviewing as a research method is common in the social sciences, it is more limited in the case of economics, where there is a preference for indirect observations of (market) behaviour. The development of environmental/ecological economics has led to a wider use of different research methods, including an increasing use of questionnaires, best exemplified in the proliferation of Contingent Valuation surveys. Although the use of such questionnaires has raised a number of issues surrounding the presence of biases (Bateman and Turner, 1993) and their consequent reliability, it is evident that in relation to observing the behaviour of individuals there is no alternative means of eliciting the information. Moreover, the use of interview techniques can provide a rich source of information and data that would otherwise be unobtainable. Furthermore, in order to assess whether an individual is using a normatively operational criterion to guide behaviour, there is no alternative to simply asking him or her (Katzner, 1995).

The choice of interview techniques was another factor for consideration in the design of the research methodology. The use of interviews in environmental economics has been limited to the use of formal questionnaires designed to elicit quantitative information, as in the case in Contingent Valuation surveys or market research surveys. While such an approach is useful in obtaining specific data that are suitable for quantitative analysis, it does limit those being interviewed in terms of the response and interpretation of the original question (Schoenberger, 1991). Equally, it was foreseen that, in terms of operationalizing the Shackle model in the context of the case study, a number of problems would arise that would mean that a purely quantitative approach would be inadequate. As a consequence of these concerns, the interviews utilized a mixture of questions designed to elicit both qualitative and quantitative data. The two approaches were specifically designed therefore with different, yet complementary aims in mind.

Research was carried out in Belize and Washington from June to September 1997, and interviews were conducted with 38 decision makers in the Governement of Belize, IDB and DFID. A number of interviews were also carried out with decision makers in the World Bank.

## 7.3   DESIGN OF THE QUESTIONNAIRE FOR THE BELIZE SOUTHERN HIGHWAY PROJECT[2]

There were two main parts to the questionnaire which was directed at decision makers involved in the evaluation of the Southern Highway Project. The first part (questions 1–6) was structured in a way that allowed the decision maker to respond as freely as possible to the particular issue raised on a purely qualitative basis (see Appendix 1). As well as gaining specific information, by starting with the less formal and loosely structured questions a rapport was built up with the decision maker, before the more formal and more demanding section of the questionnaire was started. Another more general aim of the first part of the interview was to ensure that the decision maker's attention was fixed on the Southern Highway Project and in particular the evaluation process.

More specifically, question 1 and question 2 were designed to provide details of the decision-making context and the role of the individual in the decision-making process. Questions 3 to 6 were designed to gain qualitative information on the extent to which uncertainties surrounding the project had been identified, how they had been evaluated, and the extent to which they had affected the decision-making process. These questions not only reminded the decision maker of the way that he/she had evaluated the Southern Highway Project (which was important for the second part of the questionnaire), but also allowed the respondent to give answers without assuming the existence of a particular model of decision making under uncertainty.

The second part of the questionnaire (questions 7–20, Appendix 1) involved the use of a more formal questionnaire based on a number of scenarios presented to the decision maker (see Appendix 2). The questions were specifically designed to elicit a mix of qualitative data and quantitative data that would provide information on: 1) the way that the individual evaluated the uncertainty surrounding the possible gains and loss associated with the Southern Highway Project (questions 7–13, qualitative only); and 2) to provide data that would allow a number of propositions derived from the key elements of the model to be tested (questions 14–20, qualitative and quantitative). On the basis of this, the usefulness of the model as a means of explaining the way in which uncertainty is evaluated in the decision-making process could be ascertained.

### 7.3.1   Preparation of the Hypothesized Outcomes/Scenarios

After the key elements of the model had been theoretically developed, attention turned to how the main elements of the model could be practically operationalized in relation to the case study of the Belize Southern Highway.

The methodology focused, therefore, on the construction of the potential surprise function of the individual and the specification of his or her ascendancy function. Both of these elements required that a set of possible gain and loss scenarios, with corresponding valuations, be identified. This had not been done in a formal manner in any of the project documents or reports. It was the construction of possible gain and loss outcomes that could occur as a result of the rehabilitation of the Belize Southern Highway, that formed the basis of the design of the formal questionnaire.

Although it would have been interesting to allow the decision makers to construct their own list of possible gain and loss outcomes (as was done in Ford and Ghose, 1995c), the requirement that a gain and loss value be specified in relation to each possible outcome of the road project precluded this for practical reasons (notably the length of interview required to enable the decision makers to construct the scenarios and place valuations, as well as access to information). For these reasons it was decided that a range of gain and loss outcomes, which reflected as far as possible the information available to the decision makers at the time, would be prepared in advance of the interviews and presented within the formal questionnaire. The construction of the different outcomes was based on the project documents that had been received prior to the commencement of fieldwork in Belize and were modified slightly in Belize, after additional information had been collected, and prior to the scheduling of the interviews with the decision makers. The key design concern was to make the different scenarios reflect as fully as possible the information available to the decision makers at the time. In particular the reports were used to describe possible scenarios which could occur as a result of the road. The tendency of the different reports to separate the possible positive and negative impacts of the road facilitated this. As was stated earlier, in terms of the negative impacts of the road, the focus was on the indirect consequences, particularly those related to environmental effects. At this stage it was decided that a total of 10 scenarios, five gains and five losses, would be sufficient to encapsulate the range of hypothesized outcomes (see Appendix 2). A further practical consideration was that, because a detailed description was to be provided for each scenario, any more scenarios would require a longer period of time for the respondent to go through. The next stage was to attach estimates of the possible gains and losses associated with each scenario in the form of monetary values. This necessitated the detailed information in the project reports on the economic feasibility of the road.

### 7.3.1.1 The gain scenarios
Identifying the monetary values associated with the road was relatively simple for the gains as opposed to the losses, due to the availability of the analysis carried out in the Kocks Consult (1993) feasibility study. However,

the DHV (1994b) study of the agricultural benefits of the road was not available initially. The different scenarios gradually increased in value from the base case, which only included road benefits derived from savings made in terms of vehicle operating costs, to those scenarios where significant benefits were derived from increased agricultural productivity and tourism. All the figures, in keeping with the feasibility studies, were discounted at 12 per cent over the time span of the project, which was 1993–2015.

Scenario 4 included a hypothesized estimate of the increases in tourism, as well as the health and education benefits, which were not estimated in the Kocks Consult (1993) study. The last gain scenario (5) was estimated from the previous scenario, with the addition of an estimate of unanticipated social and economic benefits. This incorporation of unanticipated benefits in the last gain scenario captured Shackle's notion of a residual hypothesis (a similar approach is taken in the last loss scenario), and reinforced the idea that the set of scenarios was not assumed to be exhaustive. It should be stressed that, in estimating valuations for the different scenarios, the emphasis was purely in relation to the possible outcomes, reflecting the information detailed in the project reports, with which the decision makers were familiar. The focus was then on the use of the scenarios in terms of the evaluation of the uncertainty or 'surprise' that the decision maker attached to the occurrence of the outcome, rather than the outcome value *per se*. Consequently the aim was not to produce the most accurate figures possible; indeed an element of the exercise was to incorporate a certain degree of uncertainty into the different possible gain scenarios.

### 7.3.1.2 The loss scenarios

The construction of the loss scenarios, because of their focus on the possible environmental losses, was more complicated. Although the environmental assessments carried out for the project (DHV, 1994a; BECCA, 1995) together with the environmental summary (IDB, 1997a), provided a large amount of information on which the descriptions of the loss scenarios could be based, there was no attempt in any of the reports to quantify the monetary value of the possible losses associated with the loss of key ecosystem functions or services. As a result, once the five loss scenarios were described qualitatively, the estimation of environmental valuations for the different possible negative outcomes of the road project had to be made.

The first stage of this process was to calculate the areas of the different key ecosystems in the area affected by the road. From these maps, which encompassed the area affected by the road, as well as the accompanying reports, the area and dominant ecosystem type was specified for different land systems and sub-units according to the classification used by King *et al.* (1986, 1989). On the basis of this data, the different areas of five key ecosystems/biomes were

*Table 7.1    Total ecosystem areas, in area of influence of the Southern
Highway*

| Tropical broad leaf forest | Savannah | Pine | Swamp/ wetlands | Mangroves |
|---|---|---|---|---|
| 549,638 ha | 434.1 ha | 633.32 ha | 508 ha | 295 ha |

identified, namely 1) tropical broad leafed forest, 2) pine forest, 3) savannah, 4) marsh/mangroves and 5) swamps/flood plains. In identifying the different eco-systems, only the areas where there was no or very limited agriculture or development were included. When the different sub-units were grouped together the total areas of the different systems were as given in Table 7.1.

The next stage involved the estimation of the area losses associated with the different scenarios to be presented to the decision maker. This was done by first hypothesizing different incremental area losses for the individual areas of the various ecosystem types/biomes present, based on the extent of development described in the scenario. The type of ecosystem affected was dependent on the type of development induced by the road. So, for example, agricultural expansion was assumed to cause deforestation. In terms of pro-jecting the different areas, another assumption made was that areas closest to the road would be most vulnerable and would therefore be affected first.[3] Once the total area destroyed in each biome was calculated, these figures were converted into percentage terms for ease of description in the loss scenarios presented to the decision maker (see Appendix 2). In the case of scenario 6, the first loss outcome, this contained only the direct costs of building the road and thus encompassed no destruction of the main ecosys-tems. As in the case of gains scenario 10 included unanticipated losses, but it was also not quantified in terms of percentage losses of ecosystem type.

The next step was to attach estimated monetary values to the loss scenarios in terms of the hypothesized destruction of the key ecosystem types identi-fied. Again the estimation of the values attached to the different scenarios was not the main concern of this book. As a result, some of the major issues raised earlier in this book with regard to valuation are side-stepped, with the focus remaining on the model of decision making under uncertainty, which requires the gain and loss values to facilitate its operationalization in a behavioural sense. The use of environmental valuation reflects the focus on environmental uncertainty.

Once the five loss scenarios had been developed from information derived from the different reports available, valuation estimates were attached to the different scenarios. For the first loss scenario, scenario 6, because no environmental degradation was hypothesized, this cost figure represented the total cost of all sections of the Southern Highway Project.[4] The loss scenarios 7, 8 and 9 were based on this total cost figure plus the valuations attached to the hypothesized loss of the area of the various ecosystems under the different outcomes.

The environmental valuation data, which were used to come up with environmental loss figures for scenarios 7–9, were derived from the study by Costanza *et al.* (1997b). This large study presented estimates of the average global value of annual ecosystem services in 1994 US$ per hectare for the different ecosystem systems grouped by biome. However, the study recognized that 'there are many conceptual and empirical problems inherent in producing such an estimate' (Costanza *et al.*, 1997b: p. 255). In particular, there are a large number of dangers inherent in the extrapolation of point estimates to global totals, as well as the uncertainties inherent in the estimates produced. Even so, given that at the time of the fieldwork no valuation studies had been carried out specifically in relation to Belize, the Costanza *et al.* study was by far the most comprehensive and best source of estimates of the possible valuations of different ecosystem functions.

The study, therefore, presented a source of annual ecological valuations of different biomes (see Table 7.2) which could be used, in conjunction with the area data collected on the different sub-units present in Belize, to estimate the economic value of hypothesized destruction of the different biomes in the scenarios. The overall value given to the different biomes was based on valuations of specific ecosystem functions, such as climate regulation, erosion control, nutrient cycling and genetic resources.

The next step was to calculate the total gross discounted costs for scenarios 7, 8 and 9. This was based on adding the direct costs of the roads (in scenario 1) to the total lost value of the flow of ecosystem services over the lifetime of the project for all the biomes which were projected to be affected in the different scenarios.

For the last scenario (10), no specific areas were specified. Instead large losses for all the different biomes were assumed to occur, including sea grass beds and corals. The latter two could not be given valuation estimates because, although value data existed in the Costanza *et al.* (1997b) study, no area figures could be obtained for sea grass or coral in the area affected by the road. Further losses were hypothesized to occur from unanticipated losses of ecosystem services. A very conservative estimate was made for this scenario. Again it should be emphasized that these valuations relate to the marginal value of the different biomes, rather than the total value. Further caveats related to using the valuation data are detailed in Costanza *et al.* (1997b). Nevertheless, despite these problems, the attachment of environmental values

*Table 7.2  Summary of global value of annual ecosystem services*

| Biome | low | | high | | average | |
|---|---|---|---|---|---|---|
| | ha-1 yr -1 US$ | ha-1 yr -1 BZ$ | ha-1 yr -1 US$ | ha-1 yr -1 BZ$ | ha-1 yr -1 US$ | ha-1 yr -1 BZ$ |
| Estuaries | 12 150 | 24 300 | 33 833 | 67 666 | 22 832 | 45 664 |
| Sea grass | 10 002 | 20 004 | 28 002 | 56 004 | 19 002 | 38 004 |
| Coral reefs | 613 | 1 226 | 11 537 | 23 074 | 6 075 | 12 150 |
| Tropical forest | 1 175 | 2 350 | 4 052 | 8 104 | 2 007 | 4 014 |
| Temperate/pine forest | 261 | 522 | 344 | 688 | 302 | 604 |
| Grasslands/savannah | 232 | 464 | 232 | 464 | 232 | 464 |
| Marsh/mangroves | 7 906 | 15 812 | 15 469 | 30 938 | 9 990 | 19 980 |
| Swamps/floodplains | 9 865 | 19 730 | 30 331 | 60 662 | 19 580 | 39 160 |

*Source:*  Adapted from Costanza *et al.*, 1997b and accompanying notes.

to the different scenarios provided a good basis on which to test the operationalization of the Shackle model in relation to environmental uncertainty.

### 7.3.2 Designing the Questions Relating to the Gain and Loss Scenarios[5]

It is convenient to separate this second part of the interview based on the scenarios into two sections. The first section, consisting of questions 7–13, was designed to allow the respondent to be as unconstrained as possible in his/her description of the way in which they would go about evaluating the uncertainty surrounding the scenarios, before any restrictions were placed on the format of responses necessary to assess the model quantitatively. The second section, consisting of questions 14–20, was designed to ascertain whether the decision maker's behaviour was consistent with the key propositions of the model. This was also important in indicating whether the model could be practically operationalized in a normative manner.

On the basis of the gain and loss scenarios generated, the formal questionnaire included a number of qualitative questions, which were asked once the decision maker was read a note explaining the different scenarios (see Appendix 2), and given time to read over the gain and loss scenarios. The questions 7–13 (Appendix 1) were asked before any of the different elements of the Shackle model were applied. These questions allowed the decision maker to draw on the evaluation of the project in the decision process and provided information on the approach which he/she would have taken. The information gained from the answers could then be analysed in relation to its general consistency with the Shackle model as opposed to, say, an expected utility approach. At a more basic level information on the extent to which the particular institution/organization explicitly recognized the existence of uncertainties surrounding the road was also gained.

Questions 14–20 presumed the existence of the key elements of the model of decision making under uncertainty developed in Chapter 5, namely the potential surprise function and the ascendancy/weighting function. The aim of the questionnaire was then to provide data which could be analysed in order to assess whether the individual's behaviour was in fact consistent with the different elements of the model. The purpose was therefore not to provide evidence on the choice of uncertainty variable (as in Ford and Ghose, 1995c) or weighting procedure, but to assess whether, if the decision makers were asked to assign a degree of potential surprise and weight to the different outcomes, they would do so in a manner consistent with the Shackle model. The only way that such a methodology could be designed was by using an existing model of decision making under uncertainty. Such a deductive framework was adopted, because the only alternative methodological approach to this would have involved being present at all the different meetings in which uncertainties related to the road were discussed and evaluated. Although this would have overcome some of the difficulties encountered in the use of a formal questionnaire to elicit direct responses to a series of questions it was not practically feasible, nor would it provide data that would lend itself to assessing in a more detailed manner the key propositions of the model.

The first assumption made in questions 14–20 was that gains and losses could be separated, as proposed by the Shackle model. This proposition is arguably the least controversial of the main elements of the Shackle model. Moreover, evidence of the separation of the gains and losses at a qualitative level was found in the report documents.[6] On the basis of the gain and loss scenarios, question 14 was designed to derive a measure of the potential surprise that the decision maker attached to the alternative outcomes. Building on the experiments by Ford and Ghose (1994a, 1994b, 1995a, 1995b and 1995c), the potential surprise values for the decision makers were elicited directly from the respondents by asking question 14 (see Appendix 1).[7]

After the potential surprise allocated to each of the five gain and five loss outcomes by the respondent was recorded, attention turned to the ascendancy function. First of all a series of qualitative questions (questions 15 and 16) were designed to gain information on whether, as consistent with the Shackle model, the respondent would sift through the different gain and loss scenarios and focus on one loss outcome and one gain outcome. Similarly questions 17 and 18 were used to identify on a qualitative basis the outcome which would be weighted highest out of the gain scenarios and the outcome which would be weighted highest out of the loss scenarios (corresponding to the focus gain and focus loss in Shackle's model).

The method used to elicit the ascendancy function, namely the means by which the decision maker is presumed to evaluate the outcome and the corresponding degree of surprise, was more complicated. It should also be reiterated that the emphasis in the interpretation of the Shackle model given in Chapter 5 is on the ascendancy function as a means by which the decision maker weights the various $(x, y)$ elements (see Section 5.5.3) and is in no way related to the concept of utility. Theoretically, in the Shackle model, the ascendancy function is derived from a series of indifference curves. One approach akin to that taken in utility analysis involves attempting to elicit a series of ascendancy indifference to elicit trade-offs between different pairs of elements. However, the problem with using this method is that it is time consuming (an issue of particular concern in relation to interviewing senior decision makers) and also can be unreliable. This is due to the fact that decision makers find making specific (hypothetical) trade-offs over a large number of element pairs very difficult (Edwards, 1977). Because of these methodological concerns, as well as the argument advanced in Chapter 5 that the specification of ascendancy indifference curves was not necessary for the operationalization of the Shackle model, attention turned to eliciting the ascendancy function directly.

The advantage of eliciting the ascendancy function directly was that the decision maker would only have to consider the five gain (gain, surprise) pairs and the five loss pairs rather than the far larger volume of information required in order to generate the ascendancy indifference curves. In order to specify the function, and in light of the theoretical interpretation given to the Shackle model, the ascendancy function was interpreted as a weighting function, by which the decision maker would then allocate a subjective weight to each pair which reflected the weight that s/he would give to the outcome and its associated degree of surprise in the decision-making process. Thus, after reading a short paragraph to the interviewee explaining the scaling of the weights to be allocated (see Appendix 1), questions 19 and 20 were designed in order to gain the weights that the decision makers would give to the different gain/loss uncertainty pairs.

## 7.4   DATA ANALYSIS

The analysis of the data involved three elements. First the documentary evidence was read over a number of times to assess the extent to which and way in which the decision process had evaluated environmental uncertainty. The second element involved the analysis of the qualitative questions asked in both the specific and general interviews and the third aspect involved the econometric analysis of the quantitative data.

It is to an analysis of the results from the application of the case study that we now turn.

## NOTES

1. An excellent range of experiments that have been carried out and attempt to provide evidence on the choice by individuals in respect of the different measures of uncertainty put forward by alternative models detailed in Ford and Ghose (1994a, 1994b, 1995a, 1995b, 1995c). A possible means of distinguishing between the use of the Shackle model and the expected utility model is found in Ford and Ghose (1998).
2. This section deals exclusively with the questions detailed in Appendix 1.
3. See Chomitz and Gray (1996) for a model of road induced development applied to Belize, which also makes this assumption.
4. This total cost figure was derived from an unpublished document, although it is very similar to that contained in the Kocks Consult (1993) feasibility study.
5. This section deals exclusively with Appendix 1, questions 7–20.
6. The documentary evidence will be analysed in more detail in the following chapter.
7. This question was adapted from that used in the questionnaire detailed in Ford and Ghose (1995c: p. 17).

# 8. Results of the application of the Shackle model

## 8.1 INTRODUCTION

This chapter presents evidence of whether the behaviour of the individuals interviewed is consistent with the key propositions of the model. These propositions centre on the evaluation of the outcomes in terms of degree of potential surprise as well as the existence of an ascendancy function. In terms of potential surprise the specific assumptions on which evidence is provided include: that potential surprise reflects the belief that the individual has in the occurrence of the outcome; the extent to which any of the axioms for potential surprise (as described in Section 5.4.1.1) are supported; and whether potential surprise was treated as a continuous or binary measure of uncertainty. In terms of the existence of the ascendancy function, evidence is provided on: the consistency of the coefficients of the potential surprise and outcome variables with that of theory; the overall explanatory power of the ascendancy function; the difference between the ascendancy/weighting function over gains and losses; the difference of the coefficients between the individuals; the significance of the potential surprise and outcome variable; and the role of the ascendancy function as a sifting device by means of which the individual decision maker focuses on one gain and one loss outcome respectively.

In Section 8.3 the Shackle model is then applied at a more general level in an attempt to explain the way that uncertainty is evaluated in institutions such as the Inter-American Development Bank and the World Bank. In this chapter the results from the specific interviews will be interpreted in a broader context and will be supplemented by the more general interviews carried out with decision makers, which did not solely focus on the Southern Highway. By drawing together the wider implications of the theoretical arguments that have been developed throughout the course of this book, as well as the information gained from the interviews, the aim is to help to explain in a broader context the evaluation of uncertainty within the decision-making process. Thus, while the application of the Shackle model focused on the evaluation of uncertainty at an individual level, the recognition that the decision-making process involves the interaction of a number of key actors necessitates a broader analysis of decision making under uncertainty developed in this book. As such, it is argued that within the decision-making process the different actors effectively contest different competing focus outcomes. It is at this stage that, if no explicit evaluation of hard uncertainty has been made, there is a danger that it has not been adequately dealt with.

## 8.2 EVIDENCE OF THE KEY ELEMENTS OF THE SHACKLE MODEL IN THE SOUTHERN HIGHWAY PROJECT

This section focuses more specifically on the key elements of the Shackle model as interpreted in Chapter 5. The separation of gains and losses is discussed, before evidence surrounding the evaluation of uncertainties is analysed. The bulk of this section, however, focuses on the testing of a number of propositions with respect to the use of potential surprise and the role of the ascendancy or weighting function.

### 8.2.1 Separation of Gains and Losses

The first element of the Shackle model on which some evidence from the reports and interviews was gained was the separation of gains and losses. Although this was not formally tested, as were the other elements relating to potential surprise and the ascendancy function, it is arguably the least controversial aspect of Shackle's theory. Evidence of the separation of costs and benefits was evident in the project reports, which formally separated the two (either costs and benefits or positive and negative impacts) (Kocks Consult, 1993; DHV, 1994a; BECCA, 1995; IDB, 1997a). The respondents were also comfortable with the separation of gains and losses in the scenarios presented to them as part of the questionnaire (see Appendices 1 and 2). Thus during the interviews the respondents tended to focus on the gains and losses separately, sometimes giving more attention to one than the other. For example one decision maker stated:

I would start with the worst case scenario.[1]

### 8.2.2 The Quantification of Uncertainty

Before the decision makers were asked to assign the degree of surprise they would feel at the occurrence of the individual outcomes, preliminary evidence was gained on possible measures of uncertainty used by decision makers when they were assessing the uncertainty surrounding a particular outcome. This provided an interesting insight into how the decision makers evaluated the uncertainties on an individual basis. Overall only two of the total of 23 respondents interviewed with respect to the Southern Highway started to talk about uncertainties in terms of probability. One of these individuals, when asked if she would attempt to quantify the nature of the uncertainty faced in the project, responded:

> I'm not sure that there were any attempts to quantify the uncertainties … having said that I'd probably build a probability curve starting with the worst case scenario and moving on to what I would call a more likely scenario.[2]

The use of probability was framed in terms of the likelihood of a particular effect such as sedimentation. However, when the same decision maker was asked about whether she would attempt to estimate a probability curve for the consequences of a particular effect she replied:

> I am willing to venture that we have never done that, because it is very difficult, you have to have so much data, you could do it in a very conceptual way.[3]

The decision makers' interpretation and use of probability is rather interesting, however, and will be returned to in Section 8.3.2. Only one other individual mentioned probability in relation to one of the scenarios introduced, with regard to the weighting of the scenarios.

The rest of the respondents made no mention of probability as a possible measure and indeed other notions of measures were used. For example one individual stated:

> The Southern Highway is one of those projects where there is a large measure of uncertainty on a range 1–5, 1 being minimal uncertainty to 5 being some maximum.[4]

Another stated:

> using as scale 1–10, I would definitely be about 70–80% uncertain.[5]

Other respondents talked about the surprise they would feel at the occurrence of a particular outcome, while another talked in terms of likelihood, and another in terms of the realism of particular scenarios and whether or not they were believable. A number of individuals referred to the possibility of a particular event occurring. This would appear to indicate that individuals may base their expectation in relation to an uncertain event on more than one criterion such as belief or realism (see Section 5.4.1.1). Whether the use of different criteria corresponds to different types of uncertainty is difficult to conclude from the evidence obtained in the interviews, although one decision maker stated that:

> high levels of surprise reflect the huge uncertainties that I feel are running through the process.[6]

Overall, however, the majority of decision makers stated that they had not quantified or attempted to assign some scale to the level of uncertainty that they faced. Again this indicates that no normative framework had been adopted. However, the use of certain scales or criteria such as belief, reality and surprise, indicates that on an individual basis some informal assessment of the outcomes of the project was made.

### 8.2.2.1  Potential surprise

The replacement of probability by an alternative measure of uncertainty is a key element in the Shackle model. While the analysis did not test the use of potential surprise as opposed to other measures such as probability (as in Ford and Ghose, 1994b), the results do provide evidence of whether, if adopted as a measure of the decision makers' degree of uncertainty as to the outcomes of the road (in terms of the different gain and loss scenarios presented to them), the assignment of potential surprise by the decision maker is broadly consistent with what would be expected in theory. In addition, some indication of its applicability as a measure of uncertainty in a normative manner can also be assessed. At a theoretical level its superiority as a measure of hard uncertainty of the kind faced in the Southern Highway project has already been demonstrated.

The focus of this section is on question 14 (Appendix 1). The results for the individual respondents are presented in Appendix 3. The majority of respondents when asked the question seemed comfortable with the concept of surprise and the scale of 0–10 used, although one respondent initially required the concept to be explained to him in greater detail. The interpretation of potential surprise as a measure of uncertainty was perhaps more varied. In Shackle's theory, potential surprise is seen as reflecting the degree of possibility that the individual thinks resides in the realization of the alternative outcomes. As such, it is a measure of the belief that a particular outcome is possible. This is captured by axiom A1 which states that degree of potential surprise is dependent on the extent to which an individual believes that a particular outcome is possible. Zero degree of surprise indicates that the individual believes that it is perfectly possible that the outcome will occur, while the absolute maximum degree of surprise $\bar{y}$ indicates that the individual believes the occurrence of the outcome to be impossible (see Section 5.4.1.1).

Evidence of the interpretation of potential surprise was articulated in a number of cases. For example, one decision maker stated with reference to the different scenarios:

> Because [scenario] 10 would be a total surprise as would [scenario] 6. [Scenario] 6 would be a total surprise. Okay in fact what I am saying is that for me [scenario] 6 and [scenario] 10 would be totally unrealistic, [scenario] 9 would be very unrealistic. Can I put the same surprise to more than one of them?[7]

This statement would tend to support the interpretation of surprise which was broadly consistent with the model. Namely, the fact that the decision maker asked if she could assign the same degree of surprise to two outcomes (which she had started to do) would indicate some consistency with, for example, axiom A5 which states that the degree of surprise assigned to any outcome need not depend on the degree of surprise attached to the occurrence of its rivals (see Section 5.4.1.1). However, in terms of allocating numerically a degree of surprise, the same respondent when talking about scenario 6 stated:

> I don't think scenario 6 is a realistic one as far as we are concerned.

Yet, she went on to allocate a zero degree of surprise to the same outcome (see respondent I, Appendix 3), which could be interpreted that, although the decision maker did not believe the outcome to be realistic (or have a high degree of possibility), nevertheless she would not be surprised as to its occurrence. At a more general level this would appear to be in line with some of Carter's (1953) criticisms that, while an individual may believe that the possibility of an outcome is low (or unrealistic), they would still not be surprised were it to occur.

The two respondents who mentioned the use of probability are interesting in that although they both allocated degrees of surprise, in the course of the interview they repeatedly referred to probability. While the comments of one of the respondents will be left to the following section, the behaviour of respondent E will be considered here. When the respondent was allocating the degree of surprise to the different scenarios she also talked about the probability of the different outcomes occurring. In particular with respect to the gain scenarios (1–5), she allocated a probability of 40 per cent to scenarios 1, 2 and 3, which corresponded to a degree of surprise of 3, a probability of 25 per cent to scenario 4 which was equivalent to a degree of surprise of 5, and a probability of 1 per cent to scenario 5, equivalent to a surprise of 10. The use of probabilities and their conversion to potential surprise could in certain respects have more in common with the approach taken by Ford (1983), although in this case the probability is replaced by potential surprise. However, in specifying the probability of the scenarios, she did so in a manner which was not consistent with probability theory which would require that the probabilities sum to 100 per cent. This would appear to demonstrate a greater consistency with Shackle's theory and in particular the proposition that the measure should be non-additive. None of the other respondents mentioned the use of probability in the exercise, which is interesting given the theoretical hegemony of probability in academic studies.

Where no verbal description was offered of how decision makers interpreted their allocation of degrees of surprise to the different scenarios, their behaviour in terms of the allocation of the degree of surprise could be interpreted by analysing their potential surprise values. This was done by producing a graph of all the potential surprise values allocated by the individual decision makers to the different scenarios (see Appendix 3). The most revealing aspect of the graphs is the shape of the potential surprise function. Although Shackle's theory indicates that there are numerous shapes that the potential surprise function could take, where the function is generally smooth, as opposed to having a number of peaks and troughs, this appears to indicate that potential surprise has been interpreted as a continuous variable. The majority of the graphs do tend to a smooth continuous shape, indicating that potential surprise is revised gradually in accordance with the magnitude of the gain and loss values, which is consistent with theory.

There are a number of exceptions, which would appear to indicate an interpretation of potential surprise as binary, namely that the decision maker is either surprised or not. Respondents D and K are the most obvious example of this. The graphs for respondents B, C, O, and S interestingly appear very similar to the shape of the potential surprise function sketched by Shackle (see Figure 5.1). What is perhaps unclear is the relationship between potential surprise and the extent to which the individual believes there is a high degree of uncertainty surrounding the occurrence of a particular outcome. So, for example, in terms of scenario 6 (the first cost scenario) which reflects the direct costs of the project, eight respondents allocated this outcome a low (relative to the other cost scenarios) or zero surprise, which indicated they would be not be surprised at all if the scenario was to occur because at a minimum these costs would be incurred. However, the other respondents gave a higher degree of surprise for scenario 6, indicating that, because they felt that there would be greater costs than those encapsulated by the first cost scenario, they would feel a greater degree of surprise at its occurrence.

In terms of interpreting the data it should be emphasized that a fair amount of caution must be exercised. The results cannot explain exactly how the uncertainty associated with a particular scenario is evaluated by the different individuals. Even so, in terms of assessing the consistency of the behaviour of the individuals with that suggested by theory, the results suggest that the allocation of degree of surprise by the decision makers is broadly in line with that which would be expected in the model. In particular the evidence would suggest that potential surprise was defined as a non-additive variable by the majority of respondents. In addition most of the decision makers did assign the degree of surprise in a continuous manner. However, a significant number of individuals did appear in contrast to interpret degree of surprise in a binary manner, suggesting that some individuals did not interpret degree of surprise in a fashion consistent with the Shackle model. As well as providing evidence in relation to potential surprise as an element in the Shackle model, an important aspect of eliciting the potential surprise variables was to facilitate the modelling of the ascendancy function to which we now turn.

### 8.2.3 The Ascendancy or Weighting Function

The next stage of the analysis involved the modelling of the ascendancy or weighting function. The purpose was to gain evidence of whether the behaviour exhibited by individuals, when they were asked to weight the different scenarios, was consistent with the model outlined in Chapter 5.

#### 8.2.3.1 Preliminary evidence of a sifting or editing process

In Shackle's theory the ascendancy function encapsulates the editing or sifting process by which the decision makers arrive at one focus outcome on the gain side and one focus outcome on the loss side. Before the function in relation to the gain and loss scenarios presented to the decision maker was elicited from the decision makers, the individuals were asked to assign a weight to the different scenarios (see Appendices 1 and 2). Specifically questions 15 and 16 were asked in order to gain some evidence of the respondents' willingness to discard any of the scenarios and exclude them from any further consideration in the evaluation process. Although this cannot be directly equated with the ascendancy or weighting function, it highlighted whether individuals would at a preliminary stage find it useful to discard some of the scenarios. This would suggest the basis of a sifting or editing process as described in Chapter 5. In total in response to questions 15 and 16, 14 or 62 per cent of the 21 decision makers included in the analysis stated that they would discard one or more scenarios at the initial stage of the evaluation process. The details of how many and which scenarios were excluded are shown in Tables 8.1 and 8.2.

Overall it was the highest gain and highest loss scenarios that were the most likely to be excluded by the decision makers. Interestingly enough only one scenario on the gain side (scenario 2) and one on the loss side (scenario 7) was not excluded by any of the decision makers. This is consistent with the next section in which in no cases were these scenarios allocated a weighting

*Table 8.1   Number of scenarios discarded*

| Number of scenarios excluded | 0 | 1 | 2 | 3 | 4 | 5 | 6 | Total |
|---|---|---|---|---|---|---|---|---|
| Number of respondents | | 8 | 1 | 4 | 3 | 3 | 1 | 1 | 21 |

*Table 8.2   Frequency of scenarios discarded*[8]

| Scenario number | 1 | 2 | 3 | 4 | 5 | 6 | 7 | 8 | 9 | 10 |
|---|---|---|---|---|---|---|---|---|---|---|
| Number of respondents who discarded the scenario | 3 | 0 | 1 | 2 | 4 | 5 | 0 | 4 | 8 | 9 |

of zero, which would appear to indicate that in the sifting out process, scenarios 2 and 7 survived to the latter stages.

#### 8.2.3.2   Modelling the ascendancy/weighting function
In order to model the ascendancy or weighting function for the individuals, a functional form had to be specified. From Chapter 5, the general functional form of the ascendancy function was assumed to be:

$$\phi = \phi(x, y) \tag{8.1}$$

Three specific functional forms, consistent with Shackle's theory, were then identified:

$$\phi = ax^{0.5} - by^2 \tag{8.2}$$

$$\phi = ax - by^2 \tag{8.3}$$

$$\phi = ax^{0.5} - by \tag{8.4}$$

with $\phi$ indicating the level of ascendancy (or weight) on a scale 0–10, $x$ the absolute gain or loss, measured in US$, $y$ is potential surprise measured on a scale 0–10, and $a$ and $b$ are coefficients for the outcome value and the degree of surprise respectively. These coefficients can be different over gains and losses. Equation 8.3 has been used theoretically by Ford (1994). The signs of the coefficients are consistent with Shackle's arguments that the absolute value of the outcome will increase the ascendancy or weight of that outcome in the mind of the decision maker, whereas potential surprise will have a negative effect on the weight or ascendancy given to the outcome. All three differ with respect to the combinations of the power attached to the outcome value and the degree of potential surprise. So, for example, a power of 0.5 attached to the size of the outcome is consistent with the theoretical assumption that the contribution of the magnitude of the gain or loss outcome makes to the overall weight given will decline marginally. A power of 2 attached to the degree of potential surprise assumes that the (negative) contribution that degree of surprise makes to the overall weight is marginally increasing. Although the model was intrinsically linear and additive, the use of the power terms reflected Shackle's assumption that the outcome value and the degree of surprise are non-linearly (negatively in the case of potential surprise) related to the weighting/level of ascendancy.

Once the different functional forms were specified, the weight given (elicited from questions 19 and 20, Appendix 1), $\phi$ was regressed against the value of the outcome (derived from the scenarios) and the degree of surprise (elicited from question 14) for the whole sample (21 $\times$ 10 observations), over gains and losses (21 $\times$ 5 observations), as well as for each of the individual decision makers. On the basis of the results of the OLS regressions, equation (8.2) was chosen as the most appropriate. This decision was based on the theoretical considerations outlined above and in Chapter 5, as well as the statistical diagnostics produced for each of the individual regressions. Because the potential surprise values used in the regression for each individual represent the degree of surprise associated with that outcome value, it was important to check for multicollinearity.

The theoretical model assumes no intercept. A first step therefore was to run regressions for the individual respondents which included an intercept term. In 14 out of the 21 individuals in the sample (66 per cent of the respondents) the intercept term was not significant. This confirmed at a general level that the theoretical assumption of no intercept term could be accepted, and indicates that the ascendancy functions of the individual decision makers were broadly consistent with that of the theoretical model represented by equation (8.2).

On the basis of the OLS regressions carried out for the functional form specified in equation (8.2), the data obtained from the modelling of each individual in respect of gains and losses jointly, as well as gains and losses separately, were analysed. The results of the regression and the diagnostics tests are summarized in Appendix 4. Although the individual regressions passed the majority of the diagnostic tests, for some there were a number of possible problems identified with the individual models. However, because the aim was to compare the propositions of a theoretical model with actual behaviour, rather than to attempt to define closely the specification of the weighting/ascendancy function, no attempt was made to define the best fitted function for each individual. Instead the diagnostics were used as a further check on the consistency of individual behaviour with the theory.

Another concern was that, although the modelling of the individuals' weighting function allowed the analysis to take place at the individual level and provided comparative data for the qualitative information collected, for the gain and loss regressions there was an issue of statistical reliability due to the small sample sizes (5). This re-emphasized the importance of making sure that the general characteristics of the overall data set were consistent with the requirements necessary for carrying out the OLS regression.

Overall the weighting/ascendancy functions for each decision maker over gains and losses jointly and gains and losses separately pass most of the diagnostic tests. The most common problem indicated by the diagnostics was the possibility of multicollinearity or possible mis-specification indicated by an inconclusive Durbin–Watson statistic. As such the regression models for the majority of the individuals would appear to be fairly reliable. The explanatory power of the individual models in terms of the R-squared values is also relatively high (see Appendix 4). However, where the diagnostic statistics have indicated a number of problems such as is the case for respondent M, less weight should be given to the R-squared value for the individual. Overall, the theoretical model of the ascendancy function seems to have captured fairly well the behaviour of the individual respondents. If the ascendancy functions for gains and losses are taken, for example, the majority of the adjusted R-squared values are higher than 60 per cent, with a large number in the 80 per cent and 90 per cent regions. These figures allow us to proceed in relative confidence to the more detailed analysis of a number of further propositions relating to the Shackle model.

### 8.2.3.3  Testing the propositions of the ascendancy/weighting function

Modelling the weighting/ascendancy function permitted a number of further propositions relating to the model to be tested. A summary of the key results is presented in Table 8.3.

The first proposition that can be tested is whether or not the sign of the coefficients of the individuals' weighting function is consistent with the theoretical requirements. In Shackle's model the absolute value of the outcome, $x$, is expected to contribute positively to the weighting assigned, while the degree of surprise, $y$, is expected to affect negatively the weight assigned to an outcome. For all of the respondents, in respect of the ascendancy function over gains and losses jointly and gains and losses separately, the coefficient of $x$, namely $a$, was positive, showing perfect consistency with the Shackle model (see Appendix 4). The fact that the coefficient for the absolute value of the loss outcomes was positive also confirms that none of the respondents interpreted the weighting function in terms of utility, because if

Table 8.3  *Summary of key results from the modelling of the ascendancy function*

| | Percentage with negative coefficient sign for $b$ | Percentage of significant equations (F test sig. = 0.05) | Percentage of significant $x^{0.5}$ (T-test sig. = 0.05) | Percentage of significant $y^2$ (T-test sig. = 0.05) |
|---|---|---|---|---|
| All | 77% | 100% | 90% | 43% |
| Gain | 57% | 76% | 52% | 24% |
| Loss | 80% | 52% | 43% | 38% |

| | No. of respondents with negative coefficient sign for $b$ | No. of respondents where weighting function is significant (F test sig. = 0.05) | No. of respondents where $x^{0.5}$ is significant (T-test sig. = 0.05) | No. of respondents where $y^2$ is significant (T-test sig. = 0.05) |
|---|---|---|---|---|
| All | 16 | 21 | 19 | 9 |
| Gain | 12 | 16 | 11 | 5 |
| Loss | 17 | 11 | 9 | 8 |

this were the case, then it would be expected that as the loss became larger its utility would decrease.

The analysis of the signs of the coefficient of potential surprise, $b$, for the individual respondents would also appear to be consistent with theory. For the ascendancy function grouped together for all respondents for gains and losses jointly, as well as for gains and losses separately, the coefficients had a negative sign in the main (see Appendix 4). In terms of the gains and losses jointly for 77 per cent of the respondents a negative sign was exhibited. For the gain function this figure was less, with approximately 12 or 57 per cent of the decision makers having the expected sign. For losses considered separately the figure was higher with 17 or 80 per cent of the respondents having negative coefficients for potential surprise. This would appear to suggest some difference in respect of gains and losses. However, on further inspection of the function for gains and losses jointly, in all but one of the respondents' ascendancy functions for whom $b$ was positive, the $y$ term was not significant (see Table 8.4).

*Table 8.4  Individual ascendancy function for gains and losses jointly*

|  | Total no. | No. where $y^2$ not significant (0.05) | % where $y^2$ not significant (0.05) |
|---|---|---|---|
| Sign of $b$ positive | 5 | 4 | 80% |
| Sign of $b$ negative | 16 | 7 | 44% |

In respect of gains all the coefficients that were positive (9) were not significant (see Table 8.5). For losses, for all but one of the respondents, for whom the coefficient of potential surprise was positive, $y$ was not significant (see Table 8.6). When tested statistically, it was also found that there was no significant difference between the coefficients of $y$ or $x$ for the separate gains and losses weighting functions. This would suggest that there was no significant difference between the ascendancy function over gains and losses and would suggest that the estimated individual ascendancy functions for gains and losses jointly could be considered reliable. Thus, although Shackle's theory allows room for the gain and loss ascendancy function to differ in terms of the effect of the degree of surprise on the weight attached to a particular outcome, in the case of the decision makers sampled for the Southern Highway there was no difference in the effect of potential surprise over gains and losses on the weighting function.

The lack of difference between the size of the coefficients $a$ and $b$ in respect of the separate gain and loss functions can be shown by comparing

*Table 8.5    Individual ascendancy function for gains*

|  | Total no. | No. where $y^2$ not significant (0.05) | % where $y^2$ not significant (0.05) |
|---|---|---|---|
| Sign of *b* positive | 9 | 9 | 100% |
| Sign of *b* negative | 12 | 7 | 58% |

*Table 8.6    Individual ascendancy function for losses*

|  | Total no. | No. where $y^2$ not significant (0.05) | % where $y^2$ not significant (0.05) |
|---|---|---|---|
| Sign of *b* positive | 4 | 3 | 75% |
| Sign of *b* negative | 17 | 11 | 65% |

the rolling regression plots of the coefficients for the gains and losses jointly (see Figures 8.1a and 8.1b), gains separately (see Figures 8.2a and 8.2b) and losses (see Figures 8.3a and 8.3b). If Figures 8.1a, 8.2a and 8.3a are analysed, it is apparent that there is very little difference in the range of values of the coefficients for the individuals. Likewise, if Figures 8.1b, 8.2b and 8.3b are compared, the gain and loss coefficients for *y*-squared are broadly within the same range, although it is evident that in comparison with gains, for losses a higher number is negative. Two respondents, D and W, were excluded from the rolling regression due to the coefficients for their equations being outside the range shown in Figures 8.1–8.3 (see Appendix 4 for the size of the coefficients of respondents D and W).

With the exception of decision makers D and W, generally the size of the coefficients is within a relatively narrow range, showing a degree of similarity amongst the individual decision makers in the way that the outcome value and the degree of potential surprise affect the weighting of a particular outcome.

Although overall it would appear that gains and losses were not treated differently in relation to the effect of outcome and degree of surprise on the overall weighting given to the outcome in the course of the interviews, some of the respondents suggested that they would treat gains and losses differently. Although this behaviour is still consistent with the Shackle model, it is worth highlighting as an insight into the evaluation process of one of the individuals who was one of the two decision makers who had at the earlier stages talked about the concept of probability. The following excerpt is inter-

Coefficient of XALLHALF and its two S.E. bands based on rolling OLS

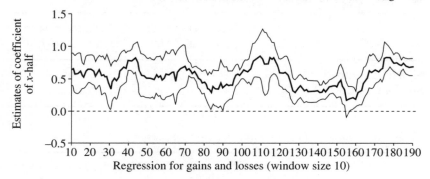

*Figure 8.1a    Rolling regression plot of a for the ascendancy function for gains and losses jointly*

Coefficient of YALLSQ and its two S.E. bands based on rolling OLS

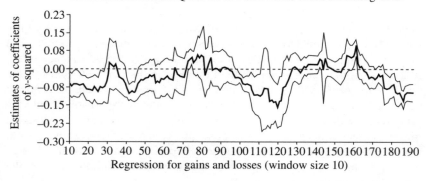

*Figure 8.1b    Rolling regression plot of b for the ascendancy function for gains and losses jointly*

esting not only as an insight into the weighting process but also with regard to the interpretation given to probability which was very different to that given in a conventional expected utility approach. Thus, the respondent stated:

The approach towards benefits is very different to the approach towards costs. Uncertainty in terms of costs, I guess from an environmental side has an element of irreversibility. So even though this is improbable, it has a low probability, the 9 here (gains) is not equivalent to the 9 here (losses). Although this would surprise me, I have more uncertainty towards this, and there is an element of irreversibility, which magnifies, it sort of exacerbates the uncertainty, … I was saying that the probability here is different to the probability here. Here its like what I call dream

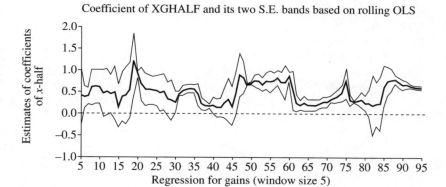

*Figure 8.2a*  *Rolling regression plot of* a *for the ascendancy function for gains*

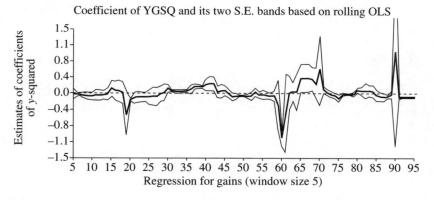

*Figure 8.2b*  *Rolling regression plot of* b *for the ascendancy function for gains*

land. Here it has maybe a 1% probability because it assumes all these things about the government wanting to manage the whole process. Whereas here even although it is a worst case scenario, you may in fact be as high as 15%. I'm trying to make a sort of relationship, it is not a quantitative thing, but the 9 does not reflect well, the degree of surprise on the loss side. That would affect my weighting. That's what I'm trying to say, in terms of weighting, In terms of how much attention you would give to a worst case scenario is maybe even a 7.[9]

The weighting function for this individual clearly therefore fulfils an important role in allowing the decision maker to weight higher a loss out-come with the same degree of surprise as a gain outcome.

Coefficient of XLHALF and its two S.E. bands based on rolling OLS

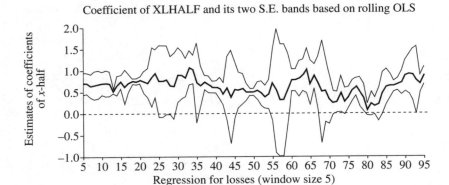

*Figure 8.3a    Rolling regression plot of a for the ascendancy function for losses*

Coefficient of YLSQUARE and its two S.E. bands based on rolling OLS

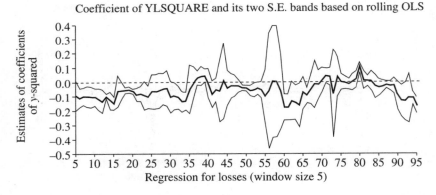

*Figure 8.3b    Rolling regression plot of b for the ascendancy function for losses*

The significance of the variable in the modelled ascendancy functions for the decision makers has already been touched on in relation to testing whether there are any differences between the way that weights were assigned to the different gain and loss scenarios. The significance of the outcome variable and the degree of potential surprise is also important in that it partly indicates the importance of that variable in the weighting process, and as such gives an insight into the evaluation of hard uncertainty surrounding the environmental consequences of the road. In terms of the ascendancy functions for the individual decision makers for gains and losses considered jointly, for all but two of the individuals the outcome variable, $x^{0.5}$, was significant. For gains, only for 10 out of the 21 was the outcome variable significant. For losses, in 20 out of the 21 respondents the outcome variable was significant (see Table 8.3). The significance of potential surprise in the individual ascendancy function is less for gains and losses considered jointly, $y^2$ is significant in nine out of 21 cases, while for gains in only five cases is $y^2$ significant, and for losses the equivalent number of cases is eight (see Table 8.3). The difference between the significance of the outcome and potential surprise variables does suggest some inconsistency with the theoretical model. Part of the difference can be partly explained by the instances where the coefficient of the potential surprise variable is positive and non-significant (see Table 8.5), as well as there being problems with the small sample size. In contrast, for the model for all the respondents grouped together, both the outcome and potential surprise variables are highly significant. At the same time the relatively low number of cases in which potential surprise is significant could also suggest that potential surprise, as a measure of hard uncertainty, was not a significant factor in the weighting of the outcome. Instead the decision makers focused purely on the outcome value alone. This position would appear to be consistent with the views of a significant minority of decision makers, who in the course of their interview, gave the impression that they did not consider hard uncertainty to be a major concern in the evaluation process. In other words where the potential surprise variable is insignificant, this may be seen either in terms of the quality and sample size of the data, or in the interpretation that the surprise that the decision maker felt at the occurrence of the outcome was to a large degree ignored.

A further proposition of the Shackle model that could be assessed by the modelling of the ascendancy function related to its role in editing or sifting the different outcomes to arrive at a focus gain, representing the best outcome to be hoped for, and a focus loss value, representing the worst outcome to be feared. A simple way of testing this proposition was to look at the weighting of the gain and loss scenarios and to identify whether only one gain value and one loss value was identified. In 19 out of the 21 cases only one gain outcome was given the highest weighting. For losses, 15 of the respondents gave their highest weighting to one outcome. Overall, 14 out of the 21 decision makers identified only one outcome value and one loss value, suggesting that generally the behaviour of the decision makers in terms of the ascendancy as a focusing device was in a manner consistent with that expected in theory.

Where only one outcome on the gain side and one loss outcome is identified when the graph of the ascendancy function is drawn with respect to the absolute value of the outcome, then the ascendancy function has one peak (see Appendix 3) and has an appearance similar to that drawn by Shackle (see Figure 5.3). In terms of the identification of the focus gain value, scenario 5 was by far the modal choice (see Table 8.7). In terms of losses the spread was

*Table 8.7   Identification of focus gain*

| Scenario | 1 | 2 | 3 | 4 | 5 | Total |
|---|---|---|---|---|---|---|
| Frequency | 2 | 1 | 3 | 3 | 10 | 19 |

*Table 8.8   Identification of focus loss*

| Scenario | 6 | 7 | 8 | 9 | 10 | Total |
|---|---|---|---|---|---|---|
| Frequency | 3 | 4 | 4 | 3 | 1 | 15 |

more even, with scenarios 7 and 8 being the most common choice of focus loss (see Table 8.8).

### 8.2.4   Summary of Results

The case study of the Belize Southern Highway provides an interesting insight into the way in which uncertainty is evaluated in the decision-making process. The application of the Shackle model to the case study also demonstrates that the model is indeed operational, and that a number of its key propositions could be tested. From the application of the model, it would appear that the decision makers felt comfortable with the separation of gains and losses, a position which is also reflected in the project documents. The use of potential surprise as a measure of uncertainty seems to be broadly consistent with the theoretical model, although in a number of cases it was interpreted as a binary measure. In terms of the modelling of the individual ascendancy/weighting functions, the functional form chosen would appear to capture the behaviour of the decision makers relatively well, as indicated by the high R-squared values, the overall significance of the equations and the fact that the individual regression models passed the majority of the diagnostic tests. The signs of the coefficients are also broadly consistent with the Shackle model, although interestingly there was no difference in the way in which gains and losses were evaluated, indicating that a separate ascendancy function over gains and losses was not necessary. Indeed the individual decision makers showed a large degree of similarity in the way that they weighted the different outcomes based on the outcome and potential surprise values.

In terms of the significance of the variables, the outcome variable is significant in a large number of cases. However, the potential surprise variable is less so, indicating some inconsistency with the Shackle model. Although some of these cases can be explained statistically, an alternative interpretation is that some of the decision makers effectively ignored any uncertainties that they felt at the occurrence of the different outcomes, as indicated by their degree of surprise. The last proposition tested was that of the behaviour of the individuals in terms of the ascendancy/weighting function acting as an editing or sifting device. The results obtained would suggest that the behaviour of the individuals was consistent with the model, with the majority of respondents focusing on one gain outcome (the focus gain) and one loss value (the focus loss).

Overall the results would therefore appear to offer some support for the Shackle model, although clearly some reservations apply, as would be expected from the necessity of using small data sets for the individuals. The more general explanations which the model can offer in terms of the way in which uncertainty is dealt with in the decision-making process is now looked at in the following section.

## 8.3   AN INTERPRETATION OF THE EVALUATION OF UNCERTAINTY IN THE DECISION-MAKING PROCESS

While the evidence presented in the previous section does suggest a certain degree of consistency in the behaviour of individuals as regards the Shackle model, a further step can be taken in applying the Shackle model as a framework for explaining the decision-making process at a more general level. This is useful in that it provides an understanding of the way that within institutions uncertainty is dealt with in the decision-making process. Moreover, in terms of using elements of the model to help to develop a normative framework for improving the way that environmental uncertainty is dealt with in the decision-making process, its behavioural application at a more general level helps to give further evidence on the applicability of a number of its key propositions.

### 8.3.1   The Role of Individual Decision Makers

The Shackle model as a model of individual decision making under uncertainty was applied on an individual basis to decision makers involved in the evaluation of the Belize Southern Highway Project. However, in relation to the overall decision-making process it is apparent that individuals will play different roles within this process. Consequently it will be important to consider the interaction of individuals in terms of the decisions made and the evaluation of uncertainty at an institutional level. As one senior decision maker pointed out:

> with an institution as complex as this, with certain different departments and divisions, that are in charge of certain things ... within that you have very random results when you mix all the private interests and sub interests in a decision ... theoretically you see many tools that decision makers put out on paper, you see analytical and logical frameworks to attain certain aims. But along the way they are kind of damaged in a way, hidden within a not very clear set of roles.[10]

Within the institutions, therefore, different individuals may focus on different issues within the decision-making process. Often, for example, this involved limiting their role to that defined by their position. Thus one environmental specialist pointed out that she felt that part of this job entailed assessing the worst case scenario of any project.[11] In another case, an individual involved in the assessment of the environmental aspects of the project pointed out that s/he had been involved in several instances where they were asked not to comment on non-environmental issues.[12] In addition, decision makers at different levels in the decision-making structure played different roles. As one senior decision maker commented:

> at a decision making level, most of these people perhaps at one point in their career are technical people but they aren't really technical people any more, you apply your common sense, ... there is a certain point where you have to trust your technical people and you go a lot frankly by the reputation of the people that are doing the work.[13]

### 8.3.2   Contesting Focus Outcomes

Recognizing the different roles that the individuals play in the decision-making process provides a platform on which it is possible to assess at a more general level another key proposition of Shackle's theory, namely that the possible outcomes of any action, such as a development project or policy are sifted out, on the basis of the consequences of the outcome (which can be expressed in monetary terms) and the extent to which the outcome is expected to occur, until one outcome on the gain side and one outcome on the loss side are focused on. While, on an individual basis, this sifting out process is represented by the ascendancy function, at a more general level a similar process within the IDB, GoBl, DFID and World Bank can be described. Accordingly in such an interpretation, while at the evaluation stage a number of possible outcomes are assessed, by the time the project reaches the final stages of the decision-making process, only one scenario or focus outcome is presented. As one decision maker in the World Bank outlined:

By the end, by the time you are appraising a project, before you even think about sending it to the Board, you have one scenario. A sifting down of the scenarios takes place between the concept stage and the decision stage.[14]

One senior decision maker confirmed this process, in that he argued that the top managers did not want to consider three possibilities, but that the decision-making process pressured the evaluation team to come up with one scenario.[15]

At the earlier stages, before the agreed project scenario was approved, a process could be seen whereby a number of focus outcomes were contested, within the institution, and in the case of a project like the Belize Southern Highway Project, between the different institutions, such as between the IDB and the GoBl. Within the different institutions the role of the individual decision makers was clearly important, with individual decision makers pushing a particular outcome depending on their position, for example as an environmental specialist or economist. The contesting of different focus outcomes between the different institutions involved in a project would also appear to be an important aspect of the negotiation of the project, so for example it was apparent that at initial stages in the Southern Highway project there was a contrast in the focus outcome advanced by the IDB and the GoBl. The differences in the scenario focused on were highlighted by one decision maker in the GoBl who argued that:

> the external agencies go with a much exaggerated impact in terms of the impacts and the scenarios. When you could easily make a more reliable projection.[16]

However, while it was clear that at the evaluation stage a number of possible outcomes were considered, the project was then designed in a manner which aimed to reduce the possible negative outcomes of the project, again with the emphasis being on a solution-based approach:

> when somebody works as a specialist in a project they look for certain parameters and after you have looked at these you kind of narrow down, to one or two choices. We get a feeling that this will work, or this will not. After that you basically keep on narrowing down to the end, where you come with one choice and you then develop it in the feasibility study.[17]

Another decision maker involved in the evaluation of projects outlined a similar process:

> my objective is to relatively quickly in the project ascertain what is a probable scenario. ... Given that what is accepted as what is going to be the project, I would try to figure out what is going to be a probable scenario, starting with the worst case scenario and gradually moving towards, as you get more information, what is a probable scenario.[18]

However, as has been indicated this sifting basis was done on the basis of professional judgement rather than with the use of any formal framework. As one senior decision maker confirmed:

> There is no formal methodology that we use to sift through them, we tend to sift through the possible alternative outcomes, based on the project officers, and the team's assessment of the risks involved, some risks seemed higher than others. How do we determine these? How do we determine this, mostly I would say this is based on experience on what is most likely, the most likely scenario.[19]

By the end of the process a single focus outcome has been developed, and the project based on this outcome is presented to the higher tier of decision makers, at which stage the emphasis is on questioning the assumptions made in that scenario. As one senior decision maker pointed out attention was placed on questioning the likelihood of the outcome presented:

> how much do I believe in those assumptions? What do I think, do I think that those assumptions are correct or not, or do I think that they exaggerate? I would question each one of the assumptions.[20]

The evidence would suggest, therefore, that rather than taking an averaging approach as would be suggested by expected value and utility theory, the decision-making process is designed at an early stage to sift through the range of possible outcomes and to focus on one outcome. However, while the decision-making process results in the focus on one outcome, the evidence suggests that to a large extent the weighting of the different outcomes takes place predominantly on the extent to which the individual decision makers, and the institution as a whole, expect an outcome to occur.

Although the focusing approach would seem consistent at a general level with Shackle's theory, it is not obvious that the sifting process is done in the manner theorized in the form of the ascendancy function. In particular the question arises of whether this sifting process evaluates both the uncertainty associated with a particular outcome, as well the consequences of the outcome, in the manner theorized by Shackle or whether in essence the uncertainty is filtered out with the focus on one particular outcome. The lack of formal mechanisms to evaluate explicitly the uncertainty (which will be highlighted in the following chapter), as well as evidence presented in the previous chapter, in which for a number of the individual regressions the potential surprise was not significant, would to a large degree point to the latter explanation.

While caution must be exercised in any interpretation, an explanation of the decision-making process can be advanced in which, rather than uncertainty being explicitly accounted for, it is filtered out and only dealt with in terms of designing solutions to reduce the effects of any negative consequence of the resulting outcome which is focused on. This could even be explained in a manner similar to that suggested by Ford and Ghose (1994b), namely, that while the possibility of the occurrence of the outcome is assessed in terms of the expectations of the individual or institution, this in itself results in an early sifting process, before any consideration is made of the extent to which the decision maker would be surprised or confident that the outcome would occur. In a normative sense there is a danger, therefore, that such an approach does not explicitly consider the full range of possible uncertain consequences of a particular project, and indeed there could be a tendency for a confusion between the most likely and the most desired outcome. Furthermore the emphasis on a solutions-based approach may result in only those outcomes for which possible 'solutions' or mitigative measures can be designed being advanced as focus outcomes. Possible hard uncertainties surrounding outcomes for which the uncertain consequences would not be so easily solvable (such as the passing of a threshold in an ecosystem) are in effect excluded from the final decision stages. Thus hard uncertainties which, if explicitly considered, could affect a decision to proceed with a particular project or policy, may not actually reach the final stage of the decision-making process. Consequently in such an interpretation it can be argued that only outcomes with uncertain consequences that are solvable (and by their very nature are more likely to be soft rather than hard uncertainties) are focused on and presented at the final decision-making level. Such a process, by designing measures which attempt to ensure that the identified outcome is the one that occurs, would only deal indirectly with the uncertainty surrounding the other possible outcomes. As one senior decision maker pointed out:

> The starting point of a decision-making process that is self seeking and is seeking the objective ... should mean that you are able to redesign, re-adapt, re-shuffle project design.[21]

He went on to provide an interesting analogy in terms of how the 'uncertainties' were dealt with:

> Think of it in a general way like ... you are throwing a dice, and before you are going to throw the dice, you call all the clairvoyants in the world and pay them tons of money, i.e. consultants and tell them, this is the way it should go, I want a six on the table, two sixes. And the guys come in and they put Vaseline on your hands and they grease the cup, and say don't do it like this, do it like that. And then sometimes you get a couple of fives, sometimes you get a six, a six and a five. Depending on the way that you do it.[22]

This explanation would appear to be further supported by the recognition in the different institutions that there has been a tendency for projects to be excessively optimistic in their projections (Pohl and Mihaljek, 1992; Mathur, 1994; DFID, 1998). Part of this problem could be accounted for by the lack of explicit evaluation of hard uncertainty within the decision-making process.

This process would also appear to be reinforced by the higher stages of the decision-making process, whereby the final scenario or outcome developed in the feasibility study is questioned in terms of its assumptions. The scenario with the least uncertain assumptions is therefore pushed forward. This process may exclude from explicit consideration the uncertainties involved. In terms of environmental decision making, there is therefore a danger that particularly the negative environmental consequences of a project are not given sufficient weight in the decision-making process precisely because they are conditioned by hard uncertainty. In recognition of this issue, attention is turned in the following chapter to assessing why existing practical mechanisms do not ensure the explicit consideration of hard uncertainty as well as the design of a normative framework which gives adequate attention to these concerns.

## NOTES

1.  Interview with senior decision maker.
2.  Interview with senior decision maker.
3.  Interview with senior decision maker.
4.  Interview with senior decision maker.
5.  Interview with decision maker.
6.  Interview with decision maker.
7.  Interview with senior decision maker.
8.  One of the decision makers did not specify the specific scenario numbers that he would discard.
9.  Personal communication with senior decision maker.
10. Personal communication with senior decision maker.
11. Personal communication with decision maker.
12. Personal communication with decision maker.
13. Personal communication with senior decision maker.
14. Personal communication with senior decision maker.
15. Personal communication with senior decision maker.
16. Personal communication with senior decision maker.
17. Personal communication with senior decision maker.
18. Personal communication with senior decision maker.
19. Personal communication with senior decision maker.
20. Personal communication with senior decision maker.
21. Personal communication with senior decision maker.
22. Personal communication with senior decision maker.

# 9. Discussion: A framework for the evaluation of hard uncertainty in environmental decision making

## 9.1 INTRODUCTION

In the previous chapter the Shackle model was applied as a tool to help to explain the way in which uncertainty was dealt with at an individual as well as an institutional level within the decision-making process. An explanation was forwarded, in which although the decision-making process did result in the sifting out of the possible outcomes of a project or policy, the presence of hard uncertainty did not appear to have been dealt with in a manner consistent with that outlined in the Shackle model. This chapter therefore, in analysing why this may be the case, assesses the existing conceptualization of uncertainty at an institutional level as well as the practical (rather than theoretical) mechanisms currently used to deal with uncertainty. It is argued that to a large extent only a limited conceptualization of uncertainty is given which results in none of the existing mechanisms applied within the decision-making process giving adequate attention to hard uncertainty. Building on the theoretical development of the Shackle model in this book, and its application in a behavioural sense to the case study of the Southern Highway, a normative framework for dealing with hard uncertainty is advanced.

Correspondingly this chapter is organized into two main sections. In the first section the different conceptualizations of uncertainty within the different institutions are analysed both in relation to the case study as well as at a more general level. Then the mechanisms which are designed to deal with uncertainty in the decision-making process are assessed in a normative manner. In the second section the application of a normative framework to ensure the explicit evaluation of hard uncertainty in environmental decision making will be forwarded.

## 9.2    THE CONCEPTUALIZATION OF UNCERTAINTY IN ENVIRONMENTAL DECISION MAKING

A key contribution of this book has been the assertion that there are a number of different modes of uncertainty, and that this recognition has a number of implications for the decision-making process. An important issue, therefore, is the extent to which the evidence gained from the interviews supports or refutes the proposition that adequate attention is given to this in the decision-making process. In terms of the case study of the Belize Southern Highway, it would appear that in both the GoBl and the IDB no formal explicit recognition was given to distinguishing between the types of uncertainty faced. In particular, the presence of what has been termed hard uncertainty or any similar conceptualization of uncertainty, rather than soft uncertainty, in environmental projects was not explicitly recognized.

The lack of recognition in the Southern Highway case study of the presence of hard uncertainty with respect to the environment, was evident for a number of decision makers. For example one decision maker in the IDB stated that:

> you are perturbing some sort of equilibrium in an ecosystem and once you bring in a road, it doesn't take too many hours of experts of knowledge to arrive at a list of possibilities. No, it doesn't take much time to assume which of the impacts are going to have the highest likelihood of occurring.[1]

Another decision maker in the GoBl highlighted a high level of confidence in what the implications of the road would be in terms of its environmental impacts:

> I think that the degree of uncertainty is mostly in the area of the extent rather than the nature of the impacts. We know what will happen.[2]

While a number of decision makers had characterized the Southern Highway project in a manner similar to what has been defined as soft uncertainty, the overriding impression at an individual level, and perhaps more importantly at an institutional level was that no distinction was made between the type of uncertainty faced. For example, a decision maker in the GoBl argued:

> We definitely evaluate risks, but uncertainties, I think that we generalise them all as risks. But the risks we do address.[3]

Another decision maker in the IDB confirmed this position:

I don't know of any systematic effort to distinguish between the two in the Bank. In fact the word uncertainty is not used much in the Bank. The word risk is used, there is an actual category on risks.[4]

In a number of cases, however, in the project reports reference is made to uncertainty:

There is considerable uncertainty with regards the magnitude of the negative indirect impacts. (IDB, 1997a: p. 34)

When questioned on this, the same decision maker, who had made the previous statement, responded:

I was using it in that sense, it is uncertainty … in other words I really mean uncertainty, when it is a risk you can really assess it … to me risk is very different from uncertainty. In the land use context, like I explained to you in the beginning, we were dealing with uncertainty.[5]

This conceptualization would appear to be similar to that of what has been termed hard uncertainty. Thus, although no formal framework was present in the GoBl and the IDB which distinguished between the type of uncertainty faced and so the approach to decision making, some individuals did make a distinction similar to that highlighted in Chapter 3.

While in a number of cases a distinction was made between the type of uncertainty faced, in a large number of cases the term 'risk' was used by decision makers to describe the negative impact of a particular outcome. The lack of clear formal conceptualization and definition of uncertainty at an institutional level has led to a potentially misleading situation whereby many decision makers in the institutions assessed in the case study implicitly appeared to assume that by identifying the potential negative outcomes of a project or 'risks', they were in effect dealing with uncertainty within the decision-making process. This lack of formal recognition at an institutional level resulted in a lack of attention being paid to uncertainty *per se*. As one senior decision maker, who was aware of this problem stated:

Many people don't tend to see uncertainty and make it explicit as something that is legitimate.[6]

The lack of legitimacy and formal recognition of uncertainty in practice was highlighted by one decision maker in the IDB who pointed out:

Every one of our profiles has a section called risk, and what we try to do is to list those risks, and for each risk we have to show how we are going to manage that risk, and if we can't manage it say why. But as far as uncertainty goes I don't believe there has ever been a big discussion about that.[7]

One senior decision maker, who had declined to be recorded, went as far as to say that the reality of uncertainty in the IDB was that, in the projects looked at by management, uncertainty was given little weight. Another consultant, who was at the time working for the Government of Belize (GoBl) and who had had experience of working on a number of development projects, confirmed this view that no distinction was made in the type of uncertainty faced.

In terms of the British Development Division in the Caribbean (BDDC)/ DFID, from the more limited evidence gained, the focus again appeared to be in terms of soft uncertainty (or risk), as opposed to hard uncertainty. However, there did appear to be some confusion in the use of the term 'risk' which in some cases was used to refer to what has been termed soft uncertainty, and in other cases has referred to the negative impacts of a particular outcome. So, for example, in the Office Instructions which give guidance on the completion of DFID project reports, (the actual DFID Southern Highway project report was not available at the time of the fieldwork) within the section which must be completed on risks, the interpretation seemed to cover both definitions of 'risk'. However, it was indicated by a senior decision maker that an assessment had been made of the 'risk' or soft uncertainties and it did appear that a distinction had been made between 'risk' and 'uncertainty', or what has been defined as soft uncertainty and hard uncertainty in this book. Indeed, it was indicated that in the project report, an assessment of the 'risks' or soft uncertainties associated with the road project was made. Although this assessment was not publicly available for analysis, the assessment followed the procedures set out in a technical note on risk (DFID, 1998). This document is interesting in that it seems to address in part the need to distinguish between the interpretation of risk as the negative consequences of a possible outcome, which appeared to be prevalent in previous reports, and an interpretation of 'risk' which recognized uncertainty:

> project submissions have hitherto carried descriptions of the main risk factors identified in project frameworks. But little attempt is generally made to assess how seriously these factors are likely to affect project outcomes. (DFID, 1998: p. 4 of 28)

Clearly, therefore, there has been a recognition of the need to deal more explicitly with the uncertainty *per se*. Again interestingly, a distinction is made between the type of uncertainty faced, in terms of quantifiable and unquantifiable uncertainties, but the term 'risk' is used to cover both these categories. The procedures do, however, seem to recognize that in many cases a mode of uncertainty similar to that defined as hard uncertainty is present:

the word 'risk' is used to broadly encompass both quantifiable and unquantifiable uncertainties about outcomes. In only a very few, specialised, cases can the characteristics of outcome variability be accurately quantified. In general the main threats to outcomes can be identified and qualitatively characterised, but with only intuitive indications of probabilities. In some cases our state of knowledge is so preliminary that we cannot initially tell what the range of possible outcomes will be nor what the principal risk factors are. (DFID, 1998: p. 7 of 28)

Within this definition of risks, further characteristics are recognized in terms of the nature of the uncertain outcome. For example key considerations include whether it is catastrophic or non-catastrophic, the extent to which the outcome is reversible or non-reversible, the degree of controllability, the extent to which the 'risk' can be insured or mitigated against and whether or not it is quantifiable. While the last characteristic, namely whether or not it is possible to quantify the mode of uncertainty, is similar to one of the charac-teristics used in Chapter 3, the other characteristics would appear to influence the weighting given to that uncertain outcome. Although the DFID proce-dures do incorporate an explicit evaluation of the uncertainty involved, which will be assessed in greater detail shortly, the extent to which these procedures were applied consistently at a decision-making level could not be deter-mined, due to the limited contact with DFID. The methods adopted to evaluate 'risks' or soft uncertainties will be looked at in the next section.

In terms of the World Bank, the evidence gained from interviews and reports confirmed a similar position to that of the IDB, in that there was no real formal distinction made in the type of uncertainty faced, with in many cases the term 'risks' being used to describe the negative consequences of a possible outcome. So, for example, even although in the World Bank *Envi-ronmental Assessment Sourcebook* (1991) a formal distinction was made:

Risks are involved when probabilities can be assigned to the likelihood of an event occurring ... Uncertainty describes a situation where little is known about future impacts and where no probabilities can be assigned to certain outcomes, or where even the outcomes are so novel they cannot be anticipated. (World Bank, 1991: pp. 149–50)

the same manual goes on to state that in practice the assessment of risk and uncertainty is grouped together through the use of sensitivity analysis (World Bank, 1991). This lack of distinction in practice was confirmed by a decision maker in the Bank who stated:

in terms of distinguishing between risk and uncertainty, I think that's not some-thing we have gotten into on a systematic policy basis.[8]

Instead a more case-by-case approach was outlined:

Most types of considerations are brought in on a case-by-case basis. Let's say there is a feeling that an environmental assessment has identified serious risks, but there is great uncertainty as to whether or not, you know situations will be actually in place that will trigger that risk to actually materialise then you have to deal with that, but that is only at a case-by-case basis, it is not systematically factored in … we don't take that step of trying to distinguish between risk and uncertainty.[9]

Overall, although a number of individuals did appear to distinguish between the mode of uncertainty faced, with the exception of the DFID, a general lack of attention appears to have been paid to conceptualizing uncertainty at the preliminary stage in the decision-making process. This lack of recognition of the need to make explicit and define the uncertainty faced has clearly influenced the way that uncertainty has been dealt with at a project level in the GoBl, the IDB and the World Bank, in that attention was placed on identifying solutions or ways of managing the 'risks' within the decision-making process, rather than explicitly dealing with the uncertainty *per se* when evaluating the merits of a particular project. One decision maker neatly characterized this process by stating:

risk is manageable uncertainty. You take certain risks as long as you know that they are manageable. I think it is implicit, no distinction is made explicitly in the decision making process.[10]

Indeed arguably this has resulted in no clear recognition of hard uncertainty at an institutional level. Overall, this has had a major impact on the way in which environmental uncertainty has been evaluated within the decision-making process.

### 9.2.1   The Evaluation of Uncertainty in the Southern Highway Project

The way in which uncertainty is conceptualized at an institutional level is important in that it influences the way in which uncertainty is evaluated within the decision-making process. This section highlights this by drawing on evidence gained from the interviews conducted as part of the case study. In particular, the focus was on whether any formal or informal approaches were used to evaluate the uncertainty in the decision-making process. In terms of the evaluation of uncertainty in the Southern Highway Project, it was generally raised in the reports in an impressionistic manner with no attempt made to use some measure of uncertainty; instead qualitative statements were used. So, for example, in relation to uncertainty surrounding a number of key factors, typical statements in the Environmental Summary for the project were:

The indirect effects of highway rehabilitation on logging activities are also unclear. (IDB, 1997a: p. 35)

it is difficult to foresee the most likely scenario. (IDB, 1997a: p. 35)

Although no attempt was made in the decision-making process to quantify or measure in any formal sense the uncertainty faced, evidence of a distinction in the level of uncertainty faced was made at an individual level by a number of decision makers. Accordingly one decision maker responded:

I'm not so sure that there were attempts to quantify the uncertainties, but when the focus shifted onto indirect effects, because when we started talking to people we realised that the magnitude of indirect effects was likely to be considerably larger than direct effects both in time and true magnitude.[11]

Another decision maker in the IDB stated in relation to uncertainties regarding the consequences of the project:

I don't think we tried to quantify them, I think them we ranked them, we tended to rank them ... To quantify that uncertainty, that would be difficult. What we would do, the country team would look at these issues and ask whether or not it was convincing, was it believable, was it realistic based on the expertise of the team members, again impressionistic.[12]

Further recognition of the uncertainty (rather than risk) faced in the project is highlighted in one of the project documents:

substantial indirect effects are expected given the growth projected in sectors such as tourism, agriculture and coastal aquaculture. The proposed improvements to the Southern Highway will contribute to accelerated expansion of these operations along with a variety of other land use changes which will bring on indirect environmental costs associated with increased rates of deforestation, increased sedimentation in coastal areas and other types of biophysical changes. In the absence of reliable projections on potential land use changes in the southern region, uncertainty is leading to highly differing opinions with respect to the geographic scope and magnitude of such potential negative impacts. (IDB, 1997a: p. 34)

However, although a recognition was made in the project reports of the presence of uncertainty, this was not reflected in the approaches used to evaluate the uncertainties involved. Indeed it became clear in the conversations with the decision makers within the GoBl and the IDB that there were no formal approaches used to evaluate the uncertainty. Instead it was by means of the mechanisms and procedures which formed the basis of the decision-making process that uncertainties were identified. Therefore, the evaluation of uncertainty in the case of the GoBl was carried out within the overall evaluation of the project by means of the project reports, the assessment of the project by NEAC and ESTAP as well as by consultation with the stakeholders of the project.[13]

Within the IDB, again no formal framework was evident for evaluating environmental uncertainty *per se*. However, other mechanisms and procedures forming part of the overall *ex ante* evaluation of the project raised issues of uncertainty. In particular, the use of a logical framework, which makes clear all the assumptions of the project as well as allowing a separate section on 'risks', was the closest to a formal framework that existed in the Bank. The use of a logical framework was also prominent in the BDDC evaluation of the project.[14] Another important mechanism in which uncertainties were raised in the IDB was the project evaluation by the CESI committee and the approval by the loan committee. Once any uncertainties were raised, both the GoBl and the IDB tended to rely on the studies conducted in order to identify the uncertainties, as one senior decision maker pointed out:

> the mechanism that we used to handle uncertainty in those environmental areas were basically studies.[15]

Although therefore a number of mechanisms were in place, which did raise (often indirectly) issues of uncertainty relating to the Southern Highway, there was no overall formal framework that was used for evaluating the uncertainty either in the IDB or the GoBl,[16] and certainly no evidence of the use of expected value or expected utility approaches.

In the case of the GoBl the absence of a formal framework for evaluating the uncertainties surrounding the Southern Highway led one decision maker to admit that the formal evaluation of uncertainties:

> is something certainly that I think we need to look at because there are certain of us within this government that feel there is no risk, none so ever. But then you begin to point out certain things and when you do they'll say well perhaps I do need to think about that, but prior to that they had never thought about that. They have seen a project like this one, in only one light and they have never thought that there could be risks or uncertainties, more the risks.[17]

In summary, it is evident that no formal mechanism or framework was employed to evaluate uncertainty in the decision-making process. Thus, although an economic feasibility study/cost–benefit analysis was an integral part of the evaluation process, there was no evidence of the formal application of a probability approach such as that of expected value. It was also clear that within the evaluation process no formal distinction was made between the different types of uncertainty faced. The lack of formal approaches used to evaluate the uncertainties is partly due to the limited conceptualization of uncertainty made. This in turn appears to have affected the design and thus ability of the existing mechanisms actually employed in the evaluation of projects to deal explicitly with hard uncertainty. It is to a brief discussion of these existing mechanisms that this book now turns.

### 9.2.2 Existing Mechanisms which Attempt to Deal with Uncertainty

An argument made in this book is that the type of uncertainty faced in the decision process has significant implications on the mechanism or framework used to evaluate environmental uncertainty within the decision-making process. The evidence collected, although not comprehensive, suggests that generally limited attention has been given to the presence of hard uncertainty in environmental decision making. This in turn has influenced the way that development projects have been evaluated and is manifested in the existing methods used to evaluate uncertainty. This section, therefore, reviews the main mechanisms utilized in practice especially by the IDB, the World Bank and DFID to evaluate uncertainty in the decision-making process and to assess at a normative level whether they adequately deal with hard uncertainty in projects with environmental consequences. Less attention is given to the GoBl, due to the fact that the IDB, World Bank and DFID over a long period, have a more established set of procedures, due to their role in assessing a large number of projects. This section, therefore, complements the theoretical review of approaches to dealing with uncertainty, in assessing the way that uncertainty has been evaluated in the decision-making process in practice.

Within the different institutions what was immediately apparent was the lack of evidence of the application of the theoretical approaches reviewed in Chapter 4. As the author of a World Bank paper pointed out:

> While there is an extensive literature on risk and uncertainty, even well known theoretical concepts have not been extensively incorporated into project appraisals. At the same time, it is also clear that many of the theoretical results available in the literature are not sufficiently practical to be readily applied in the appraisal of projects in developing countries. (Mathur, 1994)

Instead, in practice, it was assumed that a number of alternative mechanisms used to evaluate the project as a whole would effectively deal with environmental uncertainty. In only a small number of projects did a formal evaluation of the uncertainty take place. The most apparent mechanism, common to all the institutions surveyed in the study, was the reliance on project reports to pick up uncertainties, which were dealt with on an impressionistic basis. However, because of the lack of formal recognition of hard uncertainty at an institutional level, and with no formal mechanisms to evaluate the uncertainty, the extent to which hard uncertainty was addressed was limited to cases where the individual writing the relevant section of the report was aware of the uncertainties involved. Nevertheless even where the uncertainties were spelled out in an impressionistic basis, as was the case in the Southern Highway Environmental Summary, there was no mechanism to ensure that the uncertainties were explicitly accounted for in the decision-making process.

Another mechanism was the use of review committees, which reviewed the project, and which gave an opportunity for any concerns surrounding the uncertainties to be raised. In a large part, the committees present, for example NEAC in the GoBl and CESI in the IDB, were used to review the environmental aspects of the project before the project passed higher up in the decision-making process. In this sense they did provide a vital role. However, the extent to which they effectively dealt with hard uncertainty in the decision-making process was arguably undermined by the lack of legitimacy given to uncertainty at an institutional level, and as an indirect result of this, a lack of methodologies available to deal with hard uncertainty. This situation was illustrated by a senior decision maker in the IDB:

> What we do a lot of times at the environmental and social impact committee is to require, make requests that projects that have a degree of risk, for instance gas service plants or something like that, to run a formal risk analysis, and that they incorporate some type of contingency analysis. Yes, in many cases it is done based on a formal methodology. But what I am saying, is basically that those that are covered by that kind of methodology are less uncertain, than the uncertainties we have been talking about.[18]

When the same decision maker was asked whether, although all the risks are tackled by the risk analysis, this may detract from giving adequate attention to the other uncertainties, he responded:

> Oh yes, for sure, exactly, the uncertainties are externalised, they are spelt out as some other issue.[19]

The higher committees such as the loan committees in the IDB and World Bank, as well as the Projects and Evaluation Committee in the case of DFID, also clearly play an important role in the decision-making process. However, as will be argued in the next section to a considerable extent, a large part of any assessment of the uncertainties made will have been done before the project reaches the loan committee. Again the extent to which any hard uncertainty surrounding the environmental impacts of the project is dealt with at this level will depend on whether the uncertainties have been raised explicitly at the evaluation stages of the decision-making process. In certain projects the committees may indirectly deal with some of the uncertainties present. For example, in the case of the Southern Highway Project, the first time that the project went to the loan committee, it was rejected, due to the lack of attention given to the indirect environmental effects.[20] The committees, while not explicitly dealing with the uncertainty *per se*, did in this case act in a precautionary manner. This action only delays, however, the evaluation of the remaining uncertainties and the weighting of them in the decision process.

### 9.2.2.1  The economic analysis/CBA

A key element of the decision process is the use of economic feasibility studies or cost–benefit analysis. In Chapter 2, a decision-making framework was outlined, and in particularly the role of CBA in the decision-making context critically discussed at a theoretical level. In practice from the evidence gained from the case study, as well as at a more general level from the interviews carried out at the IDB, the World Bank and DFID, it was apparent that cost–benefit analyses that were carried out were often done on a limited basis. Moreover, although the NPV/ IRR criteria were of crucial importance, this was only one of the stages that the project had to pass in the decision-making process (see Figure 2.4). In the case of Belize, no extended CBA was carried out, so no attempt was made to incorporate the possible environmental costs of the projects in monetary terms. From the general interviews with decision makers, it was apparent that the use of environmental valuation was very limited, with often the techniques only being applied when the project had significant environmental benefits. One senior decision maker in the IDB argued that there was a reluctance to go to such a second stage of economic analysis, even where there were information gaps in the environmental damages of the project, with the focus instead on gaining a positive NPV value or a rate of return of 12.[21] As one senior decision maker stated:

> we could not go to the Board with a rate of return less than 12%. Well the cynic would say you just bumped the figures you just kept bumping them up, well maybe we did, but we tried to do it in a way, we kept digging for more benefits.[22]

This focus on the positive benefits of a project is backed up by a study based on 1015 World Bank projects, which found that there was an upward bias in the appraisal stage in rates of return (Pohl and Mihaljek, 1992). This was backed up by a senior decision maker who highlighted the difference in the *ex ante* projections and the *ex post* analysis of the project benefits. This focus on the project benefits is particularly of concern in that, as was argued in Chapter 3, it is in the realm of the environmental costs associated with a project that hard uncertainties are often of the greatest magnitude.

Perhaps partly because of the emphasis on the positive benefits of a project, in terms of the Southern Highway, as was pointed out in Chapter 6, the economic feasibility study (limited CBA) was limited in its reference to uncertainty. In general, this would also appear to be the case in other projects for which cost–benefit analyses are carried out. Thus any attempt to deal with uncertainty focused on 'soft uncertainty' with the most common approach involving sensitivity analysis. As was argued in Section 2.2.3, however, sensitivity analysis does not evaluate the uncertainty *per se* in terms of evaluating the weight that should be given to the occurrence of a particular outcome. Although it was pointed out that expected value approaches, and even expected utility approaches had been attempted in the 1980s, more recently these approaches had not been applied. Generally, as is supported by Mathur (1994), the perception was gained that the elicitation of objective and subjective probability distributions, as well as utility functions, was too difficult a task for practical applications. Thus, even excluding the theoretical concerns outlined previously, the application of such approaches, or even behaviour consistent with such approaches appeared limited.

Consequently, because a practical framework for evaluating the range of uncertainties present in a project was absent, even the assessment of the different possible alternative scenarios which could arise as a result of the occurrence of a range of uncertain factors, was rarely considered at the decision-making stage.[23] Instead this stage focused on one scenario, and the possible consequences of that scenario. As one senior decision maker in the IDB summed up the situation:

> what analysts do is they come out and use their best judgement. I think that this is the most likely scenario, so he uses that as his middle of the road, computational value, and then he varies this value up and down, to try and see how sensitive the method is, and this is as much as we do. We don't do, for all the projects this kind of study, it takes a long time.

### 9.2.2.2   Environmental assessment of projects

It we turn to the role of environmental assessment[24] in the evaluation of hard uncertainties, as was argued in Chapter 6, it is evident in the case of the Environmental Assessments carried out for the Southern Highway Project (DHV, 1994a and BECCA, 1995), that there was limited reference to hard uncertainty, with the dominant interpretation of 'risks' in terms of the negative consequences of an outcome. As such, the focus in the environmental assessments was on the identification of 'risks' (in the above sense), particularly of the direct impacts of the highway which could be mitigated. Thus, in the environmental summaries of projects, less attention was placed on considering the possible occurrence of a range of possible outcomes than on the negative outcomes presented by the scenario pushed forward in the project evaluation. As one senior decision maker in the IDB stated:

> I wouldn't say that there was any quantification of uncertainties, because personally I don't know how you would do that. I think that what we tried to do, was that, recognising that we couldn't control uncertainty, we tried to see how we could deal with it as time went on.[25]

Another decision maker in the World Bank confirmed this emphasis on policies to achieve certain goals in minimizing the impacts of uncertain outcomes rather than accounting for the uncertainty *per se*, in the overall evaluation of the project:

> we have a natural habitats policy, that is very specific about what the Bank can and can't be involved in. We can't be involved in species extinction, we can't be involved in the destruction of critical natural habitat ... for that reason we try to come up with mechanisms to avoid that from happening, and that's what we are concerned with more than deciding what form of analysis is appropriate. That is the type of thing that we can bring to the table in terms of handbooks and training, or information about good practice ... but in the end of the day it's the policies that are binding, and what we have to live up to, and they are very much goal oriented rather than process oriented.[26]

The danger of such a goal-led approach as argued in the previous chapter, however, is that the full range of possible uncertain negative outcomes may not be considered adequately in weighing up the project and as such the hard uncertainty may not be explicitly accounted for.

At a more general level where certain projects were faced with soft uncertainties, for example in the case of the possibility of flood damage in dam construction projects, where the focus was on uncertainty surrounding the occurrence rather than the consequences of the outcome, formal probability analysis has been used. However, in terms of harder uncertainties there again appeared to be a lack of applicable methods with the focus on soft uncertainties or risks. This was highlighted by an environmental specialist in the World Bank who stated that:

> Let's say there is a feeling that an environmental assessment has identified serious risks, but there is great uncertainty as to whether or not, you know situations will be actually in place that will trigger that risk to actually materialise, then you have to deal with that, but that is only at a case-by-case basis, it is not systematically factored in.[27]

One more generic approach that has been introduced in the World Bank more recently in the section on risks in project documents is the use of a simple rating system, on a scale of 1 to 4 by which:

The only purpose of that is for people to be conscious of risk, and to alert managers that this project or that project has a high environmental risk rating and needs special attention.[28]

However, again the focus would appear to be on the possible negative outcomes of the project rather than on taking into account the uncertainty surrounding those outcomes and the possible negative consequences:

We deal systematically with risk through the environmental assessment process, plus the generic risk management system that I mentioned before (using the scale 1–4). But we don't take that step of trying to distinguish between risk and uncertainty.[29]

### 9.2.2.3 Logical frameworks

Another tool used in the evaluation of projects, which is being increasingly used in institutions which evaluate projects such as the IDB, World Bank and DFID, is the 'logical framework'. The logical framework is used to evaluate the overall objectives of the project, with the emphasis being on assessing in a reasoned fashion the goal, purpose, outputs and activities of a project. These four factors are assessed by using a series of criteria: objective, indicators, means of verification and assumptions. This results in a 4 × 4 matrix or table. While a detailed discussion of the use and application of logical frameworks in project evaluation is outside the scope of this book (see IDB, 1997c for a more detailed review in the context of project appraisal), what is interesting is that by focusing on the assumptions of the project, the framework raises, albeit indirectly, the uncertainty surrounding the assumptions behind the project. As such it does represent a step forward in terms of the overall evaluation of the project. However, in its current form the tendency again is to focus on an interpretation of 'risks' as possible negative consequences:

The objective is not to list every conceivable contingency, but to identify reasonably likely possibilities. (IDB, 1997c: p. 7 of 12)

Thus, it is identifying the possible positive and negative consequences of what is seen as the most likely scenario that is the main concern, rather than the evaluation of the uncertainties surrounding the consequences. Therefore, again it does not explicitly provide a framework or mechanism to allow the decision maker to consider both the uncertainty and range of possible consequences of a particular project.

### 9.2.2.4 Specific methods for dealing directly with uncertainty

It is apparent that, although the above decision-making tools are often assumed to account adequately for uncertainty, uncertainty is only dealt with indirectly on the basis of a limited conceptualization. As a result, although an implicit assumption is made in the decision-making process that uncertainties are dealt with, in practice it is evident that hard uncertainties in environmental decision making are not adequately considered. The lack of distinction between the types of uncertainty faced and lack of legitimacy given to hard uncertainty has resulted in a lack of formal approaches to the problem. One possible exception is in the case of DFID where a set of procedures which identify two methods for evaluating uncertainty have been drawn up (DFID, 1998). The methods are interesting in that they appear to distinguish between different types of uncertainty and, when combined with other rules of thumb, provide a mechanism for evaluating both the uncertainty surrounding the possible occurrence of an outcome, as well as the consequences of that outcome. The two methods proposed are distinguished in terms of the uncertainty faced, in a way similar to the distinction made between soft uncertainty and hard uncertainty, although no explicit distinction between the type of uncertainty faced is made. The technical note (DFID, 1998) highlights the basis of the distinction between the two methods:

> The first (Method A) is a general descriptive one, which should be applied both to projects where there are major uncertainties about the relationship between project inputs and outcomes or about the impacts and probabilities of risk factors ... The second [method] in which impacts and probabilities of risk factors are quantified ... should be attempted where quantification of impacts and probabilities is thought to be meaningful. (DFID, 1998: p. 25 of 28)

The second method, if applied exclusively to cases of soft uncertainty, is not contended (although clearly if no correct conceptualization of uncertainty takes place it could be applied incorrectly to cases of hard uncertainty), so attention will focus on the first method, and in particular in its applicability to cases of hard uncertainty. The following procedures for Method A are stated in the technical note:

A.  identify a quantifiable or otherwise verifiable success criterion (e.g. a net present value figure, a physical quantity, a percentage, a development achieved by a specific time, or a 'yes/no' answer to a question);
B.  set a minimum standard of acceptable project performance;
C.  identify and describe the key risk factors. (This should normally be done in compiling the project framework);
D.  using an impact probability matrix, discuss the potential impact of each factor on project success and the probability of its occurrence;
E.  Review mitigatory measures already taken, and those contingent measures which could be taken if required;
F.  (where method B assessment is not attempted) classify the project on the basis of professional judgement about stages D and E above, as being 'low', 'medium' or 'high'. (DFID, 1998: p. 25)

In terms of the evaluation of the uncertainty, therefore, the reliance in this method is still on probability, albeit in a subjective manner. Indeed this approach does not even require an actual quantification of a subjective probability, just a categorization in terms of low, medium or high, which is made on the basis of:

> purely informal, judgmental methods, i.e. by informed guess work. (DFID, 1998: p. 16)

In relation to the weighting of the outcome, as well as the uncertainty surrounding the outcome, a number of rules of thumb are used. The identification of a minimum standard in essence sets a threshold, beyond which the decision maker is not willing to consider the project. In relation to Shackle's theory this, for example, might encompass a minimum series of gain values, below which no weight would be given. After this an impact/probability matrix is drawn up, based on the categorization of the probability and the impact on the success of the project. An example is shown in Figure 9.1, where the crosses represent a particular impact.

After the probability matrix is drawn up, the potential impacts are reviewed in terms of the extent to which they can be minimized and then an overall judgement, called the assessment of the overall risk of project failure is made on basis of stages D, E and F, with the resulting project classified as low, medium or high risk (DFID, 1998). The technical note then goes on to advise that projects with at least one high impact factor with a high probability should be classified overall as 'high risk' projects. Those with more than one high impact factor with a medium probability should also be classified as 'high risk' projects. If there is only one medium impact factor with high

| Impact / Probability | Low | Medium | High |
|---|---|---|---|
| Low | x | x | |
| Medium | | | xxx |
| High | | xx | |

*Figure 9.1   An example of an impact/probability matrix*

probability of occurrence, the project should be considered to be a 'medium risk' project. Projects where there are only medium or low impact factors with low probabilities, would be given a 'low risk' rating (DFID, 1998: p. 255).

Such a method is clearly an improvement, in that it does suggest a practically applicable framework for evaluating the uncertainties. As such, it also recognizes the need when evaluating a project or policy, to take into account both the uncertainty associated with a particular outcome, as well as the consequences of the outcome. However, it could be improved by better conceptualization and distinction between the mode of uncertainty faced at a preliminary stage. Furthermore, although the assessment of the occurrence of the outcome is done on subjective categorization of probabilities, by remaining within a probability framework, the theoretical problems outlined in this book in using probability in cases of hard uncertainty, remain.

## 9.3   A NORMATIVE FRAMEWORK FOR THE EVALUATION OF ENVIRONMENTAL UNCERTAINTY IN THE DECISION-MAKING PROCESS

It is evident from the information gathered in relation to the Southern Highway Project as well as at a more general level, that existing mechanisms do not adequately deal with hard uncertainty in environmental decision making. Consequently as well as applying and developing the Shackle model in a behavioural sense in order to explain the way in which decisions have been made, an additional aim of this book has been to develop a normative framework which will address these concerns. In achieving this aim it has been recognized from an early stage that while theories may be developed in a purely behavioural sense, they are often looked at as a starting point in terms of providing prescriptions to decision making, and that the normative assumptions in a theoretical model are often looked at as a first stage to guiding 'rational' behaviour in decision makers.

From the evidence of the case study as well as the more general investigation of the Shackle model in terms of the evaluation of development projects, it is apparent that there are a number of elements of the theory which are useful in explaining the way in which decisions are made in the presence of uncertainty. This would suggest that some of its behavioural assumptions could be extended to the model's application in a normative manner. Consequently, in this final section of this chapter a normative framework for dealing with hard uncertainty in environmental decision making will be outlined. Again it should be reiterated that the focus is on improving the procedural rationality of the decision-making process. Another caveat is that, while the aim of the frame-

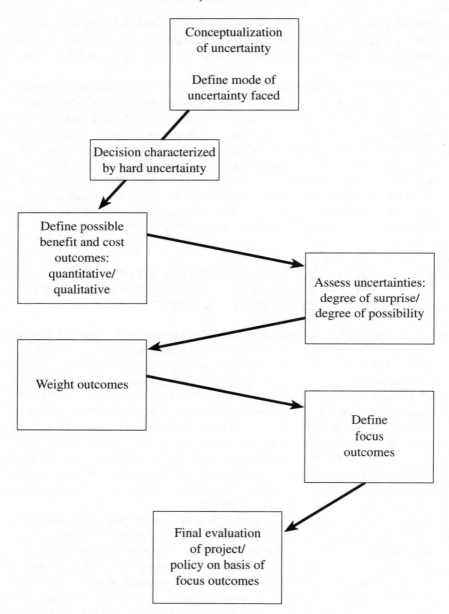

*Figure 9.2    A framework for the evaluation of hard uncertainty in
environmental decision making*

work is to improve the decision-making process, it should be recognized that there are other agendas and issues (which can be rational or non-rational) which will influence the process, and that, while not the focus of this book, should be given explicit attention (see Richardson, 1996 for example).

The general framework developed in this section concerns itself, however, with the evaluation and weighting of hard uncertainty in environmental decision making. The specifics of such a framework, however, would depend on the institutional and decision-making context. A number of stages in such a framework can be outlined, and are presented in Figure 9.2.

1.  The first step requires that the nature of the uncertainty faced in the particular decision is adequately conceptualized. In particular, based on the different characteristics presented in Chapter 3, Figure 3.2, an important step is to distinguish explicitly between hard and soft uncertainty. Where the dominant mode of uncertainty is that of soft uncertainty, the use of probability-based approaches may be applicable.[30] If, however, the dominant mode of uncertainty is characterized as hard uncertainty, as has been argued is the case in many environmental decisions, an alternative approach will have to be taken.

2.  In cases of hard uncertainty, the next stage will be to consider as full a range (although necessarily non-exhaustive) of the possible benefit and cost outcomes which could occur as a result of the project or policy under consideration. This stage will involve at least some quantification of the costs and benefits. However, while the use of specific quantitative values (and thus environmental valuation) was necessary in order to model the ascendancy/weighting function for the case study of the Belize Southern Highway, in order to operationalize the model in a normative sense, specific values would not be necessary. This is because in practice the weighting of the outcome and the uncertainty associated with an outcome is done on a subjective basis. Thus, while valuations attached to the occurrence of an outcome will aid the decision maker, they are not a prerequisite in such a framework. An alternative would be to describe as fully as possible with the use of qualitative indicators the possible consequences of an uncertain outcome. However, given the important role that CBA plays within the decision-making process, where theoretically and practically possible, environmental valuation could play an important role at this stage. What should be accepted is that any valuation estimates will necessarily involve a large degree of uncertainty, as was highlighted in Chapter 3, which will have to be explicitly considered in the next stage rather than within the decision-making process (see Section 4.4.1).

On a more qualitative, descriptive level it is also important to consider the nature of the consequences of the possible outcomes of a project or policy. In the case of decisions with significant negative environmental consequences, in relation to ensuring the sustainability of a project or policy, whether the consequences of a particular action are irreversible, and the extent to which the ecological services which could be potentially lost are substitutable are important criteria. Similarly an additional consideration would be whether an action could lead to the possibility of a potentially catastrophic outcome, such as the collapse of ecosystem resilience. Another aspect is the extent to which the negative consequences can be mitigated. This stage will of course rely on all the uncertain outcomes being made explicit, as well as a recognition that the mitigative measures may themselves be associated with a large degree of uncertainty, which needs to be evaluated. An important consideration will therefore be the extent to which the consequences of an uncertain outcome are within the control of the decision makers (DFID, 1998).

3.  The third stage involves the evaluation of the uncertainty surrounding the occurrence of the possible gain and loss outcomes associated with any project or policy. What is evident from this book is that, at both a theoretical and practical level, probability is not an appropriate measure of uncertainty. The case study, in its operationalization of potential surprise, demonstrated the possible applicability of the use of degree of potential surprise, in which the degree of potential surprise associated with each gain and loss outcome could be allocated a value on a scale of 0–10 by the decision maker. Potential surprise is a suitable measure in that it exhibits the crucial properties in relation to the evaluation of hard uncertainty in being a non-additive, non-distributional variable. Even so, some problems were encountered in the case study, where potential surprise was constructed by some individuals as a binary variable, by which the decision maker would be either surprised or not at the occurrence of a particular outcome.

As a result of this concern an alternative two-stage approach[31] could be used. This would involve first assessing the possibility[32] of the different outcomes occurring (where degree of possibility would be constructed as a non-additive, non-distributional variable) and then assessing the extent to which the decision makers would be surprised at the occurrence of the outcome. The most important point lies in the use of any measure by which the uncertainty surrounding the non-exhaustive set of possible outcomes is explicitly evaluated. Another issue in the choice of variable would be the extent to which the decision makers are comfortable with a measure. In a normative sense, as long as the measure of uncertainty possesses the crucial features of being a non-additive, non distributional variable, then its nomenclature is irrelevant.

4. The next stage is the weighting mechanism. The importance of this stage is that both the uncertainty surrounding an outcome, as well as the consequences of the outcome, are weighted together on a judgemental basis in terms of the attention the decision makers would give to a particular outcome in the decision-making process. Again this weighting could be on a simple 0–10 scale, as was done in the application of the case study, or on another more simple categorization. The advantage of such a process is that the decision makers are forced to evaluate and sift all the possible outcomes before arriving at a focus gain and loss. In terms of the weighting procedure, some of the assumptions of the Shackle model could be interpreted in a normative fashion and stated explicitly at an institutional level. So, for example, as surprise values get increasingly larger they would be expected to reduce the weight given to that outcome. Similarly, increasing benefits or costs (quantitatively or qualitatively expressed) would increase the weight given to that outcome. Where a two-stage approach was taken to the evaluation of uncertainty, it would be expected that while the degree to which an outcome was thought possible would increase the weight given, the degree of surprise would again negatively affect the weighting. A statement of the position of the institution towards hard uncertainty on an explicit basis, as is suggested by DFID (1998), would also appear important in clarifying the role of decision makers within the overall decision-making process.

   In some cases this process would result in the clear identification of one focus gain and one focus loss, as is consistent with the Shackle model. However, the evidence from the case study suggested that while a sifting or editing process is a key element in the decision-making process, it may not always result in the identification of one focus gain and one focus loss value. Recognizing this, where more than one outcome is weighted highest, then all the outcomes which are weighted highest should be carried forward to the next stage.

5. The last stage involves the evaluation or overall judgement of the project on the basis of the focus gain outcome(s) and focus loss outcome(s). In essence these focus values represent the best to be hoped for and the worst to be feared in any project. At this stage it is evident from the preceding chapters that any form of optimizing decision rule will not be appropriate in cases of hard uncertainty. As a result the decision on the overall merits of the project will have to be done on a more judgemental basis, with other (for example political) considerations being considered. At this stage particular attention would be focused on the weighting given to costs and benefits. For example, the institution may be particularly averse to irreversible environmental costs. Again the explicit use of positional policies will help to guide the resulting decision.

The application of such a framework cannot guarantee that the hard uncertainty present in many environmental decisions will be comprehensively dealt with. However, if a systematic set of rules of thumb is provided and applied, by which both the uncertainty surrounding the possible outcomes of a project or policy, and the consequences of those outcomes can be evaluated, more explicit attention could be given to uncertainty, providing a better basis for making environmental decisions.

## NOTES

1.   Personal communication with senior decision maker.
2.   Personal communication with senior decision maker.
3.   Personal communication with senior decision maker.
4.   Personal communication with senior decision maker.
5.   Personal communication with senior decision maker.
6.   Personal communication with senior decision maker.
7.   Personal communication with senior decision maker.
8.   Personal communication with decision maker.
9.   Personal communication with decision maker.
10.  Personal communication with senior decision maker.
11.  Personal communication with decision maker.
12.  Personal communication with senior decision maker.
13.  Personal communication with senior decision maker.
14.  The use of logical frameworks will be looked at in closer detail in the following section.
15.  Personal communication with senior decision maker.
16.  Because of the lack of material collected from the BDDC/ DFID relating to the evaluation of uncertainty in the case of the Southern Highway, the procedures used to evaluate uncertainty will be discussed in a more general fashion in the following section.
17.  Personal communication with senior decision maker.
18.  Personal communication with senior decision maker.
19.  Personal communication with senior decision maker.
20.  Personal communication with senior decision maker.
21.  Personal communication with senior decision maker.
22.  Personal communication with senior decision maker.
23.  Personal communication with senior decision maker.
24.  An extensive review of an EIA methodology is outside the scope of this book, and is left to the extensive literature on the topic. See World Bank (1991) for a review of environmental assessment techniques and procedures.
25.  Personal communication with decision maker.
26.  Personal communication with decision maker.
27.  Personal communication with decision maker.
28.  Personal communication with decision maker.
29.  Personal communication with decision maker.
30.  Due to the focus on hard uncertainty in this book, the applicability of the various probability approaches in cases of soft uncertainty has not been assessed.
31.  Such an approach is similar to Keynes' weight of evidence theory (1921), as well as a similar two stage approach suggested by Ford and Ghose (1994b).
32.  See Ford and Ghose (1994b) which analyses the results from an experiment on alternative measures of uncertainty.

# 10. Conclusions

## 10.1 CONCLUSIONS

This book has focused on the need to deal adequately with uncertainty and particularly what has been termed 'hard uncertainty' in environmental decision-making. The premise for this research is based on the assertion made that, if projects or policies are to be consistent with sustainable development objectives, then uncertainty is a key concern that must be addressed. The importance of the need to deal adequately with uncertainty is emphasized by a number of key issues, such as the complexity and interconnectedness of the ecological economic system, the public good nature of many environmental services, the substitutability of ecological functions, the issue of irreversibility, and the dynamic rather than static nature of the ecological–economic system.

The research carried out has yielded a number of theoretical and empirical findings which enable several key conclusions to be made. Before these key conclusions are made it will be useful to recap the four main research hypotheses set out in Chapter 1:

1. Existing conceptualizations of uncertainty and in particular environmental uncertainty do not reflect the full range of uncertainty faced in decision making.
2. By recognizing that there are in fact a number of different modalities of uncertainty, it is argued that the use of utility maximizing models, based on the notion of probability, do not adequately deal with the range of environmental uncertainty faced by decision makers.
3. The Shackle model better explains the way that decisions are made in face of uncertainty, and in the context of improving the procedural rationality of the decision-making process can be fruitfully employed in a prescriptive sense.
4. Building on this, it is hypothesized that the Shackle model can be operationalized in a real world decision context, as is done in the case study focusing on the Belize Southern Highway Project.

Given the need to address the issue of uncertainty, the research answers the first hypothesis by demonstrating that an alternative conceptualization to the dominant conceptualization of uncertainty in the literature will need to be taken. In particular, it has been demonstrated that in terms of the evaluation of uncertainty a number of different modes can be characterized, with the distinction between 'hard' and 'soft' uncertainty of crucial importance. On the basis of this conceptualization it can be concluded that, due to the presence of what has been termed ecological uncertainty and valuation uncertainty, determining both the ecological consequences as well the value of those changes to society of a particular action or policy, is largely conditioned by hard uncertainty.

The existence of different modalities of uncertainty means that notions of optimizing decision rules become meaningless in decisions characterized by hard uncertainty, with attention instead focusing on the way in which decisions are made or the procedural rationalization of the decision-making process. *Ex ante* it is not possible in conditions of hard uncertainty to know what the optimum decision is. An acceptance of this point is crucial, as it results in a re-assessment of the way in which decision-making models are evaluated. With regard to the assessment of decision-making models in relation to uncertainty, another step that has been taken is to accept that it is not advantageous to separate completely behavioural and normative interpretations of the models. The assumption that individual decision makers behave in a 'rational' manner is inevitably tied up in normative assumptions of how the decision maker should behave in the face of uncertainty, and indeed what 'rational' behaviour should be. Accepting this position is also important in facilitating better links between the theoretical and practical applications of decision-making models.

The recognition of hard uncertainty not only changes the way that decision-making models of uncertainty are assessed, but poses a number of problems for the application of traditional models of decision making under uncertainty in respect of environmental decisions, which are typically characterized by hard uncertainty. Thus, in relation to the second hypothesis, attempts to deal with uncertainty within the valuation stages by means of option value or quasi option values are not applicable on a theoretical or practical basis. Moreover, it has been forcefully argued that expected value and expected utility models are not appropriate in cases of hard uncertainty, first because of their reliance on objective or subjective probability as a measure of the uncertainty and second because of their reliance on a weighting mechanism which does not weight or attach utility to both the uncertainty as well as the value of the outcome. From a normative perspective weighting the outcome alone in expected utility models would appear not to adequately account for the presence of uncertainty surrounding the outcome. Consequently, where expected utility models or their variants are applied to environmental decisions conditioned by hard uncertainty, they may lead to unacceptable outcomes.

The failure of the dominant paradigm based on expected utility approaches to adequately explain, as well as to provide the basis for practical normative frameworks to be developed in environmental decisions, points to the need for an alternative framework. The third and fourth hypotheses contend that an alternative model based on the work of George Shackle not only better explains the way that decisions are made in the face of hard uncertainty, but also can be practically operationalized in both a behavioural and a normative manner. First, the relevance of the Shackle model at a theoretical level in relation to environmental decisions is demonstrated by developing an interpretation of the Shackle model that retains a number of its strongest elements, such as the replacement of probability with an alternative measure of uncertainty based on potential surprise, as well as the existence of an ascendancy or weighting function. In contrast, the interpretation advanced dispenses with other elements of the original model, such as the standardization of the focus outcomes and the existence of and application of a gambler's preference map. By interpreting the Shackle model in a slightly different fashion, and solely in the context of hard uncertainty (rather than all types of uncertainty), a large number of the most prevalent criticisms of the model have been addressed and a better platform arrived at, upon which the model can be operationalized.

Building on this, the book demonstrates that the Shackle model can be operationalized successfully. In Chapter 5, the most attractive normative features of the model, namely the explicit attention given to uncertainty, and the weighting of the value of an outcome as well as the uncertainty surrounding it are highlighted. In the application of the model to the case study of the Belize Southern Highway, the model's practical operationalization to a real world decision has also been demonstrated. Moreover, the evidence presented would appear to show that the majority of decision makers, when asked to go through the various stages of the model, did so in a manner consistent with the model's main propositions. Even so, as is often the case in real world experiments, a fair amount of caution has to be taken in the statistical interpretation of the results. The use of the more qualitative evidence gained does, however, assist in the more general interpretation of the results. In particular, the use of potential surprise in evaluating the uncertainty associated with a particular outcome was largely done in a manner which can be explained by the Shackle model. However, in a number of cases it would appear that for some individuals potential surprise was defined as a binary measure. In terms of the presence of the ascendancy or weighting function, the majority of individuals did behave in a manner broadly consistent with the theory, with the sign of the coefficients of potential surprise being negative and the absolute gain or loss value positive in the majority of cases. Generally, there was little difference in the size of the coefficients, which could suggest the importance of interpreting the behaviour of the individual decision makers at a wider institutional level.

Overall, the ascendancy function did provide evidence that the majority of decision makers utilize it as a means of sifting out the different outcomes, providing backing to Shackle's arguments that, rather than taking a weighted averaging approach, the decision makers are inclined to sift through the outcomes and arrive at one focus gain outcome and one focus loss. However, at a qualitative level the importance of retaining as wide a range of outcomes as possible in the early stages of evaluation was emphasized. One aspect of the results, which was inconsistent with the theory, was evidence that in a relatively large number of cases potential surprise was not significant. Although a number of statistical reasons could partly account for this, another interpretation could be that some decision makers effectively ignored the surprise that they felt at a particular outcome occurring. Clearly, if this is the case, this could have important consequences in environmental decision making.

Drawing together the evidence from the application of the Shackle model to the Southern Highway Project, and the information on the way in which uncertainty was evaluated in practice in the different institutions, a more general interpretation was outlined of the way in which hard uncertainty is or is not dealt with in the decision-making process. First, it is argued that, while the Shackle model is applied on an individual level, individual decision makers will play different roles and represent different agendas within the decision-making process. The evidence from the interviews carried out would appear to support this claim. Second, a sifting process could be outlined in which different outcomes are contested within the decision-making process until eventually discussion is narrowed down to one scenario representing the focus gain and focus loss. Evidence from the interviews carried out gives weight to the idea that such a process, similar to that articulated by Shackle actually, occurs.

However, while there is evidence to suggest that this process arrives at a focus outcome in the way Shackle envisaged, an alternative explanation indicates that instead a preliminary sifting out of the original set of outcomes is made, on the basis of the degree to which the outcomes are perceived to be possible. Accordingly, the resulting outcomes left by this process are then judged on the basis of the outcome itself, and an overall weighting obtained. If a two-stage process in the evaluation of uncertainty is envisaged, it could be that while the decision makers initially evaluate the possibility of the outcome occurring, they do not consider the extent to which they would be surprised by any of the other possible outcomes. In other words they may not consider the uncertainty surrounding the possibility of the occurrence of the outcome. Such an interpretation would appear to be consistent with the evidence from the case study. This tendency by decision makers to focus on the possibility of the occurrence of a particular outcome or scenario, rather than explicit considerations of any hard uncertainties which may affect the possibility of the outcome occuring, could have worrying consequences in environmental decision making. Thus the evidence from the interviews would appear to point to a perception at an institutional level that the possibility of the outcome occurring could to a large degree be controlled within the design of a particular project or policy. The result of this may be that only scenarios for which any negative uncertain outcomes can be 'solved' or mitigated are advanced to the latter stages of the decision-making process. In essence therefore, the hard uncertainty is extracted or removed from the process, which, rather than considering the full range of possible uncertain consequences of an action, instead focuses on increasing the possibility of the most desirable outcome occurring. It is evident that such a goal-led rather than process-led approach to decision making does not deal sufficiently with the hard uncertainty present in many environmental decisions.

The research also provides evidence, at a more general level, of the way in which institutions such as the IDB, the World Bank and DFID evaluate uncertainty within the decision-making process. When used in conjunction with the evidence from the case study this can help to explain the way in which uncertainty is actually evaluated in practice within the decision-making process. An important conclusion was that there was insufficient attention given to the conceptualization of uncertainty at an institutional level. In particular, no explicit attention was given to distinguishing between hard uncertainty and soft uncertainty, or any other similar definitions. Moreover the tendency was to group all uncertainties as risks, with 'risks' often being interpreted solely in relation to the negative consequences of an outcome. This confusion over the definition of uncertainty may have resulted in a lack of legitimacy given to hard uncertainty in the decision-making process. The consequences of this were manifested in the approaches taken by the different institutions. Overall there was a clear lack of formal frameworks for evaluating hard uncertainty and largely the tools and mechanisms used appeared to fail in dealing explicitly with the hard uncertainty present in a decision. The one possible exception was the approach detailed by the DFID, which even though a significant improvement on other methods, remained within a subjective probability framework. Given the huge number of projects in developing countries that these institutions evaluate on an annual basis, the environmental consequences of failing to deal adequately with hard uncertainty could be significant.

Given the theoretical and practical evidence, which would suggest that uncertainty and especially hard uncertainty is not adequately dealt with within the decision-making process, the final contribution of the book was to advance a normative framework for dealing with hard uncertainty in environmental decision making. The normative framework in building on the behavioural evidence presented in this book, as well as the normative interpretation of the Shackle model, also answers the claim made in Chapter 1 that it was possible to operationalize the Shackle model normatively in order to arrive at such a framework. The framework itself, which addresses both the theoretical and practical concerns raised by this book, identifies six important stages required to improve the way in which hard uncertainty is dealt with. First, the importance of conceptualizing and defining the type of uncertainty faced is stressed. Second, a list (which is recognized as non-exhaustive) of possible outcomes must be identified, and where possible the consequences quantified (for example in monetary values) or given qualitative descriptions. Third, the hard uncertainty surrounding the occurrence of the separate outcomes should be explicitly evaluated. Fourth, it is necessary to weight the different outcomes, taking into account both the consequences of a particular outcome as well as the uncertainty surrounding the occurrence of the outcomes. Fifth, on the basis of this weighting, the outcomes should be evaluated and a sifting process carried out in order to arrive at a focus gain and focus loss. In the last stage the final evaluation and decision regarding a project can be made on the basis of the focus outcomes.

In summary, this book demonstrates that the application of the Shackle model is a useful tool in terms of explaining the way decisions are made in the face of uncertainty and could be fruitfully applied to other case studies involving environmental decisions, as well as other non-environmental decisions conditioned by hard uncertainty. By developing a normative framework it is also hoped that fresh impetus has been given to developing practical approaches, which will improve the way that decisions are made in the face of hard uncertainty and which will adequately address the concerns that the presence of environmental uncertainty poses to society.

# Appendix 1:   Questionnaire

*Introduction to the work: Thank you for your time today. The research I am conducting aims to investigate the way that uncertainty about the environmental consequences of development projects is dealt with in the decision-making process. I am also assessing the use of an alternative decision-making framework for evaluating uncertainty. I would like to emphasize that the research does not seek to evaluate the Southern Highway but is restricted to a analysis of the decision-making process. The research is independently funded.*

*I would like to record this interview, if you don't object. If you want me to stop recording at any point please say.*

Q1.   Can I ask you first of all to briefly outline your position, and your responsibilities?

Q2.   Can you describe briefly your role in the evaluation of the Southern Highway rehabilitation project and the stages in the project that you have been involved in?

Q3.   Can you indicate if there are any direct or indirect effects of the project on the environment to which you or the GoBl/IDB in general felt there is a degree of uncertainty surrounding the occurrence and the possible implications of those effects?

   If so what are these effects and can you indicate what you think are the main sources of the uncertainty surrounding them?

Q4.   Could you tell me if any informal or formal approaches were used to assess any uncertainties that were identified and if there were any attempts made to quantify the uncertainties involved or evaluate their relative importance?

Q5.   In both the EIA and the feasibility study conducted for the Southern Highway a number of possible different outcomes which could result as a consequence of the Southern Highway were presented. Were any of these outcomes excluded from the decision-making process because it was felt that it was very unlikely that they would occur and was particular attention focused on one or more outcomes about which there was particular concern?

Q6.     On a more general basis would you be able to outline at all the way
        that you individually or the GoBl/IDB would go about evaluating
        possible costs or benefits of a project when there is any uncertainty
        surrounding the occurrence and the scale of these costs or benefits?

*The respondent is given the separate sheets containing the gain and loss
scenarios and read the accompanying explanatory notes (see Appendix 2).*

Q7.     As a decision maker if you had to evaluate the Southern Highway
        based on the above scenarios would you be able to outline the steps
        you would go through in assessing the individual scenarios and the
        most important factors which you use in evaluating the scenarios?
        Specifically I am interested in how you would evaluate the uncertainty
        surrounding the occurrence of the different outcomes.

Q8.     Could you tell me what you perceive to be the major uncertainties
        which would influence whether or not the above scenarios would
        occur?

Q9.     Would you attempt to quantify the degree of uncertainty you feel
        about the different outcomes occurring?

Q10.    If so can you outline the steps you would go through to do this?

Q11.    What would be the most important factors you would use in order to
        distinguish between the different scenarios in terms of the uncertainty
        surrounding their occurrence?

Q12.    For the Southern Highway project do you think it is possible to
        predict all the possible effects of the rehabilitation of the highway or
        do you think that for some of the possible outcomes, at present this is
        not possible?

Q13.    In terms of the analysis and evaluation of development projects do
        you or your organization in general distinguish between risk and
        uncertainty, in terms of the possible effects of development projects
        especially in terms of the environment?

Q14.    I would like you now to consider each of the scenarios described
        above and then allocate the degree of potential surprise, which can
        range from 0–10, that you would feel at the occurrence of the differ-
        ent scenarios. A zero degree of potential surprise will imply that you
        will not be at all surprised if the outcome actually occurred, whereas
        10 would imply that you would be totally surprised if the outcome to
        which it is assigned were to occur.

Q15.   Bearing in mind the estimated benefits associated with the occurrence of the various gain scenarios and the degree of surprise you have attached to the outcomes occurrence, can you successively discard those outcomes to which you give less weight and feel it would be useful to exclude from the decision-making process?

Can you tell me for each scenario the reasons why you excluded a particular outcome? (*Ask question on the different outcomes that were excluded.*)

Why did you exclude outcome number 'x' before outcome number 'y'?

*Repeat for the different outcomes excluded. If left with more than one outcome, ask them why they found it difficult to exclude any more of the outcomes.*

Q16.   Bearing in mind the estimated costs associated with the occurrence of the various gain scenarios and the degree of potential surprise that you have attached to the occurrence of the outcomes, can you successively discard those outcomes to which you give less weight and feel that can be excluded from consideration in the decision-making process?

Can you tell me for each scenario the reasons why you excluded a particular outcome? (*Ask question on the different outcomes that were excluded.*)

Why did you exclude outcome number 'x' before outcome number 'y'?

*Repeat for the different outcomes excluded. If left with more than one outcome, ask them why they found it difficult to exclude any more of the outcomes.*

Q17.   From the set of gain scenarios, 1–5, and bearing in mind the estimated benefits associated with the scenarios of the various outcomes and the degree to which you would be surprised at the occurrence of the outcomes, can you state the outcome to which you would give most weight, or pay most attention, in assessing the benefits of the road.

Q18.   From the set of loss scenarios, 6–10, and bearing in mind the estimated costs associated with the scenarios of the various outcomes and the degree to which you would be surprised at the occurrence of the outcomes, can you state the outcome to which you would give most weight, or pay most attention, in assessing the benefits of the road.

*In this section you will be asked about how much weight you would give the following possible outcomes in evaluating the Southern Highway Rehabilita-*

*tion Project, bearing in mind the hypothesized benefit or costs and the degree
to which you would be surprised if that outcome was to occur. For example a
score of 0 would signify that you would give that outcome no weight in
evaluating the merits and the drawbacks of the rehabilitation project and a
score of 5 would signify that you would give that outcome moderate weighting and 10 would signify that you would give that outcome the highest
weight. The different outcomes can have equal or different weights.*

Q19.    Consider scenarios 1–5 for the Southern Highway. Bearing in mind
        the estimated benefits that would result if this outcome were to occur
        and the degree to which you would be surprised if the outcome were
        to occur, could you assign on a scale of 0–10 the weight or the amount
        of attention that you would give that outcome in evaluating all the
        possible outcomes for the Southern Highway Project? A score of 10
        would mean that you would weight that outcome very highly in the
        eventual decision-making process, whereas a score of 0 would mean
        that you would give no weight to that outcome.

Q20.    Consider scenarios 6–10 for the Southern Highway. Bearing in mind
        the estimated costs that would result if this outcome were to occur and
        the degree to which you would be surprised if the outcome were to
        occur, could you assign on a scale of 0–10 the weight that you would
        give that outcome in evaluating all the possible outcomes for the
        Southern Highway Project. A score of 10 would mean that you would
        weight that outcome very highly in the eventual decision-making
        process, whereas a score of 0 would mean that you would give no
        weight to that outcome.

# Appendix 2:    Gain and loss scenarios

## NOTES ACCOMPANYING SCENARIOS

*These scenarios are based on the 1993 Kocks Consult Feasibility Study, the DHV (1994) EIA, the BECCA (1995) EIA, the Southern Highway Social Impact Study and the 1997 Environmental Summary. Use was not made of the 1995 DHV feasibility study.*

*In addition the costs have not taken into account the revised costs as presented in the Environmental Summary, August 1997. They are based therefore on the original projections in the Kocks Consult Feasibility Study as well as the Draft Environmental Summary of February 1997.*

*The following possible scenarios of the project have been hypothesized from information from the feasibility study and the EIA. The valuations attached to the occurrence of the scenarios are based on estimates from the feasibility study for the benefits and from various environmental valuation studies of the value of similar environmental functions associated with a particular ecosystem affected by the road. The valuation estimates per hectare of rain forest include estimates of the value that this ecosystem provides in terms of services such as erosion control, nutrient recycling, and raw material provision. These estimates themselves will vary in the uncertainty attached to the calculations on which they were based, as well as the extent to which they capture the full value of the particular ecosystem. There are five possible hypothesized scenarios in terms of possible benefits of the rehabilitation of the road and possible environmental costs associated with the road. Either scenario 1 will occur or scenario 2 or scenario 3 or scenario 4 or scenario 5. In the case of the costs either scenario 6 will occur or scenario 7 or scenario 8 or scenario 9 or scenario 10. One benefit scenario AND one cost scenario will occur.*

*All the values are discounted at 12 per cent from 1993 and are projected until 2015. In the environmental cost scenarios 30 per cent of the ecosystem that is removed in the scenario is assumed to happen between 1998 and 2002 at a constant annual rate. After 2003 70 per cent of the percentage of ecosystem is removed until 2015 at a constant annual rate (total 23 years).*

# BENEFIT SCENARIOS 1–5

**Scenario 1:** Increased road user benefits including savings in vehicle operating costs and time and accidental costs.
**Total gross benefits (discounted at 12 per cent) estimated at US\$ 110.5 million**

**Scenario 2:** Increased road user benefits, as well as increased benefits due to value added to agricultural production as a result of agricultural development associated with the rehabilitation of the road.
**Total gross benefits (discounted at 12 per cent) estimated at US\$ 119 million**

**Scenario 3:** Increased road user benefits, increased benefits due to value added to agricultural production, as well as favourable economic climate for banana and citrus production which stimulates additional production with higher benefits due to higher bonuses paid to producers for undamaged fruit.
**Total gross benefits (discounted at 12 per cent) estimated at US\$ 135.5 million**

**Scenario 4:** Increased road user benefits, increased benefits due to value added to agricultural production, favourable economic climate for banana and citrus production with benefits due to higher bonuses paid to producers for undamaged fruit. In addition the road results in increased tourism in Toledo and Stann Creek as well as health and education benefits.
**Total gross benefits (discounted at 12 per cent) estimated at US\$ 165.5 million**

**Scenario 5:** Increased road user benefits, increased benefits due to value added to agricultural production, favourable economic climate for banana and citrus production with benefits due to higher bonuses paid to producers for undamaged fruit, increased benefits due to tourism, health and education benefits as well as other unanticipated social and economic development benefits.
**Total gross benefits (discounted at 12 per cent) estimated at US\$ 200 million**

# COST SCENARIOS 6–10

**Scenario 6:** Direct costs of constructing the road with no limited direct impact and no major indirect negative impacts on the environment, complete success of mitigation measures and planning controls results in carefully controlled agricultural development, with minimal agricultural pollution.
**Total gross costs (discounted at 12 per cent) estimated at US$ 73 million**

**Scenario 7:** Direct costs of constructing the road with some ecosystem losses to natural grasslands, with a 13 per cent loss mainly from designated agricultural and aquaculture developments. Some deforestation occurs of approximately 13 per cent of the area of influence's tropical forest and 6 per cent of pine, but most serious effects reduced by successful adoption of better agricultural practices as opposed to milpa agriculture, and protection of ecologically most important areas. Mitigation steps generally successful.
**Total gross costs (discounted at 12 per cent) estimated at US$ 95.5 million**

**Scenario 8:** Direct costs of constructing the road with increased habitat and biodiversity losses due to increased agricultural development and squatting. In addition there is serious deforestation of approximately 23 per cent of the area's tropical forest, mainly due to widespread milpa clearing and logging activities, with associated biodiversity losses and increased habitat fragmentation. Losses of approximately 12 per of pine areas and 13 per cent of grasslands also occur mainly from aquaculture developments. Pollution from pesticides and increased sedimentation as well as agricultural and tourism development result in a 15 per cent loss of swamp areas as well as 8 per cent of mangrove areas.
**Total gross costs (discounted at 12 per cent) estimated at US$ 134 million**

**Scenario 9:** Direct costs of constructing the road with unsuccessful mitigation of negative effects, large habitat and biodiversity losses due to uncontrolled agricultural developments. Concession of forests for logging, illegal logging activities as well as large-scale milpa clearing results in the clearance of approximately 31 per cent of the area's tropical forest and 28 per cent of the area's natural pine. Aquaculture and agriculture result in the loss of 22 per cent of savannah areas. Very serious erosion and sedimentation effects and reduced flood and storm control due to uncontrolled destruction of 23 per cent of mangrove areas and 33 per cent of swamp areas from shrimp farms and tourism development. These losses result in reduction in fish catches.

**Total gross costs (discounted at 12 per cent) estimated at US$ 176.5 million**

**Scenario 10:** Direct costs of constructing the road with unsuccessful mitigation of negative effects. Very large habitat and biodiversity losses associated with agriculture, logging, shrimp farming and tourism development. Degradation of coral reef and sea grass beds due to increased sedimentation and agricultural pollution. Other unanticipated losses of ecosystem services and functions with serious effects on the economy.

**Total gross costs (discounted at 12 per cent) estimated at US$ 230 million**

# Appendix 3:    Potential surprise and ascendancy/weighting functions

When the qualitative and quantitative results of the 23 respondents used in the analysis were collected together and analysed, two were discarded (respondents G&H) due to inconsistencies in the responses. In both cases the qualitative response to the questions asking them which gain and which loss scenarios they would weight highest (Q17 and Q18) was not consistent with the scenarios to which they had allocated the greatest weight quantitatively (Q19 and Q20). In both cases at the time of the interviews, in comparison to the other interviewees, much less time was taken during the weighting exercise, suggesting that little attention had been paid to the questions.

# Respondent A

| | Benefits US$ million | surprise | weighting |
|---|---|---|---|
| Scenario 1 | 110.5 | 8 | 7 |
| Scenario 2 | 119 | 7 | 4 |
| Scenario 3 | 135.5 | 5 | 3 |
| Scenario 4 | 165.5 | 10 | 3 |
| Scenario 5 | 200 | 10 | 0 |
| | Costs US$ million | | |
| Scenario 6 | 73 | 3 | 2 |
| Scenario 7 | 95.5 | 0 | 5 |
| Scenario 8 | 134 | 0 | 10 |
| Scenario 9 | 176.5 | 3 | 10 |
| Scenario 10 | 230 | 8 | 5 |

# Respondent B

| | Benefits US$ million | surprise | weighting |
|---|---|---|---|
| Scenario 1 | 110.5 | 1 | 4 |
| Scenario 2 | 119 | 2 | 5 |
| Scenario 3 | 135.5 | 5 | 10 |
| Scenario 4 | 165.5 | 8 | 4 |
| Scenario 5 | 200 | 10 | 0 |
| | Costs US$ million | | |
| Scenario 6 | 73 | 0 | 4 |
| Scenario 7 | 95.5 | 2 | 5 |
| Scenario 8 | 134 | 3 | 10 |
| Scenario 9 | 176.5 | 8 | 3 |
| Scenario 10 | 230 | 10 | 0 |

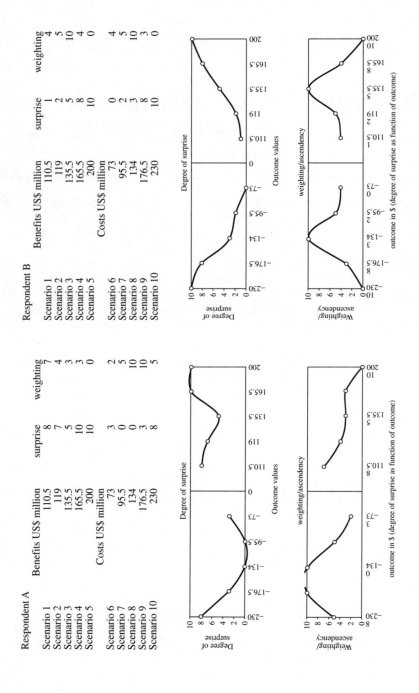

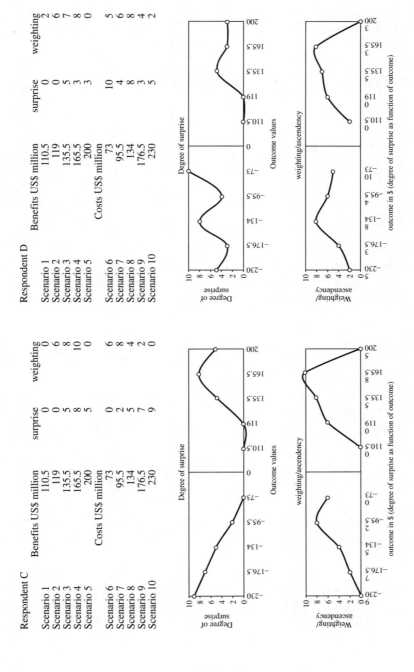

Respondent C

| | Benefits US$ million | surprise | weighting |
|---|---|---|---|
| Scenario 1 | 110.5 | 0 | 0 |
| Scenario 2 | 119 | 0 | 6 |
| Scenario 3 | 135.5 | 5 | 8 |
| Scenario 4 | 165.5 | 8 | 10 |
| Scenario 5 | 200 | 5 | 0 |
| | Costs US$ million | | |
| Scenario 6 | 73 | 0 | 6 |
| Scenario 7 | 95.5 | 2 | 8 |
| Scenario 8 | 134 | 5 | 4 |
| Scenario 9 | 176.5 | 7 | 2 |
| Scenario 10 | 230 | 9 | 0 |

Respondent D

| | Benefits US$ million | surprise | weighting |
|---|---|---|---|
| Scenario 1 | 110.5 | 0 | 2 |
| Scenario 2 | 119 | 5 | 6 |
| Scenario 3 | 135.5 | 5 | 7 |
| Scenario 4 | 165.5 | 3 | 8 |
| Scenario 5 | 200 | 3 | 0 |
| | Costs US$ million | | |
| Scenario 6 | 73 | 10 | 5 |
| Scenario 7 | 95.5 | 4 | 6 |
| Scenario 8 | 134 | 8 | 8 |
| Scenario 9 | 176.5 | 3 | 4 |
| Scenario 10 | 230 | 5 | 2 |

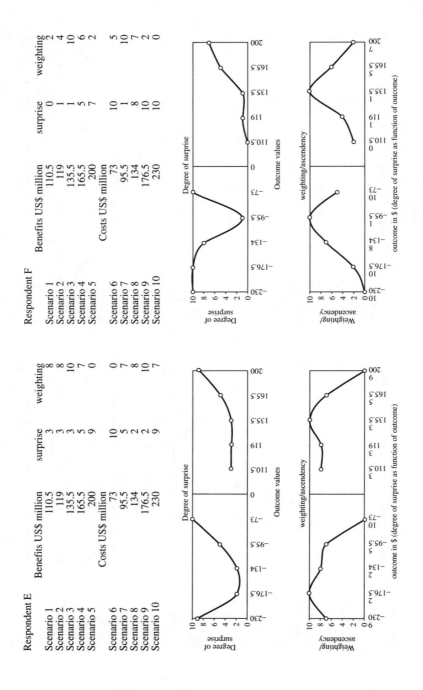

Respondent E

| | Benefits US$ million | surprise | weighting |
|---|---|---|---|
| Scenario 1 | 110.5 | 3 | 8 |
| Scenario 2 | 119 | 3 | 8 |
| Scenario 3 | 135.5 | 3 | 10 |
| Scenario 4 | 165.5 | 5 | 7 |
| Scenario 5 | 200 | 9 | 0 |
| | Costs US$ million | | |
| Scenario 6 | 73 | 10 | 0 |
| Scenario 7 | 95.5 | 5 | 7 |
| Scenario 8 | 134 | 2 | 8 |
| Scenario 9 | 176.5 | 2 | 10 |
| Scenario 10 | 230 | 9 | 7 |

Respondent F

| | Benefits US$ million | surprise | weighting |
|---|---|---|---|
| Scenario 1 | 110.5 | 0 | 2 |
| Scenario 2 | 119 | 1 | 4 |
| Scenario 3 | 135.5 | 1 | 10 |
| Scenario 4 | 165.5 | 5 | 6 |
| Scenario 5 | 200 | 7 | 2 |
| | Costs US$ million | | |
| Scenario 6 | 73 | 10 | 5 |
| Scenario 7 | 95.5 | 1 | 10 |
| Scenario 8 | 134 | 8 | 7 |
| Scenario 9 | 176.5 | 10 | 2 |
| Scenario 10 | 230 | 10 | 0 |

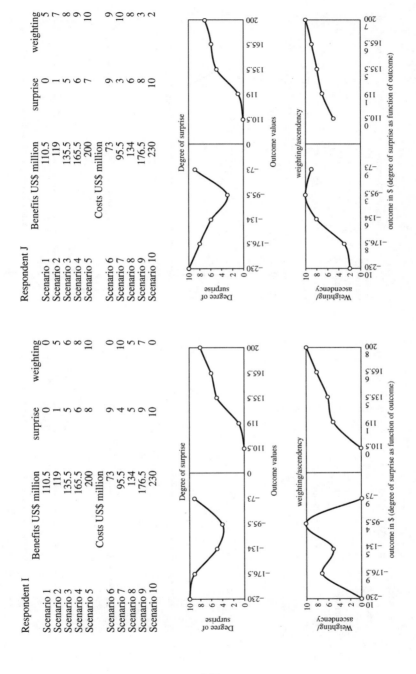

Respondent I

| | Benefits US$ million | surprise | weighting |
|---|---|---|---|
| Scenario 1 | 110.5 | 0 | 0 |
| Scenario 2 | 119 | 1 | 5 |
| Scenario 3 | 135.5 | 5 | 6 |
| Scenario 4 | 165.5 | 6 | 8 |
| Scenario 5 | 200 | 8 | 10 |
| | Costs US$ million | | |
| Scenario 6 | 73 | 9 | 0 |
| Scenario 7 | 95.5 | 4 | 10 |
| Scenario 8 | 134 | 5 | 5 |
| Scenario 9 | 176.5 | 9 | 7 |
| Scenario 10 | 230 | 10 | 0 |

Respondent J

| | Benefits US$ million | surprise | weighting |
|---|---|---|---|
| Scenario 1 | 110.5 | 0 | 5 |
| Scenario 2 | 119 | 1 | 7 |
| Scenario 3 | 135.5 | 5 | 8 |
| Scenario 4 | 165.5 | 6 | 9 |
| Scenario 5 | 200 | 7 | 10 |
| | Costs US$ million | | |
| Scenario 6 | 73 | 9 | 9 |
| Scenario 7 | 95.5 | 3 | 10 |
| Scenario 8 | 134 | 6 | 8 |
| Scenario 9 | 176.5 | 8 | 3 |
| Scenario 10 | 230 | 10 | 2 |

Degree of surprise — Outcome values

Degree of surprise

Weighting/ascendency — weighting/ascendency — outcome in $ (degree of surprise as function of outcome)

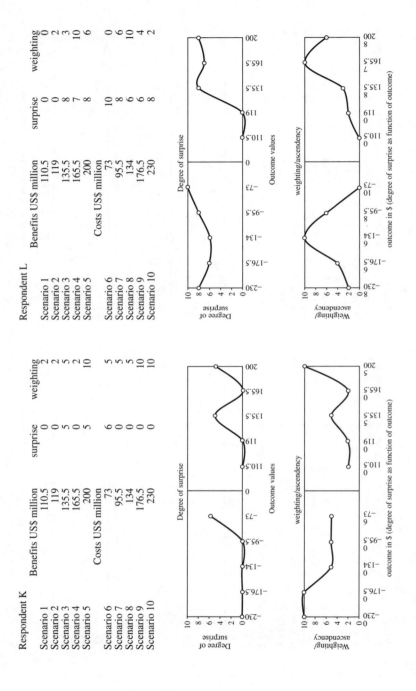

Respondent K

| | Benefits US$ million | surprise | weighting |
|---|---|---|---|
| Scenario 1 | 110.5 | 0 | 2 |
| Scenario 2 | 119 | 0 | 2 |
| Scenario 3 | 135.5 | 5 | 5 |
| Scenario 4 | 165.5 | 0 | 2 |
| Scenario 5 | 200 | 5 | 10 |
| | Costs US$ million | | |
| Scenario 6 | 73 | 6 | 5 |
| Scenario 7 | 95.5 | 0 | 5 |
| Scenario 8 | 134 | 0 | 5 |
| Scenario 9 | 176.5 | 0 | 10 |
| Scenario 10 | 230 | 0 | 10 |

Respondent L

| | Benefits US$ million | surprise | weighting |
|---|---|---|---|
| Scenario 1 | 110.5 | 0 | 0 |
| Scenario 2 | 119 | 0 | 2 |
| Scenario 3 | 135.5 | 8 | 3 |
| Scenario 4 | 165.5 | 7 | 10 |
| Scenario 5 | 200 | 8 | 6 |
| | Costs US$ million | | |
| Scenario 6 | 73 | 10 | 0 |
| Scenario 7 | 95.5 | 8 | 6 |
| Scenario 8 | 134 | 6 | 10 |
| Scenario 9 | 176.5 | 6 | 4 |
| Scenario 10 | 230 | 8 | 2 |

# Respondent N

| | Benefits US$ million | surprise | weighting |
|---|---|---|---|
| Scenario 1 | 110.5 | 4 | 9 |
| Scenario 2 | 119 | 4 | 7 |
| Scenario 3 | 135.5 | 6 | 9 |
| Scenario 4 | 165.5 | 7 | 7 |
| Scenario 5 | 200 | 4 | 9 |
| | Costs US$ million | | |
| Scenario 6 | 73 | 6 | 9 |
| Scenario 7 | 95.5 | 5 | 6 |
| Scenario 8 | 134 | 5 | 4 |
| Scenario 9 | 176.5 | 7 | 2 |
| Scenario 10 | 230 | 10 | 0 |

# Respondent M

| | Benefits US$ million | surprise | weighting |
|---|---|---|---|
| Scenario 1 | 110.5 | 10 | 2 |
| Scenario 2 | 119 | 8 | 4 |
| Scenario 3 | 135.5 | 6 | 6 |
| Scenario 4 | 165.5 | 4 | 8 |
| Scenario 5 | 200 | 2 | 10 |
| | Costs US$ million | | |
| Scenario 6 | 73 | 10 | 0 |
| Scenario 7 | 95.5 | 6 | 4 |
| Scenario 8 | 134 | 4 | 6 |
| Scenario 9 | 176.5 | 4 | 6 |
| Scenario 10 | 230 | 4 | 6 |

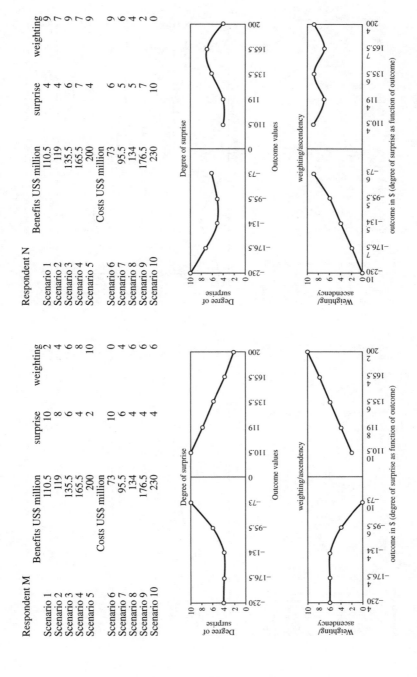

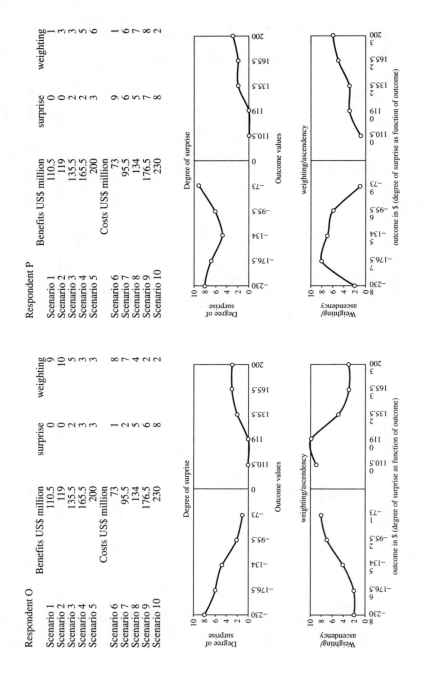

## Respondent O

| | Benefits US$ million | surprise | weighting |
|---|---|---|---|
| Scenario 1 | 110.5 | 0 | 9 |
| Scenario 2 | 119 | 0 | 10 |
| Scenario 3 | 135.5 | 2 | 5 |
| Scenario 4 | 165.5 | 3 | 3 |
| Scenario 5 | 200 | 3 | 3 |
| | Costs US$ million | | |
| Scenario 6 | 73 | 1 | 8 |
| Scenario 7 | 95.5 | 2 | 7 |
| Scenario 8 | 134 | 5 | 4 |
| Scenario 9 | 176.5 | 6 | 2 |
| Scenario 10 | 230 | 8 | 2 |

## Respondent P

| | Benefits US$ million | surprise | weighting |
|---|---|---|---|
| Scenario 1 | 110.5 | 0 | 1 |
| Scenario 2 | 119 | 0 | 3 |
| Scenario 3 | 135.5 | 2 | 3 |
| Scenario 4 | 165.5 | 2 | 5 |
| Scenario 5 | 200 | 3 | 6 |
| | Costs US$ million | | |
| Scenario 6 | 73 | 9 | 1 |
| Scenario 7 | 95.5 | 6 | 6 |
| Scenario 8 | 134 | 5 | 7 |
| Scenario 9 | 176.5 | 7 | 8 |
| Scenario 10 | 230 | 8 | 2 |

Degree of surprise

Outcome values

weighting/ascendency

outcome in $ (degree of surprise as function of outcome)

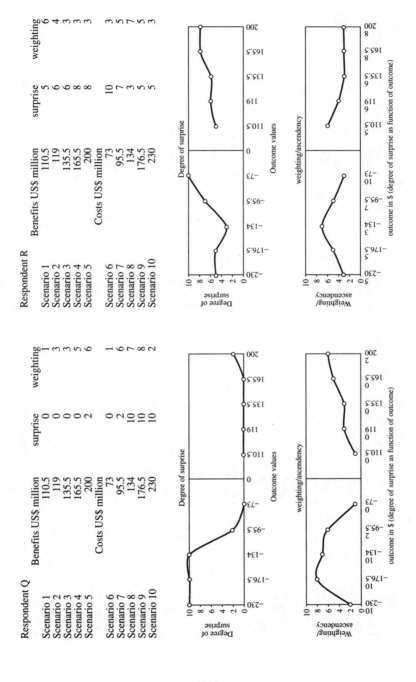

## Respondent S

| | Benefits US$ million | surprise | weighting |
|---|---|---|---|
| Scenario 1 | 110.5 | 0 | 3 |
| Scenario 2 | 119 | 0 | 3 |
| Scenario 3 | 135.5 | 6 | 4 |
| Scenario 4 | 165.5 | 6 | 6 |
| Scenario 5 | 200 | 8 | 10 |
| | Costs US$ million | | |
| Scenario 6 | 73 | 0 | 0 |
| Scenario 7 | 95.5 | 0 | 2 |
| Scenario 8 | 134 | 6 | 4 |
| Scenario 9 | 176.5 | 7 | 6 |
| Scenario 10 | 230 | 9 | 10 |

## Respondent T

| | Benefits US$ million | surprise | weighting |
|---|---|---|---|
| Scenario 1 | 110.5 | 7 | 4 |
| Scenario 2 | 119 | 7 | 5 |
| Scenario 3 | 135.5 | 5 | 4 |
| Scenario 4 | 165.5 | 8 | 6 |
| Scenario 5 | 200 | 6 | 10 |
| | Costs US$ million | | |
| Scenario 6 | 73 | 10 | 4 |
| Scenario 7 | 95.5 | 1 | 7 |
| Scenario 8 | 134 | 7 | 7 |
| Scenario 9 | 176.5 | 10 | 3 |
| Scenario 10 | 230 | 10 | 3 |

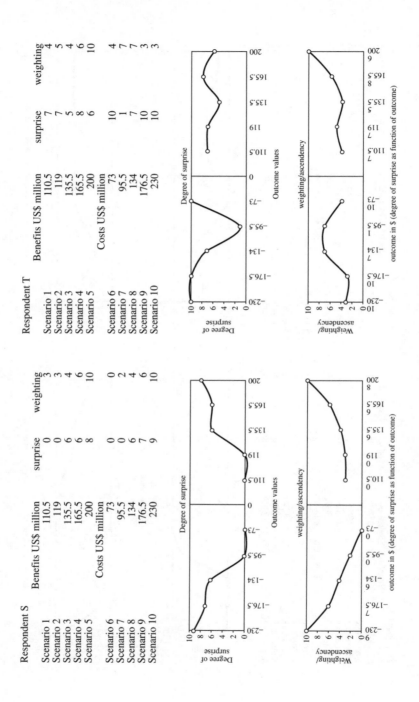

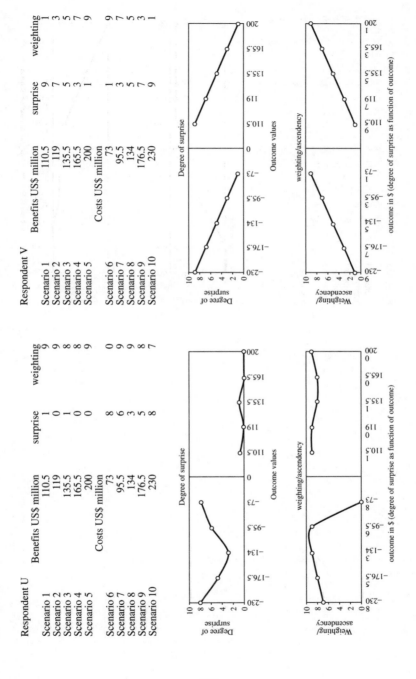

Respondent U

| | Benefits US$ million | surprise | weighting |
|---|---|---|---|
| Scenario 1 | 110.5 | 1 | 9 |
| Scenario 2 | 119 | 0 | 9 |
| Scenario 3 | 135.5 | 1 | 8 |
| Scenario 4 | 165.5 | 0 | 8 |
| Scenario 5 | 200 | 0 | 9 |
| | Costs US$ million | | |
| Scenario 6 | 73 | 8 | 0 |
| Scenario 7 | 95.5 | 6 | 9 |
| Scenario 8 | 134 | 3 | 9 |
| Scenario 9 | 176.5 | 5 | 8 |
| Scenario 10 | 230 | 8 | 7 |

Respondent V

| | Benefits US$ million | surprise | weighting |
|---|---|---|---|
| Scenario 1 | 110.5 | 9 | 1 |
| Scenario 2 | 119 | 7 | 3 |
| Scenario 3 | 135.5 | 5 | 5 |
| Scenario 4 | 165.5 | 3 | 7 |
| Scenario 5 | 200 | 1 | 9 |
| | Costs US$ million | | |
| Scenario 6 | 73 | 1 | 9 |
| Scenario 7 | 95.5 | 3 | 7 |
| Scenario 8 | 134 | 5 | 5 |
| Scenario 9 | 176.5 | 7 | 3 |
| Scenario 10 | 230 | 9 | 1 |

Respondent W

| | Benefits US$ million | surprise | weighting |
|---|---|---|---|
| Scenario 1 | 110.5 | 1 | 2 |
| Scenario 2 | 119 | 1 | 4 |
| Scenario 3 | 135.5 | 1 | 6 |
| Scenario 4 | 165.5 | 1 | 8 |
| Scenario 5 | 200 | 1 | 10 |
| | Costs US$ million | | |
| Scenario 6 | 73 | 2 | 1 |
| Scenario 7 | 95.5 | 5 | 1 |
| Scenario 8 | 134 | 8 | 0 |
| Scenario 9 | 176.5 | 10 | 0 |
| Scenario 10 | 230 | 10 | 0 |

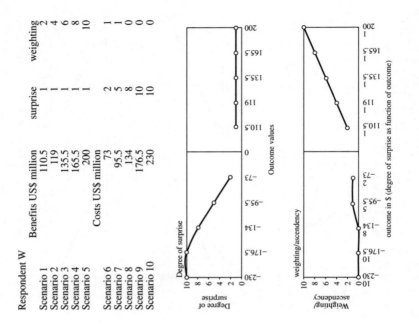

# Appendix 4:   Summary of results from regression of weighting/ ascendancy function

When the qualitative and quantitative results of the 23 respondents used in the analysis were collected together and analysed, two were discarded (respondents G&H) due to inconsistencies in the responses. In both cases the qualitative response to the questions asking them which gain and which loss scenarios they would weight highest (Q17 and Q18) was not consistent with the scenarios to which they had allocated the greatest weight quantitatively (Q19 and Q20). In both cases at the time of the interviews, in comparison to the other interviewees, much less time was taken during the weighting exercise, suggesting that little attention had been paid to the questions.

| Respondent / function | Weighting function | Equation significant F-test | Coefficient signs | Coefficients significant (0.05) | R-sq. (Adjusted R-sq.) | Model diagnostics | Intercept significant |
|---|---|---|---|---|---|---|---|
| A: all | $\phi = 0.64x^{0.5} - 0.06y^2$ | yes | correct | yes | 0.83 (0.79) | No problems | no |
| gain | $\phi = 0.41x^{0.5} - 0.03y^2$ | no | correct | no | 0.62 (0.37) | Possible multicollinearity DW inconclusive | |
| loss | $\phi = 0.70x^{0.5} - 0.09y^2$ | yes | correct | y not | 0.93 (0.87) | DW inconclusive | |
| B: all | $\phi = 0.66x^{0.5} - 0.09y^2$ | yes | correct | yes | 0.84 (0.80) | No problems | no |
| gain | $\phi = 0.62x^{0.5} - 0.07y^2$ | no (0.09) | correct | no, ($x = 0.051$) y not | 0.80 (0.66) | No problems | |
| loss | $\phi = 0.70x^{0.5} - 0.10y^2$ | yes | correct | yes | 0.91 (0.84) | No problems | |
| C: all | $\phi = 0.42x^{0.5} - 0.03y^2$ | yes | correct | no, ($x = 0.052$) y not | 0.54 (0.42) | Poss. problem with functional form | yes (0.03) |
| gain | $\phi = 0.17x^{0.5} - 0.11y^2$ | no | y not correct | no | 0.71 (0.51) | DW inconclusive | |
| loss | $\phi = 0.74x^{0.5} - 0.15y^2$ | yes | correct | yes | 0.97 (0.95) | Poss. multicollinearity | |
| D: all | $\phi = 0.31x^{0.5} + 0.04y^2$ | yes | y not correct | x yes, y not | 0.75 (0.68) | Poss. specification problem (Chow's test) | no |
| gain | $\phi = 0.28x^{0.5} + 0.12y^2$ | no | y not correct | no | 0.69 (0.49) | Poss. problem of autocorrelation (LM 0.045) | |
| loss | $\phi = 0.27x^{0.5} + 0.04y^2$ | no | y not correct | no | 0.83 (0.72) | DW inconclusive | |
| E: all | $\phi = 0.78x^{0.5} - 0.08y^2$ | yes | correct | yes | 0.94 (0.93) | DW inconclusive | no |
| gain | $\phi = 0.90x^{0.5} - 0.16y^2$ | yes | correct | yes | 0.99 (0.99) | No problems | |
| loss | $\phi = 0.78x^{0.5} - 0.06y^2$ | yes | correct | yes | 0.99 (0.99) | No problems | |

| | Equation | | | | | | yes/ no |
|---|---|---|---|---|---|---|---|
| F: | all | $\phi = 0.52x^{0.5}-0.04y^2$ | yes | correct | x yes, y not | 0.66 (0.57) | DW inconclusive | 0.048 |
| | gain | $\phi = 0.52x^{0.5}-0.09y^2$ | no (0.09) | correct | no (x = 0.057) | 0.78 (0.64) | DW inconclusive | |
| | loss | $\phi = 0.76x^{0.5}-0.06y^2$ | no | correct | no | 0.63 (0.39) | Poss. multicollinearity Possible (DW = 0.5) | |
| I: | all | $\phi = 0.58x^{0.5}-0.04y^2$ | yes | correct | x yes, y not | 0.84 (0.70) | No problems | no |
| | gain | $\phi = 0.26x^{0.5}+0.11y^2$ | yes | y not correct | no (y = 0.09) | 0.94 (0.91) | Chow = 0.047 possible specification problem | |
| | loss | $\phi = 0.90x^{0.5}+0.10y^2$ | no | correct | no (x = 0.06) | 0.77 (0.62) | Poss. multicollinearity | |
| J: | all | $\phi = 0.70x^{0.5}-0.04y^2$ | yes | correct | x yes, y not | 0.82 (0.78) | Poss. problem of heteroskedasticity DW inconclusive | no |
| | gain | $\phi = 0.57x^{0.5}+0.05y^2$ | yes | y not correct | x yes, y not | 0.99 (0.99) | No problems | |
| | loss | $\phi = 0.72x^{0.5}-0.05y^2$ | no | correct | no | 0.66 (0.43) | DW 0.5, problem of heteroskedasticity & multicollinearity | |
| K: | all | $\phi = 0.46x^{0.5}+0.05y^2$ | yes | y not correct | x yes, y not | 0.84 (0.80) | DW inconclusive | no |
| | gain | $\phi = 0.19x^{0.5}+0.20y^2$ | yes | y not correct | no (y = 0.07) | 0.92 (0.87) | DW inconclusive, problem of hetero-skedasticity | |
| | loss | $\phi = 0.62x^{0.5}-0.01y^2$ | yes | correct | x yes, y not | 0.96 (0.94) | Chow = 0.05 | |
| L: | all | $\phi = 0.36x^{0.5}+0.002y^2$ | yes | y not correct | no (x = 0.08) | 0.64 (0.54) | Poss. slight multicollinearity | no |
| | gain | $\phi = 0.17x^{0.5}+0.06y^2$ | no | y not correct | no | 0.77 (0.61) | Poss. slight multicollinearity | |
| | loss | $\phi = 0.55x^{0.5}-0.04y^2$ | no | correct | no | 0.65 (0.42) | Poss. multicollinearity | |

217

| Respondent | Weighting function | Equation significant F-test | Coefficient signs | Coefficients significant (0.05) | R-sq. (Adjusted R-sq.) | Model diagnostics | Intercept significant |
|---|---|---|---|---|---|---|---|
| M: all | $\phi = 0.59x^{0.5}-0.05y^2$ | yes | correct | yes | 0.97 (0.96) | Poss. heteroskedasticity DW 0.32, poss. mis-specification | no |
| gain | $\phi = 0.70x^{0.5}-0.06y^2$ | yes | correct | yes | 0.99 (0.99) | Poss. mis-specification problem (Chow's test) | |
| loss | $\phi = 0.50x^{0.5}-0.04y^2$ | yes | correct | yes | 0.98 (0.97) | DW inconclusive | |
| N: all | $\phi = 0.85x^{0.5}-0.11y^2$ | yes | correct | yes | 0.84 (0.80) | DW inconclusive, poss. slight multicollinearity | just sig. (0.04) |
| gain | $\phi = 0.74x^{0.5}-0.03y^2$ | yes | correct | x yes, y not | 0.98 (0.96) | Poss. multicollinearity | |
| loss | $\phi = 0.71x^{0.5}-0.10y^2$ | no | correct | no | 0.77 (0.60) | Multicollinearity, poss. mis-specification, DW = 0.70 | |
| O: all | $\phi = 0.60x^{0.5}-0.13y^2$ | yes | correct | yes | 0.81 (0.77) | Poss. heteroskedasticity | yes |
| gain | $\phi = 0.86x^{0.5}-0.98y^2$ | yes | correct | yes | 0.99 (0.98) | Poss. mis-specification Chow's 2nd test (0.008) | |
| loss | $\phi = 0.78x^{0.5}-0.17y^2$ | yes | correct | yes | 0.94 (0.89) | No problems | |
| P: all | $\phi = 0.37x^{0.5}-0.007y^2$ | yes | correct | x yes, y not | 0.78 (0.73) | DW inconclusive | no |
| gain | $\phi = 0.20x^{0.5}+0.37y^2$ | yes | y not correct | no (x = 0.053) | 0.96 (0.93) | Problem of auto-correlation & mis-specification | |
| loss | $\phi = 0.71x^{0.5}-0.007y^2$ | no (0.06) | correct | no (x = 0.07) | 0.84 (0.73) | No problems | |

| | Equation | | | | $R^2$ | Problems | |
|---|---|---|---|---|---|---|---|
| Q: all | $\phi = 0.31x^{0.5}+0.016y^2$ | yes | y not correct | x yes, y not | 0.80 (0.75) | No problems | no |
| gain | $\phi = 0.16x^{0.5}-0.13y^2$ | yes | correct | x yes, y not | 0.93 (0.88) | No problems | |
| loss | $\phi = 0.32x^{0.5}+0.014y^2$ | no | y not correct | no | 0.75 (0.59) | No problems | |
| R: all | $\phi = 0.38x^{0.5}-0.011y^2$ | yes | correct | x yes, y not | 0.86 (0.82) | Poss. mis-specification (Chow's Test) | yes |
| gain | $\phi = 0.71x^{0.5}-0.10y^2$ | yes | correct | x yes, y not (0.1) | 0.95 (0.92) | No problems | |
| loss | $\phi = 0.38x^{0.5}-0.003y^2$ | no (0.51) | correct | no (x = 0.51) | 0.86 (0.77) | DW inconclusive | |
| S: all | $\phi = 0.19x^{0.5}+0.09y^2$ | yes | y not correct | yes | 0.96 (0.95) | Poss. mis-specification | yes |
| gain | $\phi = 0.25x^{0.5}+0.08y^2$ | yes | y not correct | no (x = 0.059, y = 0.055) | 0.97 (0.95) | No problems | |
| loss | $\phi = 0.09x^{0.5}+0.10y^2$ | yes | y not correct | x not, y yes | 0.98 (0.97) | Poss. multicollinearity | |
| T: all | $\phi = 0.64x^{0.5}-0.04y^2$ | yes | correct | x yes, y not (y = 0.06) | 0.90 (0.88) | Poss. multicollinearity | no |
| gain | $\phi = 0.63x^{0.5}-0.04y^2$ | yes | correct | no (x = 0.08) | 0.94 (0.89) | DW inconclusive | |
| loss | $\phi = 0.63x^{0.5}-0.04y^2$ | no (0.053) | correct | no (x = 0.057) | 0.86 (0.76) | Poss. multicollinearity | |
| U: all | $\phi = 0.75x^{0.5}-0.07y^2$ | yes | correct | yes | 0.95 (0.94) | No problems | no |
| gain | $\phi = 0.68x^{0.5}+1.02y^2$ | yes | y not correct | x yes, y not | 0.99 (0.98) | DW inconclusive | |
| loss | $\phi = 0.88x^{0.5}-0.10y^2$ | yes | correct | x yes, y not (0.056) | 0.93 (0.89) | Slight multicollinearity, poss. mis-specification | |
| V: all | $\phi = 0.68x^{0.5}-0.10y^2$ | yes | correct | yes | 0.94 (0.92) | Possible autocorrelation, poss. mis-specification | yes |
| gain | $\phi = 0.61x^{0.5}-0.07y^2$ | yes | correct | yes | 0.99 (0.99) | DW inconclusive, poss. mis-specification | |
| loss | $\phi = 0.89x^{0.5}-0.16y^2$ | yes | correct | yes | 0.97 (0.94) | DW inconclusive | |

| Respondent | Weighting function | Equation significant F-test | Coefficient signs | Coefficients significant (0.05) | R-sq. (Adjusted R-sq.) | Model diagnostics | Intercept significant |
|---|---|---|---|---|---|---|---|
| W: all | $\phi = 0.47x^{0.5} - 0.07y^2$ | yes | correct | yes | 0.83 (0.79) | Autocorrelation, mis-specification | yes |
| gain | $\phi = 2.08x^{0.5} - 19y^2$ | yes | correct | yes | 0.99 (0.98) | Multicollinearity DW inconclusive | |
| loss | $\phi = 0.13x^{0.5} - 0.02y^2$ | yes | correct | yes | 0.92 (0.87) | Multicollinearity, poss. mis-specification | |
| All | $\phi = 0.51x^{0.5} - 0.03y^2$ | yes | correct | yes | 0.75 (0.75) | Autocorrelation, mis-specification | yes |
| All: gain | $\phi = 0.50x^{0.5} - 0.02y^2$ | yes | correct | yes | 0.79 (0.79) | Autocorrelation, mis-specification | no |
| All: loss | $\phi = 0.54x^{0.5} - 0.03y^2$ | yes | correct | yes | 0.71 (0.71) | Autocorrelation, mis-specification | yes |

# Bibliography

Abbott, L. (1955), *Quality and Competition*, New York: Columbia University Press.

Adamowicz, W.L., V. Bhardwaj and B. MacNab (1993), 'Willingness to pay and willingness to accept compensation', *Land Economy*, **69**: 416–27.

Allais, M. (1953), 'Le comportement de l'homme rationnel devant le risque, critique des postulats et axiomes de l'Ecole Americaine', *Econometrica*, **21**: 503–46.

Arrow, K.J. and A.C. Fisher (1974), 'Environmental preservation, uncertainty and irreversibility, *Quarterly Journal of Economics*, **88**: 313–19.

Arrow, K., B. Bolin, R. Costanza, P. Dasgupta, C. Folke, C.S. Holling, B. Jansson, S. Levin, K. Maler, C. Perrings and D. Pimentel (1995), 'Economic growth, carrying capacity, and the environment', *Ecological Economics*, **15**(2): 91–5.

Barbier, E.B, G. Brown, S. Dalmazzone, C. Folke, M. Gadgil, N. Hanley, C.S. Holling, W.H. Lesser, K.-G. Maler, P. Mason, C. Panayotou, C. Perrings, R.K. Turner and M. Wells (1995), in C. Perrings (ed.), 'The economic value of biodiversity', Vernon H. Heywood (ed.), *Global Biodiversity Assessment*, UNEP, Cambridge: Cambridge University Press.

Barbier, E.B., J.C. Burgess and C. Folke (1994), *Paradise Lost?: The Ecological Economics of Biodiversity*, London: Earthscan Publications Ltd.

Bateman, I. (1993), 'Revealed Preference Methods', in K. Turner (ed.), *Sustainable Environmental Economics and Management*, New York: Belhaven Press, pp. 192–298.

Bateman, I. and K. Turner (1993), 'Valuation of the environment, methods and techniques, contingent valuation method', in K. Turner (ed.), *Sustainable Environmental Economics and Management*, New York: Belhaven Press, pp. 120–91.

Bateman, I., K. Willis and J. Garrod (1993), *Consistency between Contingent Valuation Estimates. A Comparison of Two Studies of U.K. National Parks*, ESRC, Countryside Change Initiative, working paper 40.

Bator, F.J (1957), 'General equilibrium, welfare and allocation', *American Economic Review*, March: 22–59.

BECCA International Consultants (1995), *Environmental Impact Assessment of the Belize Southern Highway Project*, Government of Belize.

Bell, D.E. (1982), 'Regret in decision making under uncertainty', *Operations Research*, **30**: 961–81.

Bernouilli, D. (1738, 1954), 'Specimen theoriae novae de mensura sortis, Commentarii Academiae Scientiarum Imperialis Petropolitane, **V**: 175–82'; translated by L. Sommer (1954), as, 'Expositions of a new theory on the measurement of risk', *Econometrica*, **XXII**, January: 23–6.

Bingham, G., R. Bishop, M. Brody, D. Bromley, E. Clark, W. Cooper, R. Costanza, T. Hale, G. Hayden, S. Kellert, R. Norgaard, B. Norton, J. Payne, C. Russell and G. Suter (1995), 'Issues in ecosystem valuation: Improving information for decision making', *Ecological Economics*, **14**: 73–90.

Bird, N.M. (1997), *The Columbia Controlled Felling Programme*, Forest Planning and Management Project, Unpublished report.

Bishop, R.C. (1982), 'Option Value: an exposition and extension', *Land Economics*, **58**: 1–15.

Blaikie, P. (1996), *Grounding Biodiversity*, Paper submitted for Royal Geographical Society/Institute of British Geographers Annual Conference at Strathclyde University, 1996.

Blamey, R. and M. Common (1994), 'Sustainability and the limits of the pseudo-market valuation', in J.C.J.M. van den Bergh and J. van der Straaten (eds), *Concepts Methods and Policy for Sustainable Development: Critique and New Approaches*, New York: Island Press.

Bockstael, N.E., W.M. Haneman and C. Kling (1987), 'Estimating the value of the water quality improvements in a recreational demand framework', *Water Resources Research*, **235**: 951–60.

Bockstael, N., R. Costanza, I. Strand, W. Boynton, K. Bell and L. Wainger (1995), 'Ecological economics modelling and valuation of ecosystems', *Ecological Economics*, **14**: 143–59.

Brent, R.J. (1990), *Project Appraisal for Developing Countries*, New York: New York University Press.

Brown, G.M. (1990), 'Valuation of genetic resources', in G.H. Orians, G.M. Brown and J.E. Swierninski (eds), *The Preservation and Valuation of Biological Resources*, Seattle: University of Washington Press, pp. 203–28.

Camerer, C. and M. Weber (1992), 'Recent developments in modelling preferences: uncertainty and ambiguity', *Journal of Risk and Uncertainty*, **5**: 325–70, Kluwer Academic Publishers.

Campbell, J., J. Savage and J. Mejer (1994), 'A new species of *Eleutherodactylus (Anura: Leptodactactylidae)* of the Rugulosus Group from Guatemala and Belize', *Herptologica*, **50**(4): 412–19.

Camus, A. (1972), *The Plague*, Vintage Books.

Carnap, R. (1945), 'On inductive logic', *Philosophy of Science*, **12**: 72–97.

Carson, R.T. *et al.* (1995), *A Bibliography of Contingent Valuation Studies and Papers*, Natural Resource Damage Assessment, Inc., November.

Carter, C.F. (1950), 'Expectation in economics', *Economic Journal*, March: 92–105.

Carter, C.F. (1953), 'A revised theory of expectations', *Economic Journal*, **LXVIII**, December: 428–50.

Caulkins, P., R. Bishop and N. Bouwes (1986), 'The travel cost model for lake recreation: a comparison of two methods for incorporating site quality and substitution effects', *American Journal of Agricultural Economics*, May: 291–7.

Chew, S.H. (1983), 'A generalisation of the quasilinear mean with applications to the measurement of income equality and decision theory resolving the Allais paradox', *Econometrica*, **51**: 1065–92.

Chomitz, K. and D. Gray (1996), 'Roads, land use and deforestation: A spatial model applied to Belize', *The World Bank Economic Review*, **10**(3): 487–512.

Christensen, P. (1996), 'Classical foundations for a physiological and ecological model of sustainability', in S. Faucheux, D. Pearce and J. Proops, *Models of Sustainable Development*, Aldershot, UK: Edward Elgar.

Cicchetti, C. and A.M. Freeman (1971), 'Option demand and consumer surplus: Further comment', *Quarterly Journal of Economics*, **85**: 528–39.

Ciriacy-Wantrup, S.V. (1963) *Resource Conservation: Economics and Policies*, Berkeley: University of California.

Clawson, M. and J. Knetsch (1966), *Economics of Outdoor Recreation*, Baltimore: Johns Hopkins University Press.

Clements, F.E. (1905, 1977), *Research Methods in Ecology*, Lincoln: University Publishing Company (reprinted 1977, Arnold Press: New York).

Common, M. (1995), *Sustainability & Policy: Limits to Economics*, Cambridge: Cambridge University Press.

Common, M. and C. Perrings (1992), 'Towards an ecological economics of sustainability', *Ecological Economics*, **6**: 7–34.

Costanza, R. (1991), 'Assuring sustainability of ecological systems', in R. Costanza (ed.), *Ecological Economics: The Science and Management of Sustainability*, New York: Columbia University Press.

Costanza, R. (1994), 'Three general policies to achieve sustainability', in A. Jansson, M. Hammer, C. Folke and R. Costanza (eds), *Investing in Natural Capital: The Ecological Economics Approach to Sustainability*, Washington, DC: Island Press.

Costanza, R., L. Wainger, C. Folke and K.G. Maler (1993), 'Modelling complex ecological economic systems', *Bioscience*, **43**: 545–55.

Costanza, R., C. Perrings and C.J. Cleveland (eds) (1997a), *The Development of Ecological Economics*, Cheltenham, UK and Brookfield, US: Edward Elgar.

Costanza, R., R. d'Arge, R. de Groot, S. Farber, M. Grasso, B. Hannon, K. Limburg, S. Naeem, R.V. O'Neil, J. Paruelo, R.G. Raskin., P. Sutton and M. van den Belt (1997b), 'The value of the world's ecosystem services and natural capital', *Nature*, **387**, May: 253–60.

Cummings, R.G., D.S. Brookshire and W.D. Shulze (eds) (1986), *Valuing Environmental Goods: An Assessment of the Contingent Valuation Method*, Totowa, NJ: Rowman and Allanheld.

Dalmazzone, S. (1995), 'The economic value of biodiversity', in C. Perrings (ed.), *Global Biodiversity Assessment*, UNEP, Cambridge: Cambridge University Press.

Dalmazzone, S. and C. Perrings (1997), 'Resilience and stability in ecological economic systems', Paper presented at Department of Environmental Economics and Environmental Management, York: University of York.

Daly, H.E. (1986) 'Thermodynamic and economic concepts as related to resource-use policies: Comment', *Land Economics*, **62**(3): 319–22.

Daly, H.E. and J.B. Cobb (1989), *For the Common Good*, London: Green Print.

Dasgupta, P. and G.M. Heal (1974), 'The optimal depletion of exhaustible resources', *Review of Economic Studies, Symposium*, May: 3–28.

Davidson, P. (1996), 'Reality and economic theory', *Journal of Post Keynesian Economics / Summer 1996*, **18**(4).

de Finetti, B. (1951), 'Recent suggestions for the reconciliation of the theories of probability', in J. Neyman (ed.), *Proceedings of the Second Berkeley Symposium on Mathematical Statistics and Probability*, Berkeley and Los Angeles: University of California Press, pp. 217–26.

Devine, F. (1995), 'Qualitative methods', in D. Marsh and G. Stoker (eds), *Theory and Methods in Political Science*, London: Macmillan Press Ltd.

DFID (1998), Technical Note No. 12, *The Management of Risk in DFID Activities*. Unpublished Document.

DHV (1994a), *Environmental Impact Assessment, Southern Highway Rehabilitation Project, Belize*, (Atn/ NE -4463–BL), Final Report, DHV Consultants BV.

DHV (1994b), *Economic Feasibility Study of the Agricultural Development related to the Southern Highway Rehabilitation Project Belize*, Final Report, DHV Consultants BV.

Dodds, S. (1997), 'Towards a "science of sustainability": Improving the way ecological economics understands human well-being', *Ecological Economics*, **23**: 95–111.

Dorfman, R. (1955), Review of C.F. Carter, G.P. Meredith and G.L.S. Shackle first edition (1954) *Review of Economics and Statistics*, **XXXVII**, August: 314–16.

Dow, S. (1993), 'Uncertainty about uncertainty', *Discussion papers in Economics 93/97*, Stirling: University of Stirling.

Dunham, P.S. and P. Wanyerka (1994), *The Southern Highway Archaeological Assessment: Field Reconnaissance and Field Guide to Archaeological Remains in Stann Creek and Toledo Districts*, Report to the Inter-American Development Bank.

Earl, P. (1983), *The Economic Imagination*, Armonk, New York: Wheatsheaf Books, M.E. Sharpe Inc.

Edwards, W. (1955), 'The prediction decisions among bets', *Journal of Experimental Psychology*, **50**: 201–14.

Edwards, W. (1977), 'The use of multi-attribute utility measurement for social decision making', in D. Bell, R. Keeney and H. Raiffa (eds), *Conflicting Objectives and Decisions*, New York: John Wiley and Sons.

Ehrlich, P. (1994), 'Ecological economics and the carrying capacity of earth', in A. Jansson, M. Hammer, C. Folke and R. Costanza (eds), *Investing in Natural Capital: The Ecological Economics Approach to Sustainability*, Washington, DC: Island Press.

Ellsberg, D. (1961), 'Risk, ambiguity and the Savage axioms', *Quarterly Journal of Economics*, **75**: 643–69.

Escobar, A. (1996), 'Constructing nature: elements for a post-structural political ecology', in R. Peet and M. Watts (eds), *Liberation Ecologies: Environment, Development and Social Movements*, London: Routledge, pp. 46–68.

Faucheux, S. and G. Froger (1995), 'Decision-making under environmental uncertainty', *Ecological Economics*, **15**: 29–42.

Faucheux, S., D. Pearce and J. Proops (1996) (eds), *Models of Sustainable Development*, Cheltenham, UK and Brookfield, US: Edward Elgar.

Fishburn, P.C. (1983), 'Transitive measurable utility', *Journal of Economic Theory*, **31**: 293–317.

Fisher, A.C. and W.M. Hanemann (1987), 'Quasi option value: Some misconceptions dispelled', *Journal of Environmental Economics and Management*, **14**: 183–90.

Fairclough, H. (1995), *Critical Discourse Analysis: The Critical Study of Language*, London: Longman.

Fletcher, J., W. Adamowicz and T. Graham-Tomasi (1990), 'The travel cost model of recreation demand', *Leisure Sciences*, **12**: 119–47.

Forbes, S.A. (1880), 'On some interactions of organisms', *Bulletin of the Illinois State Laboratory of Natural History*, **1**: 3–17.

Ford, J.L. (1983), *Choice Expectation and Uncertainty: An Appraisal of G.L.S. Shackle's Theory*, Oxford: Basil Blackwell (Martin Robertson).

Ford, J.L. (1987), *Economic Choice Under Uncertainty: A Perspective Theory Approach*, Aldershot, UK and Brookfield, US: Edward Elgar.

Ford, J.L. (1994), *G.L.S. Shackle: The Dissenting Economist's Economist*, Aldershot, UK and Brookfield, US: Edward Elgar.

Ford, J.L. and S. Ghose (1994a), 'Shackle's axiom system for potential surprise: some preliminary experimental evidence', *Rivista Internazionale di Scienze Economiche e Commerciali (RISEC)*, **XLV**(3): 417–41.

Ford, J.L. and S. Ghose (1994b), 'Belief, credibility, disbelief, possibility, potential surprise and probability as measures of uncertainty: some experimental evidence', *University of Birmingham Department of Economics Discussion Paper*, 94–22.

Ford, J.L. and S. Ghose (1995a), 'Ellsberg's urns, ambiguity, measures of uncertainty and non-additivity: some experimental evidence', *Applied Economics Letters*, **5**: 147–51.

Ford, J.L. and S. Ghose (1995b), 'Shackle's theory of decision-making under uncertainty: the findings of a laboratory experiment', *University of Birmingham, Department of Economics Discussion Paper*, 95–108.

Ford, J.L. and S. Ghose (1995c), 'The primitive construct: possibility, potential surprise, probability and belief: some experimental evidence', *Metroeconomica*, **49**(2), 1–26.

Ford, J.L. and S. Ghose (1998), 'Lottery designs to discriminate between Shackle's theory, expected utility theory and non-expected utility theories', University of Birmingham, Paper to be published in a special edition of the *Annals of Operations Research*, 1998.

Freeman, A.M. (1985), 'Supply uncertainty, option price and option value', *Land Economics*, **60**(2): 176–81.

Freeman, A.M. (1986), 'Uncertainty and environmental policy: The role of option and quasi option value', in V.K. Smith (ed.), *Advances in Applied Micro-economics: Risk, Uncertainty and the Valuation of Benefits and Costs*, Greenwich, CT and London: JAI Press Inc.

Freeman, A.M. (1993), *The Measurement of Environmental and Resource Values*, Resources for the Future, Washington, DC.

Friedman, M. (1953), 'The methodology of positive economics', *Essays in Positive Economics*, Chicago: University of Chicago Press, pp. 3–43.

Friedman, M. and L.J. Savage (1948), 'The utility analysis of choices involving risk', *Journal of Political Economy*, **56**: 279–404.

Froger, G. and E. Zyla (1994), 'Decision-making for sustainable development: orthodox or system dynamics models', Paper presented at the International Symposium: 'Models of Sustainable Development. Exclusive or Complementary Approaches of Sustainability?' Paris, 16–18 March.

Frost, T.M., S.R. Carpenter, A.R. Ives and T.K. Kratz (1994), 'Species composition and complementarity in ecosystem functioning', in C. Jones and J.

Lawton (eds), *Linking Species and Ecosystems*, New York: Chapman and Hall.

Funtowicz, S.O. and J.R. Ravetz (1991), 'A new scientific methodology for global environmental problems', in R. Costanza (ed.), *Ecological Economics: The Science and Management of Sustainability*, New York: Columbia University Press.

Georgescu-Roegen, N. (1973), 'The entropy law and the economic problem', in R. Costanza, C. Perrings and C.J. Cleveland (1997), *The Development of Ecological Economics*, Aldershot, UK and Brookfield, US: Edward Elgar.

Georgescu-Roegen, N. (1979), 'Methods in economic science', *Journal of Economic Issues*, **13**: 317–28.

The Government of Belize (1995), *Environmental Protection, Environmental Impact Assessment Regulations, 1995. Statutory Instrument No. 107 of 1995*, Ministry of Tourism and the Environment, Department of Environment.

The Government of Belize (1996), *Belize, National Environmental Action Plan*, 4 June 1996.

The Government of Belize (1997), Personal interview with senior official (1), July.

Graaff, J. de V. and W.J. Baumol (1949), 'Three notes on expectations in economics, II, *Economica*, **XVI**, November: 338–42.

Graham, D.A. (1981), 'Cost–benefit analysis under uncertainty', *American Economic Review*, **71**: 715–25.

Graham-Tomasi, T. (1995), 'Quasi-option value', in D.W. Bromley (ed.), *The Handbook of Environmental Economics*, Oxford: Basil Blackwell.

Green, J. (1988), 'Ordinal independence in non-linear utility theory', *Journal of Risk and Uncertainty*, **1**: 355–87.

The *Guardian* (1998), Saturday 7 November, News Focus Hurricane Mitch, pp. 4 and 5.

Hanley, N. (1989), 'Valuing rural recreation benefits: An empirical comparison of two approaches', *Journal of Agricultural Economics*, **40**: 361–74.

Hanley, N. (1995), 'The role of environmental valuation in cost–benefit analysis', in K.G. Willis and J.T. Corkindale, *Environmental Valuation New Perspectives*, Wallingford: CAB International.

Hanley, N. and C. Spash (1993), *Cost–Benefit Analysis and the Environment*, Aldershot, UK and Brookfield, US: Edward Elgar.

Hanley, N., J.F. Shogren and B. White (1997), *Environmental Economics: In Theory and Practice*, London: Macmillan Press.

Harrison, J., R. Marcus and A. Weir (1995), *Belize Southern Highway Social Impact Assessment*, British Development Division, ODA.

Hartwick, J.M. (1977), 'Intergenerational equity and the investing of rents from exhaustible resources', *American Economic Review*, **67**: 972–74.

Hartwick, J.M. (1978), 'Substitution among exhaustible resources and Intergenerational equity', *Review of Economic Studies*, **45**: 347–54.

Henrot, J. and G.O. Robertson (1994), 'Vegetation removal in two soils of the humid tropics: Effects on microbial biomass', *Soil Biology and Biochemistry*, **26**: 111–16.

Hey, J.D. (1984), 'The economics of optimism and pessimism: a definition and some applications', *Kyklos*, Fasc 2, **37**: 181–205.

Hey, J.D. (1985), 'The possibility of possibility', *Journal of Economics*, **12** (1/2): 70–88.

Hicks, J. (1979), *Causality in Economics*, New York: Basic Books.

Hinterberger, F., F. Luks and F. Schmidt-Bleek (1997), 'Material flows vs. "natural capital". What makes an economy sustainable?', *Ecological Economics*, **23**: 1–14.

Hohl, A. and C.A. Tidsdell (1993), 'How useful are environmental safety standards in economics? The example of safe minimum standards for the protection of species', *Biodiversity and Conservation*, **2**: 168–81.

Holling, C.S. (1973), 'Resilience and stability of ecological systems', *Annual Review of Ecological Systems*, **4**: 1–24.

Holling, C.S. (1986), 'The resilience of terrestrial ecosystems: Local surprise and global change', in W.C. Clark and R.E. Munn (eds), *Sustainable Development of the Biosphere*, Cambridge: Cambridge University Press.

Holling, C.S. (1992), 'Cross scale morphology, geometry and dynamics of ecosystems', *Ecological Monographs*, **62**: 47–52.

Holling, C.S., D.W. Schindler, B.H. Walker and J. Roughgarden (1995), 'Biodiversity in the functioning of ecosystems: an ecological synthesis', in C. Perrings, C. Folke, C.S. Holling, B.O. Jansson and K.G. Maler (eds), *Biological Diversity: Economic and Ecological Issues*, Cambridge: Cambridge University Press, pp. 44–8.

The Inter-American Development Bank (1996), *Basic Facts*, Washington, DC: The Inter-American Development Bank.

The Inter-American Development Bank (IDB) (1997a), *Southern Highway Project, Environmental Summary* (Working Draft), January.

The Inter-American Development Bank (IDB) (1997b), *Belize Southern Highway Project (BL-0001) Environmental Summary*, August.

The Inter-American Development Bank (IDB) (1997c), *Evaluation: A Management Tool for Improving Project Performance*, Inter-American Development Bank Evaluation Office (EVO).

The Inter-American Development Bank (IDB) (1999), *IDB Projects Magazine: The Project Cycle*, Inter-American Development web page.

Iremonger, S. and N. Brokaw (1996), 'Vegetation classification for Belize', in NARMAP *National Protected Areas Systems Plan for Belize*, Prepared by Programme for Belize & The Inter-American Development Bank.

Iremonger, S. and R. Sayre (1993), *Draft Rapid Ecological Assessment of the Bladen Nature Reserve*, Toledo District, Belize, The Nature Conservancy Council, Audubon Society and Ministry of Natural Resources.

Jeffreys, H. (1939, 1948), *The Theory of Probability*, 2nd edn, Oxford: Oxford University Press.

Kahneman, D. and A. Tversky (1979), 'Prospect theory: an analysis of decisions under risk', *Econometrica*, **47**: 263–91.

Karmarkar, U.S. (1978), 'Subjectively weighted utility: a descriptive extension of the weighted utility model', *Organisational Behaviour and Human Performance*, **21**: 61–72.

Katzner, D.W. (1986), 'Potential surprise, potential confirmation, and probability', *Journal of Post Keynesian Economics*, **9**(1): 58–78.

Katzner, D.W. (1989a), 'The Shackle–Vickers approach to decision-making in ignorance', *Journal of Post Keynesian Economics*, **12**: 237–59.

Katzner, D.W. (1989b), 'The comparative statistics of the Shackle–Vickers approach to decision-making in ignorance', in T.B. Fomby and T.K. Seo (eds), *Studies in the Economics of Uncertainty: In Honour of Joseph Hadar*, Berlin: Springer-Verlag.

Katzner, D.W. (1993), 'Operationality in the Shackle–Vickers approach to decision making in ignorance', *Journal of Post Keynesian Economics*, Winter 1992–93, **15**(2): 229–53.

Katzner, D.W. (1995), *Time, Ignorance and Uncertainty in Economic Models*, Ann Arbor: University of Michigan Press.

Keat, R. and J. Urry (1975), *Social Theory as Science*, London: Routledge and Kegan Paul.

Kellman, M. (1979), 'Soil enrichment by Neotropical savannah trees', *Journal of Ecology*, **67**: 565–77.

Kellman, M. and K. Sanmugadas (1985), 'Nutrient retention by savannah ecosystems', *Journal of Ecology*, **73**: 935–51.

Keynes, J.M. (1921), *A Treatise on Probability*, Reprinted as vol. 8 of *The Collected Writings of J.M. Keynes* (1971), London: Macmillan.

Keynes, J.M. (1936), *The General Theory of Employment, Interest and Money*, London: Macmillan.

Keynes, J.M. (1973), *The Collected Writings of John Maynard Keynes*, vol. 13, ed. by D. Moggridge, London: Macmillan.

King, R.B., I.C. Baillie, P.G. Bisset, R.J. Grimble, M.S. Johnson and G.L. Silva (1986), *Land Resource Survey of Toledo District, Belize*, Tolworth, UK: Land Resource Development Centre.

King, R.B., I.C. Baillie, J.R. Dunsmore, D.A. Gray, J.H. Pratt, H.R. Versey and A.C.S. Wright (1989), *Land Resource Assessment of Stann Creek District*, Belize, Bulletin No. 19, Chatham, UK: Overseas Development Natural Resource Institute.

King, R.B., J.H. Pratt, M.P. Warner and S.A. Zisman (1993), *Agricultural Development Prospects in Belize*, Chatham: Natural Resources Institute, ODA, 176.

Knetsch, J. (1990), 'Environmental policy implications of the disparity between willingness to pay and compensation demanded', *Journal of Environmental Management*, **18**: 227–37.

Knight, F.H. (1921), *Risk, Uncertainty and Profit*, Chicago: Chicago University Press.

Kocks Consult GMBH (1993), *Southern Highway Upgrading and Rehabilitation Project, Feasibility Study, Draft Final Report*, Prepared for the Ministry of Economic Development, Government of Belize.

Kristrom, B. (1990), 'W. Stanley Jevons (1888) on option value', *Journal of Environmental Economics and Management*, **18**: 86–7.

Krutilla, J.V. and A.C. Fisher (1975), *'The Economics of Natural Environments*, Baltimore, MD: Johns Hopkins University Press.

Lawson, T. (1988), 'Probability and uncertainty in economic analysis', *Journal of Post-Keynesian Economics*, **11**(1): 38–65.

Lawson, T. (1997), *Economics and Reality*, London: Routledge.

Levi, I. (1966), 'On potential surprise', *Ratio*, **VIII**: 107–29.

Loomes, G. and R. Sugden (1982), 'Regret theory: an alternative theory of rational choice under uncertainty', *Economic Journal*, **92**: 805–24.

López, R. and C. Scoseria (1996), 'Environmental sustainability and poverty in Belize: a policy paper', *Environment and Development Economics*, **1**: 289–307.

Luce, R.D. (1991), 'Rank and sign dependent linear utility models for binary gambles', *Journal of Economic Theory*, **53**: 75–100.

Luce, R.D. and P.C. Fishburn (1991), 'Rank and sign dependent linear utility models for finite first order gambles', *Journal of Risk and Uncertainty*, **1**: 305–32.

Machina, M. (1982), 'Expected utility analysis without the independence axiom', *Econometrica*, **50**: 277–323.

Marie-Gren, I., C. Folke, K. Turner and I. Bateman (1994), 'Primary and secondary values of wetland ecosystems', *Environmental and Resource Economics*, **4**: 55–74.

Mars, J. (1950a), 'A study in expectations: Reflections on Shackle's Expectation in Economics: Part I', *Yorkshire Bulletin of Economic and Social Research*, **2**(2), July: 63–98.

Mars, J. (1950b), 'A study in expectations: Reflections on Shackle's Expectation in Economics: Part II', *Yorkshire Bulletin of Economic and Social Research*, **2**(3), November: 1–35.

Mason, P. (1996), 'Towards an alternative rule for the sustainable exploitation of a non renewable resource', Paper presented at the Environmental

Economics Forum, September 1996, Department of Economics, University of Lancaster.

Mathur, S. (1994), *Risk and Uncertainty: Selection Criteria for Projects Offering Net Positive Domestic Benefits*, Global Environment Co-ordination Division, Environment Department, The World Bank, Washington.

McField, M., S. Wells and J. Gibson (eds) (1995), *State of the Coastal Zone Report, Belize, 1995*, Coastal Zone Management Programme, Government of Belize.

McKendrick, J.H. (1996) (compiler), *Multi-method research in Population Geography*, A Primer to Debate (Population Geography Research Group of the Royal Geographical Society with the Institute of British Geographers).

Mooney, H.A., J. Lubchenco, R. Dirzo and O.E. Sala (eds) (1995a), 'Biodiversity and ecosystem functioning: Ecosystem analyses', in Vernon H. Heywood (ed.), *Global Biodiversity Assessment*, UNEP, Cambridge: Cambridge University Press.

Mooney, H.A., J. Lubchenco, R. Dirzo and O.E. Sala (eds) (1995b), 'Biodiversity and ecosystem functioning: Basic principles', *Global Biodiversity Assessment*, UNEP, Cambridge: Cambridge University Press.

Moore, P.D. (1982), 'Fire: Catastrophic or creative force?', *Impact of Science on Society*, **32**: 5–14.

Munasinghe, M. (1993a), 'Environmental issues and economic decisions in developing countries', *World Development*, **21**(11): 1729–48.

Munasinghe, M. (1993b), 'Environmental economics and sustainable development', *World Bank Environment Paper*, No. 3, Washington DC: The World Bank.

Munda, G. (1996), 'Cost–benefit analysis in integrated environmental assessment: Some methodological issues', *Ecological Economics*, **19**: 157–68.

Murdoch, J. and A.C. Pratt (1994), 'Rural studies of power and the power of rural studies. A reply to Philo', *Journal of Rural Studies*, **10**: 83–7.

NARMAP (1995), *Environmental Water Quality Monitoring*, Prepared by Program for Belize.

NARMAP (1996), *National Protected Areas Systems Plan for Belize*, Prepared by Programme for Belize and The Inter-American Development Bank.

Nilsson, C. and G. Grelsson (1995), 'The fragility of ecosystems: A review', *Journal of Applied Ecology*, **32**: 677–92.

Norgaard, R.B. (1984), 'Coevolutionary development potential', *Land Economics*, **60**: 160–73.

Norgaard, R.B. and R.B. Howarth (1991), 'Sustainability and the rate of discount', in R. Costanza (ed.), *The Ecological Economics: The Science and Management of Sustainability*, New York: Columbia University Press.

Norton, B.G. (1995), 'Evaluating ecosystem states: Two competing paradigms', *Ecological Economics*, **14**: 113–27.

O'Connor, J. (1988), 'Capitalism, nature, socialism: A theoretical introduction', *Capitalism, Nature, Socialism*, **1**(3): 11–38.

O'Connor, J. (1989), 'Political economy of ecology of socialism and capitalism', *Capitalism, Nature, Socialism*, **1**(3): 93–108.

ODA (1996), *The Manual of Environmental Appraisal*, London: Overseas Development Administration.

O'Riordan, T. (ed) (1995), *Environmental Science for Environmental Management*, London: Longman.

O'Riordan, T. and J. Cameron (eds) (1994), *Interpreting the Precautionary Principle*, London: Earthscan.

Oslender, U. (1997), 'Space and identity in the Colombian Pacific', unpublished undergraduate dissertation, University of Glasgow.

Pearce, D.W. (1994), 'The precautionary principle and economic analysis', in T. O'Riordan and J. Cameron (eds), *Interpreting the Precautionary Principle*, London: Earthscan, pp. 132–51.

Pearce, D.W. and C.A. Nash (1981), *The Social Appraisal of Projects*, London: Macmillan.

Pearce, D.W. and R.K. Turner (1990), *Economics of Natural Resources and the Environment*, New York and London: Harvester Wheatsheaf.

Pearce, D.W., E. Barbier and A. Markandya (1990), *Sustainable Development: Economics and Environment in the Third World*, Aldershot, UK and Brookfield, US: Edward Elgar.

Peet, R. and M. Watts (1996), 'Liberation ecology, development, sustainability and environment in an age of market triumphalism', in R. Peet and M. Watts (eds), *Liberation Ecologies: Environment, Development, Social Movements*, London: Routledge.

Perman, R., Y. Ma and J. McGilvray (1996), *Natural Resource and Environmental Economics*, London: Longman.

Perrings, C. (1987), *Economy and Environment: A Theoretical Essay on the Interdependence of Economic and Environmental Systems*, Cambridge: Cambridge University Press.

Perrings, C. (1989), 'Environmental bonds and environmental research in innovative activities', *Ecological Economics*, **1**: 95–110.

Perrings, C. (1994), 'Biotic diversity, sustainable development and natural capital', in A. Jansson, M. Hammer, C. Folke and R. Costanza (eds), *Investing in Natural Capital: The Ecological Economics Approach to Sustainability*, Washington, DC: Island Press.

Perrings, C. (1996), 'Ecological resilience in the sustainability of economic development', in S. Faucheux, D. Pearce and J. Proops (eds), *Models of*

*Sustainable Development*, Aldershot, UK and Brookfield, US: Edward Elgar.

Perrings, C. (1997a), 'Georgescu-Roegen and the irreversibility of material process', *Ecological Economics*, **22**: 303–4.

Perrings, C. (1997b), *Economics of Ecological Resources: Selected Essays*, Aldershot, UK and Brookfield, US: Edward Elgar.

Perrings, C. and H. Opschoor (1994), 'The loss of biological diversity: Some policy implications', *Environmental and Resource Economics*, **4**: 1–11.

Perrings, C. and E. Pearce (1994), 'Threshold effects and incentives for the conservation of biodiversity', *Environmental and Resource Economics*, **4**: 12–28.

Perrings, C., C. Folke and K.G. Maler (1993), 'The ecology and economics of biodiversity loss: The research agenda', *Ambio*, **22**: 201–11.

Perrings, C.A., K.G. Maler, C. Folke, C.S. Holling and B.O. Jansson (eds) (1995), *Biodiversity Conservation: Problems and Policies*, Dordrecht and London: Kluwer Academic Publishers.

Pimm, S.L. (1984), 'The complexity and stability of ecosystems', *Nature*, **307**: 321–6.

Pohl, G. and D. Mihaljek (1992), 'Project evaluation and uncertainty in practice: A statistical analysis of the rate of return divergences of 1,015 World Bank projects', *World Bank Economics Review*, **6** (2).

Popper, Sir Karl (1959–60), 'The propensity interpretation of probability', *British Journal for the Philosophy of Science*, **10**(1), 25–42.

Popper, Sir Karl (1972), *Conjectures and Refutations*, 4th revised edn, London: Routledge and Kegan Paul.

Popper, Sir Karl (1990), *A World of Propensities*, Bristol: Thoemmes.

Quiggin, J. (1982), 'A theory of anticipated utility', *Journal of Economic Behaviour and Organisation*, **3**: 324–43.

Ramsey, F.P. (1926, 1931), 'Truth and probability', originally written in 1926, reprinted in Braithwaite, B.R. (ed) (1931), *The Foundations of Mathematics and Other Logical Essays*, New York: Harcourt, Brace and Co, and London: Kegan Paul, pp. 156–203.

Randall, A. (1991), 'Total and non-use values', in J.B. Braden and C.D. Kolstad (eds), *Measuring the Demand for Environmental Quality*, Amsterdam: North Holland, pp. 303–22.

Randall, A. (1994), 'The travel cost method', *Land Economics*, **70**(1): 88–96.

Ready, R.C. (1995), 'Environmental valuation under uncertainty', in D.W. Bromley (ed.), *The Handbook of Environmental Economics*, Oxford: Basil Blackwell.

Richardson, T. (1996), 'Foucauldian Discourse: Power and truth in urban and regional policy making', *European Planning Studies*, **4**(3).

Russell, C.S. (1995), 'Are we lost in the vale of ignorance or on the mountain of principle?', *Ecological Economics*, **14**: 91–9.

Russell, C.S. (1997), *What Does Economics Have to Say About the Environment*, A draft textbook (unpublished copy).

Ruttenbeek, H.J. (1992), *Mangrove Management: An Economic Analysis of Management Options with a Focus on Bintuni Bay, Irian Jaya*, Environmental Management Development in Indonesian Project, Environmental Reports, No. 8.

Sagoff, M. (1988), 'Some problems with environmental economics', *Environmental Ethics*, **10**: 55–74.

Savage, L.J. (1954), *The Foundations of Statistics*, New York: J. Wiley and Sons.

Schill, J.L. (1997), 'The logging conflict in Belize's Toledo District', Unpublished Dissertation, Bucknell University.

Schindler, D.W. (1990), 'Experimental perturbations of whole lakes as tests of hypotheses concerning ecosystem structure and function', *Oikos*, **57**: 25–41.

Schmalensee, R. (1972), 'Option demand and consumer's surplus: Valuing price and changes under uncertainty', *American Economic Review*, **62**: 813–24.

Schoenberger, E. (1991), 'The corporate interview as a research method in economic geography', *Professional Geographer*, **43**(2).

Schulze, E.D. and H.A. Mooney (eds) (1993), *Biodiversity and Ecosystem Functioning*, Berlin: Springer-Verlag.

Segal, U. (1989), 'Anticipated utility: A measure representation approach', *Annals of Operations Research*, **19**: 359–73.

Shackle, G.L.S. (1949), *Expectation in Economics*, Cambridge: Cambridge University Press.

Shackle, G.L.S. (1952), *Expectation in Economics*, 2nd edn, Cambridge: Cambridge University Press.

Shackle, G.L.S. (1955), *Uncertainty in Economics and Other Reflections*, Cambridge: Cambridge University Press.

Shackle, G.L.S. (1961), *Decision, Order and Time in Human Affairs*, Cambridge: Cambridge University Press.

Shackle, G.L.S. (1966), *Decision, Order and Time in Human Affairs*, Cambridge: Cambridge University Press.

Shackle, G.L.S. (1969), *Decision, Order and Time in Human Affairs*, 2nd edn, Cambridge: Cambridge University Press.

Shackle, G.L.S. (1979), *Imagination and the Nature of Choice*, Edinburgh: Edinburgh University Press, p. 159.

Shafer, G. (1976), *A Mathematical Theory of Evidence*, Princeton, NJ: Princeton University Press.

Shrader-Frechette, K.S. and E.D. McCoy (1993), *Method in Ecology: Strategies for Conservation*, Cambridge: Cambridge University Press.

Simon, H.A. (1957), *Administrative Behaviour*, 2nd edn, New York: Macmillan.

Simon, H.A. (1964), 'Rationality', in J. Gould and W.L. Kolb (eds), *A Dictionary of the Social Sciences*, Glencoe, IL: The Free Press.

Simon, H.A. (1972), 'Theories of bounded rationality', in C.B. Radner and R. Radner (eds), *Decision and Organisation*, Amsterdam: North Holland Publishing Company.

Simon, H.A. (1982), *Models of Bounded Rationality*, Cambridge, MA: MIT Press.

SNH (1993), *Sustainable Development and the Natural Heritage*, Edinburgh: Scottish Natural Heritage.

Solow, R.M. (1974), 'Intergenerational equity and renewable resources', *Review of Economic Studies*, Symposium.

Solow, R.M. (1986), 'On the intergenerational allocation of natural resources', *Scandinavian Journal of Economics*, **88**(1): 141–9.

Solow, R.M. (1993), 'Sustainability: An economist's perspective', in Robert and Nancy Dorfman (eds), *Economics of the Environment: Selected Readings*, New York: W.W. Norton and Company.

Spash, C. and N. Hanley (1995), 'Preferences, information and biodiversity preservation', *Ecological Economics*, **12**: 91–208.

Suter, G.W. II, (1989), 'Ecological endpoints', in W. Warren-Hicks, B.R. Parkhurst and S.S. Baker, Jr (eds), *Ecological Assessment of Hazardous Waste Sites: A Field and Laboratory Reference Document*, EPA 600/3–89/013: 21–28, Oregon: Corvallis Environmental Research Laboratory.

Suter, G.W. II (1995), 'Adapting ecological risk assessment for ecosystem valuation', *Ecological Economics*, **14**: 137–41.

Tversky, A. and D. Kahneman (1992), 'Advances in prospect theory: Cumulative representation of uncertainty', *Journal of Risk and Uncertainty*, **5**: 297–323.

Turner, K. (ed.) (1993), *Sustainable Environmental Economics and Management*, New York: Belhaven Press.

Turner, R.K. (1995), 'Environmental economics and management', in T. O'Riordan (ed.), *Environmental Science for Environmental Management*, London: Longman, pp. 16–29.

Ulph, A. (1982), 'The role of ex ante and ex post decisions in the valuation of life', *Journal of Public Economics*, **18**: 256–76.

UNEP (1995), *Global Biodiversity Assessment*, Cambridge: Cambridge University Press.

Venn, J. (1888), *The Logic of Choice*, 3rd edn, London: Methuen.

Vercelli, A. (1995), 'Hard uncertainty and the environment', *Economics,*

*Energy and Environment, Nota di Lavoro 16.94*, Milan: Fondazione Eni Enrico Mattei.

Vickers, D. (1986), 'Time ignorance, surprise, and economic decisions: A comment on Williams and Findlay's "Risk and the Role of Failed Expectations in an Uncertain World"', *Journal of Post Keynesian Economics*, **IX** (1).

Vickers, D. (1994), *Economics and the Antagonism of Time: Time, Uncertainty, and Choice in Economic Theory*, Ann Arbor: The University of Michigan Press.

Viscusi, K. (1989), 'Prospective reference theory: Toward an explanation of the paradoxes', *Journal of Risk and Uncertainty*, **2**: 235–63.

von Mises, L. (1936, 1939), *Wahrscheinlichkeit, Statistik und Wahrheit*, 2nd edn, translated as *Probability, Statistics and the Truth*, New York: Macmillan.

von Neumann, J. and O. Morgenstern (1944), *Theory of Games and Economic Behaviour*, Princeton: Princeton University Press.

von Neumann, J. and Morgenstern, O. (1947), *Theory of Games and Economic Behaviour*, 2nd edn, Princeton: Princeton University Press.

Wagstaffe, M. and G. Moyser (1987), *Research Methods for Elite Studies*, London: Allen & Unwin.

Walker, B.H. (1992), 'Biodiversity and ecological redundancy', *Conservation Biology*, **6**: 18–23.

Warrick, J. (1997), 'Tiny Plants Threaten Bounty of Seas', *The Washington Post*, headline article, Tuesday, 23 September.

Weisbrod, B.A. (1964), 'Collective-consumption services of individual-consumption goods', *Quarterly Journal of Economics*, **78**: 471–7.

White, W., J. Raney, T. Tremblay, M. Crawford and S. Smith (1996), *Deforestation in Belize 1989/92–1994/96*, Austin, Texas: Bureau of Economic Geology and Centre for Space Research, The University of Texas.

Williams, E. and M. Findlay (1986), 'Risk and the role of failed expectations in an uncertain world', *Journal of Post Keynsian Economics*, **ix**(1).

Willig, R. (1976), 'Consumers' surplus without apology', *American Economic Review*, **66**: 589–97.

Willis, K.G. and R.T. Corkindale (eds) (1995), *Environmental Valuation, New Perspectives*, Wallingford: CAB International.

World Bank (1991), *Environmental Assessment Sourcebook*, Volume 1, World Bank Technical Paper Number 139. Environment Department, Washington, DC: The World Bank.

World Bank (1996), *Belize Environmental Report*, Report No. 15543–BEL, Washington, DC: The World Bank.

World Commission on Environment and Development (WCED) (1987), *Our Common Future*, Oxford: Oxford University Press.

Yaari, M.E. (1987), 'The dual theory of choice under risk', *Econometrica*, **55** (1): 95–115.

Young, R. (1995), 'The contingent valuation method: An application to the Waipoua Forest, New Zealand', Unpublished undergraduate dissertation, University of Glasgow.

Zisman, S. (1992), *Mangroves in Belize: Their Characteristics, Use and Conservation*, Belize: Forest Planning and Management Project.

Zisman, S. (1996), *The Directory of Protected Areas and Sites of Nature Conservation Interest in Belize*, 2nd edn, NARMAP.

# Index